The Pleasures of Babel

THE PLEASURES
OF BABEL

*Contemporary American
Literature and Theory*

JAY CLAYTON

New York   Oxford
OXFORD UNIVERSITY PRESS
1993

Oxford University Press

Oxford   New York   Toronto
Delhi   Bombay   Calcutta   Madras   Karachi
Kuala Lumpur   Singapore   Hong Kong   Tokyo
Nairobi   Dar es Salaam   Cape Town
Melbourne   Auckland   Madrid

and associated companies in
Berlin   Ibadan

Copyright © 1993 by Jay Clayton

Published by Oxford University Press, Inc.,
200 Madison Avenue, New York, New York 10016

Oxford is a registered trademark of Oxford University Press

Library of Congress Cataloging-in-Publication Data
Clayton, Jay, 1951–
The pleasures of Babel:
Contemporary American literature and theory
Jay Clayton.
p.   cm.   Includes bibliographical references and index.
ISBN 0-19-508372-5
ISBN 0-19-508373-3 (pbk.)
1. American literature—20th century—History and criticism—Theory, etc.
2. Pluralism (Social sciences) in literature.
3. Literature and society—United States—History—20th century.
4. Language and culture—United States—History—20th century.
5. Power (Social sciences) in literature.
6. Minorities in literature.
7. Narration (Rhetoric)
I. Title.
PS228.P55C57   1993
801'.95'09045—dc20   93-16129

2 4 6 8 9 7 5 3 1

Printed in the United States of America
on acid-free paper

To John B. Clayton, III and
Margaret Fooshee Clayton
and in memory of
John B. Clayton, Jr. (1900–1991) and
Marion Fresenius Fooshee (1888–1956)

Preface:
Driving through Babel

Driving through small towns with curious names is a quintessential American experience. At night, alone, with the radio tuned to some flickering country station or call-in show, I have often wondered about the lives of people in places like Hot Coffee, Mississippi, or Paradox, Colorado. But I have never had the experience of driving through Babel. Neither has anyone else as far as I know, because nowhere in this land is there a place called Babel. Get out an atlas and search all fifty states: you will finds towns called Babylon, Cain, Devil Town, Herod, Nineveh, Satans Kingdom, and even Sodom—but not Babel. Is the confusion of tongues so terrible? Evidently so.

In Genesis the people begin to build a tower on the plains of Shinar in order to "make a name for ourselves, so that we may not be scattered about the whole earth" (11:4). For their pride, they are punished with exactly the fate that they feared: "It was named Babel therefore, because there Yahweh confused the language of the whole earth. It was from there that Yahweh scattered them over the whole face of the earth" (11:9). Ever since, Babel has been a symbol of humanity's arrogance and a mythical explanation why the various peoples of this world cannot understand one another. Linguistic diversity was inflicted on the people as a curse. Difference—of language, and by extension, of culture—was portrayed as a punishment, a punishment (as the saying goes) of Biblical proportions.

Today, debates about cultuɪaɪ diversity frequently occasion wild imagery. I do not know how many times I have heard someone who is lamenting the loss of a common culture invoke the specter of Babel. It happened so often, though, that I began to question the metaphor. Perhaps the punishment of Babel has gotten bad press. Perhaps it is time to reevaluate this legendary curse. Living in Babel could not be worse than being captive in Babylon or bearing the mark of Cain. In this book, I argue that it is considerably better, that there are substantial pleasures to be found in the land of Babel and that these pleasures may ultimately benefit the nation. I argue that the United States can not only survive but prosper as a multicultural society. One of the things I discovered while writing this book is that I have been driving through Babel all the time, whenever I go to work, visit relatives or friends, cross to a different part of the city, or take a trip to another region of the country.

It is a pleasure to thank the many friends and colleagues who helped make working on this book a rewarding experience. William L. Andrews, Jonathan Arac, Susan Stanford Friedman, Margaret Homans, Michael Ryan, Cecelia Tichi, and Valerie Traub read most of the manuscript at various stages and gave me valuable suggestions. Many other people read individual chapters, which benefited from their scrutiny: Robert L. Caserio, Jean Bethke Elshtain, Alan Hunter, Gordon Hutner, Alan Liu, Nellie Mckay, Martha Minow, Julie Rivkin, Eric Rothstein, Thomas Schaub, and Nancy Walker. Other friends both encouraged and challenged me at every turn, particularly George Bradley, Edward Hirsch, and Craig Smyser.

The Robert Penn Warren Center for the Humanities provided an ideal interdisciplinary setting in which to work; I thank the other fellows, the visitors at the center, and above all, Mona Frederick for two years of stimulating dialogue and debate. The English department at Vanderbilt University is full of people who enjoy vigorous intellectual exchanges. Of many friends there, several deserve special thanks: Vereen Bell, Margaret Doody, Paul Elledge, and Laurence Lerner. I also want to thank the Graduate School and the College of Arts and Science of Vanderbilt University for research support and aid in attending conferences. I have profited enormously from my association with the Society for the Study of Narrative Literature; its annual conference always fosters lively thinking. Thanks also to audiences at Rice University, the University of Kansas Humanities Center, and Texas A & M for their probing questions. I owe a particular debt to my friends in the Draft Group at the University of Wisconsin–Madison, who were there at the genesis of this project.

Shorter versions of Chapters 3 and 4 first appeared in *Critical Inquiry* and *American Literary History* respectively. I am grateful to the editors of those journals for their hospitality to my work and for permission to reprint. It has been enjoyable to work again with Liz Maguire of Oxford University Press.

I want to conclude by thanking Ellen Wright Clayton for her presence and support; Jim and John for their presence and distraction; and my parents, to whom this book is dedicated, for their presence and for everything else.

Contents

The Pleasures of Babel

1

Culture/Narrative/Power

Humboldt was saying that Stevenson was a man of real culture, the first really since Woodrow Wilson. But Wilson was inferior in this respect to Stevenson and Abraham Lincoln. Lincoln knew Shakespeare well and quoted him at the crises of his life. . . . If you could believe Humboldt (and I couldn't) Stevenson was Aristotle's great-souled man. In his administration cabinet members would quote Yeats and Joyce. The new Joint Chiefs would know Thucydides. Humboldt would be consulted about each State of the Union message. He was going to be the Goethe of the new government and build Weimar in Washington.

SAUL BELLOW, *Humboldt's Gift* (1975)

In 1975, with the sixties drawing to a belated close, with Gerald Ford as President and the media beginning to talk about economic recession, diminished expectations, and apathy on the campus, Saul Bellow published a novel that explored the frustrations of living in a society in which culture appeared to have no real power. *Humboldt's Gift* portrays a world in which artists, writers, and thinkers have no discernible influence on the minds or hearts of those figures who appear to run the country, the leaders of government, industry, finance, and the military. This novel was Bellow's second in the decade to deal with the marginal place of culture in the United States, but unlike *Mr. Sammler's Planet* (1970), which blamed the counterculture of the sixties for bringing matters to a crisis, *Humboldt's Gift* turned back to 1952, the year of Eisenhower's election, to begin its portrait of the artist as an ineffectual *enfant terrible*. Von Humboldt Fleisher is a brilliant, self-destructive poet who responds to his political irrelevance by dreaming of how different the country would be if Adlai Stevenson became president. "He thought that if Adlai could beat Ike in the November election, Culture would come into its own in Washington" (24).

The pathos of Humboldt's fantasy lies not in Stevenson's approaching defeat, which was apparent to most observers, but in the unreality of his dream of poets helping to shape national policy. That is not how power works in the United States, not in 1952, not in 1975, and not today. Humboldt derives his notions from the nineteenth century, from its Romantic fascination with the great individual—the statesman, the general, the robber baron, and, of course, the poet. The very inadequacy of this conception, its insistence on tracing a direct line from the masterful will to the achieved event, is what leads him to despair: "Orpheus moved stones and trees. But a poet can't perform a hysterectomy or send a vehicle out of the solar system. Miracle and power no longer belong to him" (114). But Humboldt's imagery of miracle and mastery obscures other forms of influence, the diffused but omnipresent relations between culture and society that seem apparent today.

This book is about these other forms of relation and about the theories that have attempted to account for them. One of the salient features of the present moment is that these two topics are very close to being the same. The project of theory (although not the writing itself) has become hard to distinguish from the activity it supposedly describes. If in the sixties and early seventies "theory" stood for a metacritical reflection on language and textuality, "theory" in the eighties and early nineties has come to name those activities that elaborate the links between culture and society. One of the principal such activities today is literature itself. Humboldt's Romantic belief in the uniqueness of literature prevented him from seeing how his poetry was implicated in diffuse but largely hidden arrangements of power, thus encouraging him to accept the highly visible categories of power against which he railed. "He consented to the monopoly of power and interest held by money, politics, law, rationality, technology because he couldn't find the next thing, the new thing, the necessary thing for poets to do" (150). In this book the reader will encounter a surprising number of contemporary writers who *have* found the next thing, the new thing, the necessary thing to do. These writers include novelists, literary critics, philosophers, anthropologists, historians, legal scholars — and poets too. Humboldt rages against the absorption of art by intellectual discourse, but his desire to separate the two paradoxically contributes to his belief in his own futility.

Changing Conceptions of Culture

The view of culture as marginal to contemporary life is shared by the overwhelming majority of people who work in literary fields. Poets, novelists, book reviewers, literary critics, journalists, publishers, and agents all too often resign themselves to the supposed inability of culture to affect society. Everywhere one turns one hears of the superfluousness of culture, its irrelevance to the urgent concerns of modern life. Humboldt's views provide a fair sample of the usual complaints. Critics from both ends of the political spectrum raise their voices to lament the same situation. The reasons adduced for the diminished role of literature vary widely, ranging from the popularity of other media such as film and television; to the neglect of established masterpieces by educational institutions bent on expanding the canon (Bennett, Bloom, Cheney); to the disappearance of the independent intellectual, the writer unaffiliated with the university (Jacoby); to the abandonment by postmodern literature of any claim to rational understanding (Graff, *Literature*); to the view fostered by New Criticism, but prevalent in most critical movements since, that the text should be studied in isolation from politics and history (Lentricchia, *After*); to the overspecialization and rarefied discourse of the academy (Eagleton, *Function*); to the pervasiveness of fiction that celebrates only the anarchic play of desire (Goodheart); to the apostasy of novelists who have renounced their sacred imperative to write moral fiction (Gardner). The reasons may vary but the diagnosis is the same: literature (or culture) no longer counts.

These critical positions are limited by old notions of power. Laments for the vanishing intellectual or for a golden age when culture had more prestige represent a form of nostalgia. Many commentators appear to miss the old order, the one that prevailed in their youth, when they learned to love literature, or in their parents' youth (or their grandparents'). Perhaps they forget that the modern conception of culture—the one that now seems to be breaking up—is itself a relatively recent phenomenon, barely 200 years old. Perhaps they forget that culture's position in society has changed a number of times throughout history. Bards appear to have played a very different role in feudal societies from that of later court poets, who participated in a patronage system. Under modern capitalism, a still different relationship evolved. During the course of the eighteenth century, culture came to be seen as a separate, "higher" realm, a refuge from and a criticism of the everyday business of life. The category of culture itself seems to have been invented during this period, when the word began to be distinguished for the first time from the term "civilization." To a public that increasingly claimed to value the natural, the authentic, and the spontaneous, "civilized" came to mean artificial and overrefined.[1] Hence "culture" was needed as an honorific, a term for those aspects of civilization that few people wanted to do without, particularly art, literature, and the religious sense. Culture came to stand for the highest achievements of the human spirit, those monuments of unaging intellect that were to redeem readers from all that was base and mortal in their being.[2]

Culture's redemptive role in the modern era theoretically gave it a distinctive, if limited, form of power. I say "theoretically" because in practice it has always been hard to point to actual instances where art fulfilled its high mission by causing a political leader, say, to govern more humanely. Nonetheless, the implicit theory of power can be defined with precision. Humboldt's vision of cabinet members quoting Yeats and Joyce captures it perfectly. It is a liberal model in which the private individual is transformed by "his" encounter with art, and this transformation is allowed to carry over into public life. The model depends on a conception of the autonomous self and of a public realm controlled by the decisions of "great men," whether they be leaders of government or commerce. It relies on a strict division between the realm of culture and the rest of society. Humboldt's fascination with the liberal Stevenson is no accident, and another liberal eloquently put the case for this vision of culture just a few years after Stevenson's defeat. In an address at the dedication of the Robert Frost Library in 1963, John F. Kennedy celebrated the link between poetry and power in terms that Humboldt might have used. Poetry has power,

Kennedy said, by virtue of its "disinterested" questioning of society; by its ability to remain aloof from the social realm, which is the "sphere of polemics and ideology"; by its capacity to establish "basic human truths which must serve as the touchstones of our judgment." "Robert Frost coupled poetry and power. For he saw poetry as the means of saving power from itself" (Kennedy 135–6). This liberal vision is stirring, even in the face of the countless occasions in this century when poetry manifestly did not possess such power. But this vision paradoxically had the effect of marginalizing literature. Although it was intended to privilege poetry and other "high" forms as serious, spiritually uplifting, and moral, this model had the consequence of isolating culture from the other concerns of an educated citizen. In practice, literature was made dispensable to the important activities of life by the very process that attempted to exalt it.

The fact that culture has had such a circumscribed sphere of influence during the modern era may be a cause of sorrow, but it is not the reason that the relationship seems to be breaking down today. The causes of this change are profound. They lie both in our evolving sense of what constitutes culture and in the way this redefined cultural realm functions in society. The complexities of these changes make "culture," "literature," and other related terms particularly difficult to define, and uncertainty over which sense of a word is being invoked in a given argument has been a source of confusion in many contemporary debates. I will use "literature" in its accepted but now somewhat inadequate sense of poetic and fictional works of high quality. It is this sense of the word that Alvin Kernan eulogizes in his latest book, *The Death of Literature*. Although I do not share his apparent dismay at the passing away of an older, Romantic conception of literature, I think he is exactly right when he asserts that this change does not entail any diminishment of imaginative or creative energy: "If *literature* has died, *literary activity* continues with unabated, if not increased, vigor" (Kernan 5). The term "literature," in its older sense, depended on its embedded position within another construct of diminishing utility, that of "high culture." I will use this latter phrase whenever the discussion needs to distinguish between the older model of a separate aesthetic realm and the new, broader conception emerging today. The outlines of this new conception can be discerned in the way the word "culture" is used in the new field of cultural studies. In this interdisciplinary area, "culture" has expanded its reference to include a whole range of phenomena once relegated to other domains: "low" or "popular culture," the media, advertising, information technology, fashion, ritual, academic disciplines, public symbols, lifestyles, everyday practices, and more. This expanded conception of "culture," which is what I will be exploring in the remainder of the chapter, resembles the usage that has been common in anthropology for half a century. For anthropologists, culture encompasses the entire expressive dimension of communal life, anything and everything that is capable of communicating meanings, values, or beliefs. My argument about the increased power of works that were once confidently categorized as "literature" or "high culture" depends upon the way in which they participate in this new, more expansive vision of "culture."

The first sign that our conception of culture has changed is the widespread acknowledgment that it has become a battleground, a field of contention, where assumptions about personal identity, the family, gender, class, education, technology, the environment, race, religion, and a host of other topics are debated. Rather than serving as a static repository of the best that has been thought and felt in the past, the realm of high culture has become an agonistic space. Who can doubt that culture has become a hotly contested realm when a politician such as former President George Bush enters the fray over the canon in his commencement speech at Michigan, when former Vice President Dan Quayle blames the power of a "cultural elite" for the decay of "family values" in the country at large, or when Senator Jessie Helms attacks the National Endowment for the Humanities for funding arts projects that he considers obscene? The success of books such as James Hunter's *Culture Wars: The Struggle to Define America* (1991), Roger Kimball's *Tenured Radicals: How Politics Has Corrupted Higher Education* (1990), Dinesh D'Souza's *Illiberal Education: The Politics of Race and Sex on Campus* (1991), David Bromwich's *Politics by Other Means: Higher Education and Group Thinking* (1992), Henry Louis Gates, Jr.'s *Loose Canons: Notes on the Culture Wars* (1992), and Gerald Graff's *Beyond the Culture Wars: How Teaching the Conflicts Can Revitalize American Education* (1992) is further testimony to how compelling such controversy has become.

The politicians and commentators are right: we certainly do not live today in a country with a single, shared culture. (One may question whether the United States ever possessed the common body of ideas and values that some commentators look back on with nostalgia, or one may point to the exclusions of gender, race, class, and education that enabled such a comforting illusion of consensus, but these arguments transport us to a different front in the "culture wars.") The United States is splintered into vociferous and competing groups, each with its own set of sacred texts, its own narratives about reality, its own values and concerns. The nation has little common cultural experience, not even that of the mass media or advertising, as the major television networks, under competition from cable, video, and satellite broadcasting, steadily lose their grip on the national audience and as advertisers target ever more specialized markets, tailoring their messages for ever more precise demographic groups. For better or for worse, this country has become a Babel of competing cultures.

Admittedly, no culture was ever monolithic. As Raymond Williams emphasizes, no Western society has been able to achieve perfect cultural hegemony. Domination is "never either total or exclusive. At any time, forms of alternative or directly oppositional politics and culture exist as significant elements in the society" (113). But today conflict over ideas and values has grown so pervasive that most people acknowledge the loss of a homogeneous culture. Like politics, culture has become a readily available arena for reflecting, expressing, and debating differences.

The ideal of a unified culture is so deeply ingrained that commentators of very different political persuasions are disturbed by multiplicity in this sphere. Conservative critics such as Allan Bloom, William Bennett, and Lynne Cheney openly deplore the contentious, heterogeneous character of the contemporary scene. E. D. Hirsch, who does not espouse a conservative agenda, still sees mastery of a unified language of culture—the acquisition of "cultural literacy"—as the best hope for social improvement.[3] More surprising, some advocates of radical social change view our increasing cultural diversity with alarm. Many on the left worry that unchecked diversity promotes parochial interests and provides ever more specialized markets for consumer capitalism (Lasch, Genovese).[4]

Others respond to this situation positively. Perhaps the most important positive responses have been the theories of difference developed by feminists; by gay, lesbian, and antihomophobic critics; by minority scholars; and by critics in the fields of postcolonialism and cultural studies. These projects, which will be considered in subsequent chapters, have altered lives and changed the face of more than one discipline. The popularity in academic circles of Mikhail Bakhtin, who insists on a dialogical account of writing, represents another favorable reaction to heterogeneity. Finally, political criticism that emphasizes the struggle between subversion and containment, such as new historicism in America and cultural materialism in Britain, has welcomed this situation.[5] All of these movements challenge traditional ideals of consensus and assimilation in favor of a more pluralistic and democratic culture.

A second sign of the changes taking place is the erosion of the boundaries between literature and other forms of discourse. Since the mid-seventies, no trend has affected the intellectual landscape more profoundly than this blurring of spheres. Literary critics frequently identify this development as the hallmark of postmodernism. Fredric Jameson writes of the "effacement" of "some key boundaries or separations" and connects this effacement with the rise of "a kind of writing simply called 'theory,'" a writing that combines literary criticism with "political science, for example, or sociology" ("Postmodernism" 112; see also Lyotard, *Postmodern* 52). But the blurring of genres extends beyond academic writing. Today the gap has narrowed between so-called "high" literature and "low" or popular forms. Serious fiction regularly incorporates themes and techniques from detective fiction, science fiction, and romance, as well as motifs from nonliterary forms such as TV, advertising, movies, popular music, MTV, and more.[6] This trend has diminished the aura of sanctity that surrounded culture in the modern era, making it seem more heterogeneous, democratic, and accessible. Troubling as this trend is to many people, it only takes us back to an older configuration of the cultural domain. Before the late eighteenth century, the word "literature" did not refer solely to imaginative or creative works of high quality but was an omnibus term that covered all forms of writing. Samuel Johnson, for example, defined literature as "learning; skill in letters," and the term was often used to refer to any printed book.[7]

As a result of this erosion of boundaries, literary forms and methods of interpretation once associated primarily with literature are now becoming visible in a wide variety of disciplines, many of which stand in a different relation to social policy and decision making from that of literature narrowly conceived. Interpretive procedures characteristic of literary criticism now figure not only in political science and sociology but also in history, philosophy, theology, law, psychoanalysis, and other fields, so much so that the philosopher Richard Rorty has proclaimed literature "the presiding discipline of our culture" (*Consequences* 155).[8] For evidence of this development, let us turn to the social sciences. In "Blurred Genres: The Refiguration of Social Thought" (1980), Clifford Geertz identifies the rise of interpretive paradigms as part of a major "culture shift" that encompasses both anthropology and sociology (*Local* 19). The continuing force of this "interpretive turn" led two other anthropologists in 1986 to make even grander claims about the importance of literary modes: the main theoretical problems of social science today "have been most trenchantly explored by philosophical and literary theories of interpretation—thus their prominence now as a source of inspiration for theoretical and self-critical reflection in so many disciplines" (Marcus and Fischer 9). But James Clifford most closely parallels my sense of the current scene when he notes both the exchange between literature and ethnography and the growing awareness that the difference between such categories is an historical construction (*Predicament* 4–6).

Without doubt, the most impressive example of the way forms of writing once associated primarily with literature have grown in prestige is the importance narrative is assuming in "non-literary" discourses. Narrative is a cultural form, perhaps the preeminent cultural form, since the activity of storytelling is basic to all known cultures and looms large in every individual's earliest education. Narrative, an obvious formal property of literature, has become not only an object of intensive analysis for many disciplines but also a new analytic category or intellectual tool in these fields. As Edward Said comments in an article on anthropology and the humanities, "Narrative has now attained the status in the human and social sciences of a major cultural convergence" ("Representing" 221). One finds theoretical reflections on narrative not only in the work of anthropologists and sociologists but also in that of art historians — Svetlana Alpers and Richard Brilliant; cognitive psychologists — Jerome Bruner; economists — Donald N. McCloskey; historians — Hayden White and Dominick LaCapra; philosophers — Paul Ricoeur, Louis O. Mink, and Arthur Danto; physicians — Robert Coles; political theorists — William Connolly and Michael Shapiro; psychoanalysts — Roy Schafer and Donald P. Spence; theologians — Michael Goldberg and Sallie McFague; and many others.

In the final section of this chapter, I argue that the expansion of the cultural realm to include more than simply *belles lettres* has contributed to the repositioning of culture within contemporary society. I argue that this reconfigured and repositioned cultural realm has more power in today's world than it did during the previous 200 years. First, however, I want to look more closely at the way narrative is functioning in a specific "nonliterary" discipline, and I want to give more definition to a word that has already been used a number of times: "power."

Narrative and the Law

The most controversial development in legal scholarship in the last fifteen years has been the growth of Critical Legal Studies, a movement that combines interest in literary theory with a political orientation toward the law. Founded in Madison, Wisconsin, in the spring of 1977 (see Schlegel), it has grown into a large, highly publicized school, which has caused bitter divisions within some of the country's most prestigious institutions, most notoriously Harvard Law School. It has also done more than any movement in our time to get faculty of professional schools, as well as lawyers and judges outside of the academic community, to read, teach, and talk to scholars in the humanities. Humanists have begun to return the compliment, reading and writing about the law with increasing frequency.[9] Critical Legal Studies ranges from the visionary social theory of Roberto Ungar's *Politics: A Work in Constructive Social Theory* (1987) to the activism of Duncan Kennedy's *Legal Education and the Reproduction of Hierarchy: A Polemic Against the System* (1983); from deconstructions of contracts and constitutional law by Clare Dalton and Mark Tushnet to the new legal histories of Hendrik Hartog, Robert Gordon, and Joseph Singer; from the feminist theory of Catharine MacKinnon, Robin West, and Martha Minow to the widespread law-as-literature movement.[10]

Narrative theory has figured prominently in many of these projects. Clare Dalton begins her deconstruction of contracts: "Law, like every other cultural institution, is a place where we tell one another stories about our relationships with ourselves, one another, and authority" (999). Her essay looks at the way stories "limit who we can be" and at the "particular limits law stories impose on the twin projects of self-definition and self-understanding" (999). Another interesting proposal is Gerald Lopez's in "Lay Lawyering," which suggests that all persuasion, both inside and outside of the courts, depends as much on storytelling as on argument. Recently, a special issue of the *Michigan Law Review* (1989) has been devoted to the topic of "Legal Storytelling." By far the most influential of such studies has been the late Robert Cover's "Forward: *Nomos* and Narrative" (1983), which introduced the *Harvard Law Review*'s annual report on the Supreme Court decisions of the preceding year.

Cover, who spent most of his career at Columbia and Yale law schools, except for a year at the Hebrew University in Jerusalem, was the author of an important book, *Justice Accused: Antislavery and the Judicial Process* (1975), and at least two landmark law review articles — "*Nomos*" and "Violence and the Word" (1986) — as well as numerous other publications. Virtually every legal article that takes up the topic of narrative pays homage to Cover's work. Commenting on "*Nomos* and Narrative" in a special issue of the *Yale Law Journal* in Cover's honor, a critic, who is not a professor of law but of education and religion, said, "It's not the best article I've read about X or Y; it's the best article I've read about *anything!*" (Lukinsky 1836). In this article, Cover argues that "law and narrative are inseparably related" (5). Both participate in the process of creating and maintaining a normative universe. This thesis is familiar in many circles from Hayden White's often-cited essay "The Value of Narrativity in the Representation of Reality." Unlike White, however, Cover distinguishes the roles of law and narrative. In a secular society, law must struggle to maintain the coherence of its world view in the face of the proliferation of rival values, the multiplicity of meaning. Hence Cover calls our form of legal order "imperial." Imperial law must both restrict the proliferation of meaning and itself be meaningful. Narrative is the source of law's meaning; it provides the explanations, the moral justifications, the historical background, and the teleology for the rules that codify the normative order. But there is a catch. Narrative's creative capacity cannot be confined to the service of the dominant order. It continually generates rival meanings, alternative normative worlds, that threaten the state's dominion.

According to Cover, narrative is "jurisgenerative," a fertile source of new legal meaning. Just as the state has no monopoly on the proliferation of stories, it cannot control the growth of new visions of the law, new interpretations of the legal order. These interpretations inevitably put pressure on the state to create new laws. Jurisgenesis "takes place always through an essentially cultural medium" (11). Stories are the primary cultural agents for the generation of law, because they are uncontrolled, on the one hand, and are normative and communal, on the other. That is, the very multiplicity of narratives encourages competing normative orders, rival communities of interpretation, each of which agitates for the creation of legal rules appropriate to its vision. Here Cover's analysis intersects with the earlier description of our society as a Babel of competing cultures:

> We exercise rigid social control over our precepts in one fashion or another on a national level. . . . But the narratives that create and reveal the patterns of commitment, resistance, and understanding . . . are radically uncontrolled. They are subject to no formal hierarchical ordering, no centralized, authoritative provenance, no necessary pattern of acquiescence. Such is the radical message of the first amendment: an interdependent system of obligation may be enforced, but the very patterns of meaning that give rise to effective or ineffective social control are to be left to the domain of Babel. (16–17)

The courts, by contrast, are "jurispathic," according to Cover. Judges choose between two or more competing interpretations of the law; they decide which law shall govern, who has jurisdiction; they rule on the appropriate precedent. Although the courts use narrative, telling stories about the founding of our nation, about our legal tradition, and about our shared values, they most often employ narrative to maintain a normative order rather than to create new meanings. "Judges are people of violence. Because of the violence they command, judges characteristically do not create law, but kill it. Theirs is the jurispathic office. Confronting the luxuriant growth of a hundred legal traditions, they assert that *this one* is law and destroy or try to destroy the rest" (53). Cover's discussion seems a bit strained here, because what he calls "jurispathy" actually represents a continuation of certain narrative lines and the deflection of others, not their death. Furthermore, his term does not recognize the distinction between violence against people, both symbolic and actual, and textual violence, a distinction he is careful to maintain in other parts of the article. For example, Cover is more persuasive in providing an explanation for the violence of laws. Violence is inevitable, not because all states are inherently authoritarian, but because a normative order requires commitment: "a legal interpretation cannot be valid if no one is prepared to live by it" (44). Violence ratifies a community's commitment to its particular values, its own chosen narratives, either because a community approves the violence that the court exercises on its behalf or because a group is willing to pay a price for resisting the court's edict.

Even in such brief summary, *"Nomos* and Narrative" brings out many of the themes of this chapter. First, the article represents a valuable example of the kind of interdisciplinary work being done today. In particular, it testifies to the attraction of a "literary" form such as narrative for another discipline. Second, it argues for the seamlessness of culture and society. Social institutions such as those that make and administer the law should be seen as only part of a larger normative order, an order constituted in important ways by cultural forces. Third, the culture that helps to create the law in our society is anything but unified. "American political life no longer occurs within a public space dominated by common mythologies and rites and occupied by neighbors and kin" (49). It is made up of myriad competing communities, each of which must struggle to uphold the validity of its traditions. Fourth, the person who works to define or maintain a specific cultural vision is engaged in jurisgenesis, a fundamental form of political action. The literary intellectual may, in however small a degree, create the conditions for social change. Finally, narrative plays a special role in this never-ending struggle.

This last point anticipates debates that will come up in later chapters. Cover suggests that narrative is an important source of power in society but that the state has no monopoly on that power. It is the very multiplicity of stories, the breakdown of an agreed-upon canon, that allows narrative to work against a dominant social order. Narrative may play a role in shaping norms and molding communities without always being authoritarian. In Chapter 2 I discuss a number of narrative theorists who make the opposite assumption, connecting narrative with power but condemning it for the connection. There is shock value in saying that the stories a society tells control its citizens as much as do courts and prisons, but there is wisdom in also recognizing that penal institutions exercise a more direct, violent, and restrictive form of control over behavior. Cover thinks it possible to distinguish law from literature in U.S. society, for law demands the violence of commitment that literature requires only in authoritarian or fundamentalist states. This difference does not mean that culture has no power; it only suggests that the form of its power must be reimagined.

Contemporary Theories of Power

When critics speak of the power of narrative, they generally mean one of two things. The first is a psychological principle—that narratives are capable of affecting people deeply, of moving them emotionally and sometimes intellectually too. The implied model of agency is direct and immediate: one reads (or hears, or sees) a story and feels oneself responding. The second idea is political—that the stories people tell can have an influence on society. Once it was thought that the content of the story carried whatever political impact it had; a story exposing the ugliness of racial prejudice, for example, might be expected to have a socially progressive effect. Lately, it has been more common to suggest that the formal structures of narrative have political implications of their own and thus to argue that a progressive subject matter can still have conservative effects. In either case, the model of agency involves several steps: one reads a story and finds one's prevailing conceptions of the world reinforced or subverted; one then argues that such conceptions affect the way the social, economic, political, or sexual realms are organized.

In most contemporary theory, these two aspects are generally kept separate. Although the way a story moves its readers should be part of any explanation of the role it plays in their lives, a surprising number of theorists focus on only one question or the other. In the eighties and nineties the political question has dominated literary discussions of power, so much so that the psychological principle is generally recast in other terms, most often that of "desire."[11] Even when restricted to the political context, however, the word "power" presents more than its share of complications.

In political theory the concept of power has provoked such lengthy debate that some commentators have concluded that it is an "essentially contested concept," a term about which people will never agree.[12] William Connolly writes: "Disputes about the proper concept and interpretation of power . . . are part of larger ideological debates. To convert others to my idea of power is to implicate them to some degree in my political ideology" ("Forms" 128). Distinctions among theories of power, however, can still be useful. There is a rich tradition of political thought that surrounds the term, which critics often ignore when they theorize about the relation between literature and society.

The most familiar line of thinking about power among political theorists concentrates on situations where one person or group has "power over" another. From Voltaire to Weber, from Bertrand Russell to Bertrand de Jouvenel, from C. Wright Mills to Nicos Poulantzas, numerous writers have analyzed the phenomenon of power in terms of domination or coercion. Some have approached coercion in individual terms as "the possibility of imposing one's own will upon the behavior of other persons" (Weber 924);[13] others, particularly in the Marxist tradition, have emphasized the relation of groups or classes in defining power (Poulantzas 105). Some have anatomized the means of exercising control — military might, wealth, and propaganda constitute Russell's typology; others have focused on the people who possess influence, those whom Mills has named the "power elite." In all these accounts, however, power depends upon and expresses a particular hierarchical relationship—that of domination.

Another view of power comes out of the late work of Michel Foucault. In *Discipline and Punish*, the interviews collected in *Power/Knowledge*, and the first volume of *The History of Sexuality*, Foucault outlines a theory of "disciplinary power," which differs widely from most theories of "power over" or domination. According to Foucault, power is not an hierarchical relationship, not something that those on top hold over those below. Rather, everyone—the mighty as well as the humble—is positioned by networks of power that organize the social realm by shaping the way one thinks about the body, sexuality, kinship, the family, and all other contemporary modes of knowledge. In English his idea is summed up in a pun: the fact that the word "discipline" stands both for punishment and for specialized fields of inquiry indicates the way in which the organization of knowledge rules everyone's life.

This central idea has several corollaries. First, power is everywhere; it is not concentrated in the hands of a few individuals—such as the leaders of the state, the judiciary, the military-industrial complex, giant corporations, or financial institutions—but circulates throughout the entire social body. Power can be studied at countless local sites and in a multitude of different forms. Obviously, certain social positions possess more power than others, but no position is immune from the effects of power: "It's a machine in which everyone is caught, those who exercise power just as much as those over whom it is exercised" (*Power* 156). Second, power works through "micro-mechanisms" of surveillance, registration, normalization, investigation, research, and administration, not through overt coercion. The contrast with the "power over" model, which works through the rule of law, backed up by the threat of force, is great. Third, power creates its own subjects; it "subjects" us, to use another of Foucault's puns. Bodies, gestures, discourses, and desires are produced by power, not vice versa. Finally, power is productive; it creates as well as forbids. Power "doesn't only weigh on us as a force that says no"; rather, "it traverses and produces things, it induces pleasure, forms knowledge, produces discourse" (*Power* 119).

I have outlined these two contrasting models as a groundwork for a discussion of narrative's connection with power. Before proceeding, however, I need to say a few words about the issue of resistance. For each of these conceptions of power, one can identify a corresponding model of resistance or subversion. Resistance to domination from above has run the gamut from liberal individualism, with its theory of rights and entitlements, which are designed to protect the private citizen from arbitrary incursions of state power, to armed insurrection. All are ways of attempting to free oneself (or one's class) from unjust subordination, but revolution represents the most radically subversive response to power from above. It is domination's absolute opposite. By contrast, revolution does not constitute a clear opposite to Foucault's disciplinary notion of power, for any possible revolutionary movement represents only a reorganization of power and a new discipline. Liberal individualism, as well, is not an escape from domination, in Foucault's terms, but only a particular mode of subjection. Resistance to disciplinary power can only be local and strategic, never absolute. But this does not mean that resistance is futile. Although it inevitably forms a part of any arrangement of power, resistance also inevitably produces effects, causes "cleavages in a society that shift about, fracturing unities and effecting regroupings, furrowing across individuals themselves" (*Sexuality* 96). Consequently, Foucault argues for the subversive potential of "specific intellectuals," people who struggle within the institutions in which they find themselves. To counter forms of power that circulate throughout the social body, that organize subjectivity, resistance must occur "right at the point where relations of power are exercised" (*Power* 142).

In the eighties, resistance and subversion became important topics for literary and social theorists, as important as the topic of power itself. Few literary critics, however, seemed interested in asking whether or not power had a positive side, even though some traditions of political thought have taken a rosier view of this possibility. One thing that may prevent literary critics from discerning the altered political function of narrative today is their tendency to ignore any productive or socially creative uses of power. If we take a moment more to look at some of the political traditions that have emphasized the positive side of power, we may be better prepared to acknowledge the diverse political uses to which narrative is put in contemporary society.

The most common affirmative vision of power comes as a response to the "power over" model. This positive account of power
is developed in the theory of civic republicanism, versions of which
can be found in the work of Hannah Arendt, Robert Bellah, Jean
Bethke Elshtain, Alasdair MacIntyre, and others. This tradition
justifies some uses of power by stressing a conception of the "public interest" or the "common good"; it emphasizes civic virtue and
the citizen's role within a larger community. In opposition to the
sometimes atomizing language of liberalism, it employs the vocabulary of belonging and commitment. This tradition has been under-
going something of a revival in American political and legal[14] discourse, prompted in part by some strands of feminism, which seek
a more interrelational politics, and in part by dissatisfaction with
the incoherence of contemporary life. The difficulty, of course, is
coming up with a vision of the common good that does not privilege the values of some groups while excluding those of others.

Hannah Arendt has written the most thorough defense of the
republican vision of power. She begins by asserting a fundamental
principle of republicanism, that "it is the people's support that
lends power to the institutions of a country" (62). From this notion,
she derives a definition of power that emphasizes consensus and
cooperation: power is nothing more than the ability "to act in
concert" (64). Power belongs only to the group as a whole, never to
an individual. Hence Arendt must distinguish power from strength,
which is a personal attribute, and from violence and coercion,
which are merely instrumental in nature. The power of those in
authority — power over others — rests on the support of those governed, or else it becomes violence. This may seem a thin and unduly
optimistic description of power,[15] but it has the virtue of emphasizing a fact that is often overlooked in cultural criticism: that some
manifestations of power are worthy of respect, some social arrangements are better than others. Whether one endorses a republican ideal or not, it is important to keep in mind that power has a
positive as well as a negative face.

Is there a positive account of power that corresponds to Foucault's disciplinary model?[16] I think there is, and although it cannot
boast the long intellectual heritage of civic republicanism, it has
lately acquired some eloquent expositors among theorists of "practice" and "everyday life." Pierre Bourdieu and Michel de Certeau,

two of the most important of these theorists, are interested in the way ordinary people actually live amid the structures of societies. Like Foucault, Bourdieu uses the word "strategy" to characterize a type of practice that cannot be accounted for by rules. Drawing on anthropological studies of Kabylia, he examines several "practices," including marriage, gift giving, household economy, the division of the agricultural calendar, and the organization of labor. Marriage, for example, is governed by rules of kinship, eligibility, inheritance, relations between the sexes, the role of younger sons, and so on. But within these rules, strategies arise for emphasizing one's strengths and disguising one's weaknesses, playing one set of traditions off against another, and exploiting ambiguities or contradictions within the rules. Such practices are temporal in character, because they depend on the parties' ignorance of the outcome. Rules, by contrast, totalize experience, transforming a risky, improvisational, and irreversible process into an already-completed structure, and hence can be thought of as spatial.

Practice is by no means a realm of unrestricted freedom. To the contrary, practices are generated and organized by what Bourdieu calls *habitus*, "systems of durable, transposable *dispositions*," which are "objectively 'regulated' and 'regular' without in any way being the product of obedience to rules, objectively adapted to their goals without presupposing a conscious aiming at ends or an express mastery of the operations necessary to attain them" (72). The participants are often not conscious of the true meaning of their actions. Deeply embedded in the realm of the familiar, practice leaves unsaid everything that goes without saying. When agents attempt to provide an explanation of their behavior, their language "conceals, even from their own eyes, the true nature of their practical mastery, i.e. that it is *learned ignorance* (*docta ignorantia*), a mode of practical knowledge not comprising knowledge of its own principles" (19). Strategies, in fact, depend on this ignorance – or on a misrecognition (*méconnaissance*) of what is really occurring. In Kabylian gift giving, for example, the system presupposes a collective blindness to the economic, highly "interested" relations of kinship and alliance behind the supposedly disinterested exchange of presents. This misrecognition, in turn, helps to reproduce and sustain the existing conditions of domination.

There is a split, in Bourdieu's work, between the closed, perdurable systems of *habitus* and the open, unstable temporality of practice. Both give accounts of power, accounts that cannot adequately be theorized in terms of rules (or of domination from above), but *habitus* more obviously supports the status quo than the other. Both operate with what Foucault would call a disciplinary conception of power, but practice emphasizes the positive, creative side of that power. De Certeau criticizes Bourdieu for this split and argues that he uses *habitus* to tame the "sly multiplicity of strategies" (58). In the works of de Certeau, on the other hand, the positive side of a disciplinary conception of power is openly celebrated.

De Certeau explicitly locates his notion of the "practice of everyday life" in relation to Foucault's theory of power. "If it is true that the grid of 'discipline' is everywhere becoming clearer and more extensive, it is all the more urgent to discover how an entire society resists being reduced to it, what popular procedures . . . manipulate the mechanisms of discipline and conform to them only in order to evade them" (xiv). He prefers to call these popular procedures "tactics" rather than "strategies" (the word used by Bourdieu and Foucault), because "tactics" seems to capture more effectively the provisional, opportunistic character of these responses. If strategic planning implies a general outline for an entire conflict, tactics suggests isolated and independent decisions, judgments made on the spot, under the pressure of engagement, often on foreign territory. A tactic makes use of chance advantages and unexpected weaknesses; it capitalizes on surprises and small ruses; it engages in quick raids and guerrilla movements; it seizes the moment. De Certeau explores the tactical dimension in such everyday practices as talking, moving about, reading, shopping, and cooking, but he focuses on certain procedures that appear to highlight the devious creativity of the ordinary—games, gift giving, figurative language, what the French call *la perruque*, and, of special interest to this discussion, storytelling.

In all these activities, temporality takes precedence over the spatial grids of disciplines, and the weak elements in the system make use of the strong. Perhaps the most interesting of these procedures for members of a consumer society is consumption itself. De Certeau describes how ordinary habits of consumption can work against the grain of disciplinary orders and become a form of secondary production. Consumers transform the dominant economy by using products in unintended ways; by reading their own messages into the productions of the media; by colonizing certain public spaces, such as shopping malls, while ignoring others; by introducing innumerable small changes into their environment; and by "popularizing" or "degrading" elite culture. In the tactic of *la perruque*, the worker performs private tasks on the employer's time. A temporal art (the worker steals time, not goods), this activity transforms the workplace—the very heart of the established order—into a locus of free, pleasurable, and "unproductive" labor. In figurative language, a popular art of speaking distorts ordinary language, inscribing the feints, the circumventions, the displacements and delays that a rationalized, disciplinary order would deny. The practical effects of gift giving were mentioned in the discussion of Bourdieu, and I want to save the question of narrative—perhaps the most important tactic of all—for extended discussion in a later chapter.

Like Hannah Arendt's positive response to the "power over" model, de Certeau's affirmative vision of a society ruled by disciplinary power seems too optimistic. It appears to gloss over the way popular tactics can be coopted by the dominant economy. In the years since *The Practice of Everyday Life* was published, pessimistic critiques of postmodernism and of popular culture have emerged to challenge such a utopian vision. Still, one should not dismiss entirely the protean gifts of ordinary people, the ability to change tactics at the very moment when a practice has become commercialized. A more balanced account would attend to both the creative and the imprisoning power of disciplines, just as it would attend to the ideal of a common good, as well as to the frequent reality of domination from above. This position is the one I work toward in the current study. Critics must recognize that domination occurs both from above—by those with power over others—and from within—through their own cherished disciplines. Equally, critics must recognize the possibility of two kinds of resistance—overt resistance to those with power over others and local, strategic resistance to the disciplines that organize the positions subjects may take. Finally, critics should welcome the fact that both kinds of power have positive, creative uses—protecting freedoms, promoting diversity, and enhancing the quality of lives.

Power itself is neither good nor bad, positive nor negative. There are only better or worse uses of power, more or less just arrangements of society. Then why have I felt it necessary to describe some positive conceptions of power? The tendency of literary theorists to focus only on the dyad of domination/resistance has made it hard for them to see the ways in which legitimating norms can be enabling as well as constraining. Cultural norms exclude and contain, to be sure, but they also *empower*. It is important to keep both sides of this recognition in mind when considering contemporary cultural productions, particularly those of marginalized groups. The creation of counternorms through an exercise of cultural power can help open society to alternative perspectives. Minority groups have a special interest in the legitimating power of culture — its ability to legitimate the dominant ideology, of course, but also its ability to consolidate subterranean values, to preserve marginal traditions, and to confirm as subjects people who have long been denied that status.

The contrasting perspectives on power outlined above may help critics bring to their discussions of narrative a more flexible sense of its political uses. If, in today's society, there are multiple kinds of power regulating lives; multiple forms of resistance adapted to these modes of power; and multiple ways of employing each mode of power for positive ends, then critics must learn to be more subtle in assessing the political value of all cultural forms.

The Power of Culture in Today's Society

At the beginning of this chapter, I argued that both the erosion of boundaries among different forms of writing and the splintering of culture into contending groups contributed to a repositioning of the cultural realm within society. Important as these cultural changes are, they alone are not responsible for the increased prestige of narrative and other cultural forms. Equally important are contemporary changes in social and economic conditions. Two developments seem of particular relevance: the emergence of a multicultural society and of a postindustrial economy.

Perhaps the most visible, and in many circles disturbing, social change in recent decades has been the increasing activism of once marginal groups. The expression of political demands by racial minorities — such as African-Americans, Chicanos, Asian-Americans, and Native Americans — as well as by diverse social groups, including feminists, gay men and lesbians, people with disabilities, and the elderly, has resulted in a new form of politics, what has been called the "new social movements" or the "politics of identity."[17] Daniel Bell describes this trend as a "participation revolution" in which "many more groups now seek to establish their social rights — their claims on society — through the political order" (*Post-Industrial* 365, 364). Many commentators, including Bell, worry that this revolution will lead to chaos because our country will lose all sense of a shared identity and consequently the ability to coordinate policy on a national level. One need endorse neither Bell's fears nor his proposed solutions to recognize the acuteness of his analysis. He discusses the multiplication of constituencies (160); the increasing primacy of the group, rather than the individual, as a political unit (301); the changing networks of social relationships — from kinship to occupational and issue-oriented affiliations (189); the role of project grants and mission orientation in dispersing the centralized power of institutions and corporations (249); and the alteration of classic bureaucratic structure by the growth of nonprofit organizations (324). The orientation of social movements today toward specific issues cuts across older ways of organizing the social body (political party, class, etc.), and this fact applies to movements located along the entire spectrum of contemporary values: environmentalism, the peace movement, lesbian and gay rights, pro-choice and pro-life movements, the campaigns for and against gun control, and religious fundamentalism.

Since this reorganization of the social body is often labeled fragmentation and treated as one of the most intractable problems confronting our nation, it might be useful to recall some of the strengths of this new dispensation. To begin with, identity politics, which derives its power as much from a consumer economy as from a democratic polity, may succeed in changing social attitudes — and hence altering everyday practices — in patterns that are out of sync with legislative or judicial decisions from on high. The way women's roles have continued to change despite the failure of the Equal Rights Amendment is one example; the increase in visibility of lesbian and gay lifestyles despite the Supreme Court's decision in

Bowers v. Hardwick (and despite the enormous risks involved in such visibility) is another.[18] I am not suggesting that misogyny or homophobia have disappeared — not when violence toward women is as pervasive as ever and HIV infection is used as an excuse for new forms of discrimination, to say nothing of the persistence of many old forms of prejudice — but I am arguing that local practices, which are given power by an advanced capitalist economy, can offset some of the effects of domination from above. Further, I am not advocating fragmentation but only suggesting that social diversity does not have to be regarded as an unmitigated evil. What some people label fragmentation may be the sign of alternative communities that mark out greater areas of choice and freedom.

However one views the rise of new social movements and identity politics, it is clear that their advent has contributed enormously to the power of cultural forms.[19] The very term "multiculturalism," which the media have turned into both a rallying cry and a scare word, captures the centrality of cultural phenomena to political battles in the nineties.

The transformation of our economy over the course of the last three decades is the other major external cause of the altered position of culture. In the United States today, the manufacture and dissemination of information has replaced the production of goods as the primary economic activity. This shift has given us the first service economy, in which more than half of the work force is involved in neither agriculture nor industry but in providing services to other people. The dominant sector in this service economy consists of what has been called the "knowledge class": a population that includes not only writers, educators, administrators, and archivists but also the media, advertising, communications workers, and data processors; not only think tanks, consulting firms, lobbying organizations, and regulatory agencies but also the traditional professions — law, medicine, and the ministry. All these groups are involved in the production, administration, and diffusion of knowledge or expertise. As Daniel Bell puts it, "the heart of the post-industrial society is a class that is primarily a professional class"; and he adds, "A profession is a learn*ed* (i.e. scholarly) activity, and thus involves formal training, but within a broad intellectual context. To be within the profession means to be certified, formally or informally, by one's peers or by some established body within the profession. And a profession embodies a norm of social responsiveness" (*Post-Industrial* 374).[20] If Bell is correct, then many features of what was once regarded as the cultural realm—learning or scholarship, formal training, certification by degree or examination, and a norm of social responsiveness—now characterize the dominant sector of our economy.

The transition to what has variously been called the "postindustrial society," the "knowledge" or "information society," or simply "postmodernism" means that people trained in intellectual and cultural disciplines influence many apparently social or political decisions.[21] This group's power stems from "its virtual control over the society's educational apparatus, technical expertise, mass media, its demographic concentration in urban areas, and . . . its general affinities with the world view of modernity" (Wuthnow et al. 69). This power, however, differs from the customary understanding of power. It is not individual but neither is it precisely collective: it arises from one's participation in established networks of expertise, a participation that inevitably contains both individual and collective aspects. Lyotard has painted a particularly glowing picture of this situation: "a person is always located at 'nodal points' of specific communication circuits, however tiny these may be"; and "no one, not even the least privileged among us, is ever entirely powerless over the messages that traverse and position him" (*Postmodern* 15). This comment glosses over the fact that some people have vastly more power over such networks than others,[22] but it does make the point that in an information society, an important source of power is the ability to influence "messages," an ability one would traditionally describe as cultural.

Commentators who lament that contemporary intellectuals only talk to one another do not take into account the changed organization of our economy. Intellectuals have a distinctive form of power today *because* they talk to one another, because they speak to and from disciplines.[23] Nostalgia for a vanished social world, in which the individual genius spoke to a general public, will not bring back the social conditions that made that scenario possible. In the nineteenth century, if a robber baron read poetry, the only social, economic, or political effects this activity could have were indirect: he might be humanized by the experience, and as a result, he might change his behavior toward his wife (social), or change the conditions of employment for his workers (economic), or advise the President not to go to war (political). Improbable as this sequence might seem, it is the principal way that culture can be said to have had power in the modern era. In the postmodern era, when a professional working in a knowledge industry participates in cultural activities, this participation directly affects the material with which the professional works—knowledge, information (in short, the revised notion of culture). To put it another way, the realm of culture is congruent with the realm of material production. There is no division, no marginalizing split, between intellectual activity and the everyday business of life.

Some theorists agree with this description of the changed position of culture but contend that this new location only creates new opportunities for ideological conscription. Paul Bové, for example, has written an eloquent account of the political obstacles that face oppositional critics: "Even the most revisionist, adversarial, and oppositional humanistic intellectuals—no matter what their avowed ideologies—operate within a network of discourses, institutions, and desires that . . . always reproduce themselves in essentially antidemocratic forms and practices" (*Intellectuals* 1–2). This book takes another view, and the chapters that follow attempt to illustrate how the activity of novelists, critics, and scholars can have diverse political effects, some conservative, others progressive. It is the inscription of intellectual work within larger networks of "discourses, institutions, and desires" that makes culture matter today. Jonathan Arac anticipated my position exactly when he wrote in 1987: "Postmodern critics . . . can carry on a significant political activity by relating the concerns once enclosed within 'literature' to a broader cultural sphere that is itself related to, although not identical with, the larger concerns of the state and economy" (*Critical* 308). The crucial word is "can," for nothing ensures that writers will. All the same, I find it possible to sustain a cautious optimism about the power of culture today.

Other people are still more sanguine. The altered position of culture in contemporary Western societies has become so prominent that some authors now invert the old hierarchy and claim that cultural forces are more influential than economic conditions. Marshall Sahlins takes this position when he argues for the symbolic construction of both nature and practice. According to Sahlins, material forces do not determine cultural forms, because the "social existence of material force" is itself "determined by its integration in the cultural system" (206). Whereas some Marxists have talked of culture reproducing the dominant modes of production, Sahlins reverses the terms, claiming that "production is thus the reproduction of the culture in a system of objects" (178). A similar argument comes from Daniel Bell, who maintains that the changing conditions of postindustrial society have made culture "supreme" (*Cultural* 33). Finally, Mark Poster, a historian of Marxism, has suggested that the advent of the information society should force changes in Marxist views of the priority of base to superstructure (39–40).

This inversion may be a necessary corrective to the long neglect of culture by social theorists. But merely turning relations upside down seems mistaken. Many theorists have been insufficiently historical in considering these questions. A better example is the historical perspective of Pierre Bourdieu, who sees culture as crucial in reproducing social hierarchy but who also views it as functioning differently in different historical periods. In his history of what he calls "symbolic capital," culture is seen as a dominant force in precapitalist societies but as a subsidiary power in modern (industrial) capitalism. In industrial capitalism the very effectiveness of economic modes of domination makes symbolic power—in the form of myths, rituals, religious ceremonies, royal pomp, and so on—less necessary. But postindustrial societies seem to revive aspects of the precapitalist paradigm. Now that the Enlightenment project of demystification, which contributed to the spread of capitalism, has been extended to the institutions of capitalism itself, symbolic power is needed once again to reinforce the social bonds. Certainly, the renewed concern with symbolic, ritual, and narrative forms in the social sciences would suggest that the role of symbolic power is increasing in their worlds. The prominence of traditional forms and oral narrative in literary works in the eighties and nineties, which I will examine in later chapters, suggests something similar about other worlds.

Let me conclude by registering an important qualification. Nothing I have said about the new power of culture in society is meant

to suggest that this power is necessarily benign or uplifting or enno-
bling. The fact that the realms of culture and material production
interpenetrate does not mean that both are not (or may not become) cheap, degraded, or demeaning. But the responsibility is
with us. The question of how culture affects society lies in our
hands. Our practices, our interventions at the particular places
where we live or work, our effect on the messages that traverse us
will help to determine the kind of world we inhabit. As the chapters
that follow will make clear, this claim is not meant to mobilize
the liberal self for a lonely crusade against the dehumanization of
modern society. Rather, this vision of cultural power depends on
other models of agency and other conceptions of the subject. But
the potential to make a difference, for good or for ill, is here
today, as it perhaps was not for an older cultural figure of the type
Humboldt represented.

"Maybe America didn't need art and inner miracles. It had so many
outer ones. The USA was a big operation, very big" (5). So the
narrator of *Humboldt's Gift* muses, reflecting on a poet who was
never able to reimagine his relation to power. Humboldt could not
discover the "next thing, the new thing, the necessary thing for
poets to do" (150). Who has discovered the next thing? What shape
does this necessary work take? Can one point to the new thing
itself?

In the next chapter, I look at literary theorists of narrative to see
if they have an answer to these questions. I examine what a variety
of narrative theorists — structuralist and poststructuralist — have to
say about narrative's relation to society. It turns out that there is
an active, if strangely limited, discourse on this topic. In this first
chapter, however, I have already laid the groundwork for answer-
ing these questions. In one sense, the answer must be no; one
cannot single out the new thing itself. A characteristic of the next
work to be done is its anonymity. We are in a great age for literature, a great period for culture in the United States, but a feature
of that greatness is the disappearance of the old Romantic notion
of the masterpiece. Some works are better than others, some contemporary novels still move the heart to tears and the mind to
rejoice, but their power does not lie in that excellence, at least not
wholly. It lies in their participation in larger networks of discourse

and in their ability to attract, to hold, and to shape particular communities of readers. In another sense, the answer to these questions is yes; I have all along been pointing to this new work, this necessary thing, even when talking about Bellow's novel. For *Humboldt's Gift*, like all the texts in this domain of Babel, has its power too.

2

The Story of Deconstruction

Song of Solomon (1977), Toni Morrison's novel about a young black man growing up in the middle of the United States in the middle of the twentieth century, dwells on politics and poetics with equal fervor. The novel dramatizes some pressing contemporary problems—racial inequality, class conflict, terrorism, the oppression of women, and the division between generations; but it also explores some perennial aesthetic topics—the value of oral traditions, the magic of names, the nature of myth and ritual, the power of story and song. This fusion of contemporary politics and traditional narrative forms has created much satisfying fiction, not only in Morrison's hands but also in those of many other contemporary writers. So perhaps I should ask how Morrison mediates between her interest in storytelling and her political concerns. What link does her novel establish between the narrative forms it celebrates and structures of social, economic, or political power?

Midway through the novel, her protagonist, Milkman, hears that a bag hanging in his aunt Pilate's shack might be full of gold, but this news hardly interests him at all. The money represents his father's world, and it is his father who is obsessed with stealing the gold. Milkman is too confused right now to care about getting rich himself. But the moment he tells his friend Guitar about the gold, something strange occurs. He begins to grow excited. The act of telling the story seems to stimulate desire. For the first time in his life, he knows what he wants and is willing to act to possess it. In the language of contemporary theory, Milkman becomes a desiring subject. His new desire has several immediate consequences. For one, it gives him a stronger sense of self; for another, it provides him with a new social confidence. With such a story to tell, he knows he will be accepted by the older black men who congregate at Railroad Tommy's.

These developments are all welcome enough, but Morrison also registers some of the negative consequences of having a story to tell. Milkman's new desire is not his own. In order to be accepted, he has taken on the desire of others — his father's craving for money as well as Guitar's eagerness for adventure — and the self he has acquired is alien also. The more intensely Milkman feels these desires, the more completely he exposes their derivative nature. By the time he thinks he has found the gold, the terms of his desire have expanded beyond their origin in the fantasies of his father and Guitar to embrace the dreams of the culture at large. The smell of money, in Milkman's frantic metaphors, becomes an anthology of debased cultural symbols, the most shopworn coins of an acquisitive realm:

> He smelled money, although it was not a smell at all. It was like candy and sex and soft twinkling lights. Like piano music with a few strings in the background. . . . Las Vegas and buried treasure; numbers dealers and Wells Fargo wagons; race track pay windows and spewing oil wells; craps, flushes, and sweepstakes tickets. Auctions, bank vaults, and heroin deals. (250-1)

Narrative's role in constituting the subject is double-edged. It assigns Milkman a position of his own, as an adult among others in a defined social world, but it also ensures that this position is thoroughly mediated by the desires of others. Authorizing him to speak, it tends to limit his words to the already spoken. This paradox, and even the terms in which I have phrased it, are familiar to those who pay attention to poststructuralist theory, particularly deconstruction. Morrison's novel, like much recent fiction, confronts the same problems that preoccupy many literary theorists. This point lends support to Henry Louis Gates's contention that the African-American tradition has developed its own version of many of the ideas now common in poststructuralism. But it also suggests that the division between literature in general and other forms of discourse, including criticism and theory, is not as great as is often supposed.

When Morrison implies that Milkman's identity is not his own but is bound up with the cultural system of which he has just become an adult member, her insight reveals the ideological content of apparently innocent symbolic practices. This posture of suspicion, if so dramatic a characterization may be allowed for the present, is the prevailing attitude of most deconstructive thinking about narrative. Deconstructive critics, who have frequently been accused of being unconcerned with politics, were among the first writers after structuralism to articulate a political critique of narrative. By the early seventies, they were already arguing that the conventions of narrative are not neutral structures; that the formal characteristics of storytelling convey assumptions about life, independent of the content; and that the power of narrative establishes and sustains networks of power beyond the text. These assumptions now represent the largest common ground joining novelists with literary and social theorists from a wide variety of disciplines and from diverse critical schools, including some of the historicist and political criticisms that have been most vocal in attacking deconstruction.

The question of whether deconstruction is "conservative" or "radical" has been argued with great passion and for diverse polemical agendas.[1] The discovery of Paul de Man's early journalism for a collaborationist newspaper in occupied Belgium has occasioned an enormous amount of discussion about whether his mature writings contained a hidden political content.[2] I do not intend to weigh, once again, the virtually imponderable question of whether this literary theory entails one political position rather than another. But I do want to show how even a movement accused of formalism and arid intellectualism participates in the political turn of contemporary culture. This alternative goal helps clarify why versions of deconstruction have been important to some political actors engaged in specific struggles to change society: members of the Critical Legal Studies and the Critical Race Theory movements,[3] some feminist and minority critics, working in a variety of academic disciplines,[4] and even some Marxists.[5] In the process, it demonstrates one of the connections between intellectual discourse and specific social conflicts.

The title of this chapter should be taken in two ways: it implies that deconstruction has a stance toward narrative, but it also implies that deconstruction *has* a narrative, a story that organizes the positions it takes fully as much as Milkman's story shapes him. The former implication will take us into a survey of deconstruction's chief contributions to narrative theory, but the latter implication determines my answer to the question of deconstruction's politics. The narrative implicit in the practice of deconstruction in the United States over the last fifteen years inscribes its subjects in a politics and gives their position agency and power.

Intertextual Networks

The analysis of the ideological dimension of narrative represents a departure from the structuralist project that has come to be called "narratology." From its earliest phase, the investigations of Vladimir Propp into the morphology of the Russian fairytale, the question of a story's relation to the larger culture was left out. In his search for the invariant structure of a finite body of tales, Propp bracketed such considerations, maintaining that they were part of the historical and the evaluative branches of literary study but had nothing to do with elucidating formal principles (106). The now classic structuralist studies of Todorov, Bremond, Greimas, and Barthes continued this division, isolating the object of analysis as part of their search for narrative's distinctive grammar, matrix, or code. In Barthes's words, "the narrational code should be the final level attainable by our analysis, other than by going outside of the narrative-object" ("Introduction" 115).

The case of Barthes is exemplary, for his subsequent turn away from structuralism reflects the more general tendency in narrative studies since the early seventies. In his "Introduction to the Structural Analysis of Narratives" (1966) he synthesized the work of earlier theorists in an effort to present a total description of narrative structure. But a few years later he renounced this ambition, declaring that "the destruction of meta-language" should be part of any adequate theory of the text ("Work" 164). In part, his dissatisfaction with structuralism grew out of his interest in power. The search for a metalanguage involves an effort of abstraction that makes the analysis of narrative's connections with the social world difficult. Throughout his career Barthes was concerned to move beyond the limits of formal analysis, but in his structuralist phase he could see no way to accomplish such a task other than by shifting modes of analysis. "Just as linguistics stops at the sentence," he wrote, "so narrative analysis stops at discourse — from there it is necessary to shift to another semiotics" ("Introduction" 115–16). In works such as *Mythologies* he produced "another semiotics" that did not stop at the analysis of discourse but involved a reading of culture. But the gap between his structuralist studies of narrative and his cultural criticism indicated that the relationship between the two projects remained unexamined. Just a few years later, however, he published *S/Z* (1970), a work that was influential in the turn of narrative studies away from the structuralist project.

Although originally received in the United States as a continuation of Barthes's structuralist investigations, *S/Z* actually represented a radical departure.[6] This shift was announced on the very first page: "we shall, [structuralists] thought, extract from each tale its model, then out of these models we shall make a great narrative structure, which we shall reapply (for verification) to any one narrative: a task as exhausting (ninety-nine percent perspiration, as the saying goes) as it is ultimately undesirable, for the text thereby loses its difference" (3). The five codes he proposed in *S/Z* gave the appearance of being another structuralist formula but were in fact opposed to the entire enterprise. These codes were not intended to describe an invariant structure so much as to indicate the multiple ways in which a text produces its plural readings. "Hence we use *Code* here not in the sense of a list, a paradigm that must be reconstituted. . . . The units which have resulted from it (those we inventory) are themselves, always, ventures out of the text" (*S/Z* 20).

Barthes's nonstructuralist use of narrative codes can be seen to follow from the theory of textuality that he and others were developing in the late sixties, the theory that would come to be known as intertextuality. Properly understood, Barthes's new insight would undermine the structuralist project, because intertextuality calls into question the belief that any piece of writing possesses a closed, determinate structure. In his widely read essay "From Work to Text" (1971), Barthes summarized the new attitude toward textuality. Unlike the work, which is a finite, ordered unit, Text is a methodological field that is experienced as an activity, a production of plural meanings. Text does not stop at the boundaries that define a work, or even a genre, but intersects with every kind of discourse, connects via association and cross-reference with whatever falls within the cultural field. Not surprisingly, this new conception of textuality requires a new form of analysis. As Barthes put it in an essay written in the same year, "[textual analysis] conceives the text as taken up in an *open* network which is the very infinity of language, itself structured without closure; it tries to say no longer *from where* the text comes (historical criticism), nor even *how* it is made (structural analysis), but how it is unmade, how it explodes, disseminates—by what coded paths it *goes off*" ("Struggle" 126-7). The important point is that the kind of textual analysis[7] that Barthes practices in *S/Z* moves outside the "narrative-object" in an endless inventory of the story's connections with other aspects of the culture.

From its first uses, the word "intertextuality" possessed a political valence that "structure" did not have. Julia Kristeva coined the term in 1966 in an essay introducing the works of Mikhail Bakhtin to the world of French intellectuals, including her teacher, Roland Barthes. Kristeva employed the ideas of this largely unknown Russian formalist to displace semiotics, shifting it toward a more openly ideological criticism. Like many critics today, Kristeva saw in Bakhtin a chance to open linguistics to society. "Bakhtin situates the text within history and society, which are then seen as texts read by the writer, and into which he inserts himself by rewriting them" (65). Bakhtin authorizes this attention to history by shifting linguistic analysis from the grammatical, atemporal plane to that of the individual utterance, which is always caught up in a context of other utterances. A sign can never be analyzed in isolation, for its meaning is always informed by the many, often conflicting ways it has been used by other speakers. The sign, in short, is "dialogic" and must be analyzed as part of a dialogue.

At the same time that Kristeva gives "intertextuality" a political turn by her invocation of Bakhtin, she transforms some of Bakhtin's concepts by reading them in conjunction with poststructuralist ideas drawn from Derrida. For instance, she slips "text" into a paraphrase of Bakhtin: "each word (text) is an intersection of words (texts) where at least one other word (text) can be read" (66). Though the parentheses imply that Kristeva is only supplying a synonym, or at most a neutral expansion of Bakhtin's concept, this textualization of Bakhtin changes his ideas—changes them just enough to allow the new concept of intertextuality to emerge. Thus she characterizes Bakhtin's "conception of the 'literary word' as an *intersection of textual surfaces* rather than a *point* (a fixed meaning), as a dialogue among several writings" (65; italics in the original). One cannot help but see Derrida's critique of voice behind this slight shift toward a dialogue of "writings" not "utterances," particularly since Kristeva cites *Of Grammatology* on the first page of her essay. A Derridean view of "writing" supplies a dimension that was not present in Bakhtin originally, the dimension of indeterminacy, of *différance*, of dissemination. Although Bakhtin's notions of "heteroglossia" or "hybridization" might seem near equivalents to the poststructuralist concepts, Bakhtin's emphasis on the historical uniqueness of the context of every utterance distances his terms from the endlessly expanding context of deconstruction.[8]

One way of characterizing the difference between the historicist mood of the eighties and early nineties and deconstructive thinking of the late sixties and early seventies is to note how the role of indeterminacy and endless play has receded, in accounts of intertextuality, in favor of Bakhtin's earlier emphasis on social context. But the development of the term "intertextuality" was a more complex intertextual event than is often acknowledged, an event that already included the potential for a politically oriented criticism. This potential was most visible in the critical practice of a figure whose gender and whose status as a nonnative speaker made her doubly marginal to the French intellectual establishment in the mid-sixties. I shall take up the ramifications of this fact at the end of the chapter, where I explore the subject position implicit in the narrative of deconstruction.

Although Barthes's criticism did not take the historicist path, the potential was there in his work too. I said above that Barthes's dissatisfaction with structuralism stemmed from his continuing preoccupation with power. The traces of that preoccupation are everywhere visible in *S/Z*. All five of the codes elaborated in this work are used to address issues of power. Three are integral to the development of ideology. The "semic" code establishes the attributes of character and hence "is linked to an ideology of the person" (191); the "symbolic" code identifies those antitheses that organize society, the oppositions of language, gender, or money; and the "cultural" code is the repository of the collective wisdom that originates in traditional human experience. Let us take a moment to look at the symbolic code. This code creates meaning through an "appropriative violence" (130) that names things according to its oppositional logic. "Meaning is a force," Barthes declares; "to name is to subject, and the more generic the nomination, the stronger the subjection" (129–30). Such a conception of meaning makes it easy to relate the symbolic code to systems of power beyond the work. Barthes writes, "the strongest meaning is the one whose systematization includes a large number of elements, to the point where it appears to include everything noteworthy in the world: thus great ideological systems which battle each other with strokes of meaning" (154).

The other two codes describe features of the text that structuralists regarded as essentially narrative. The "hermeneutic" code records enigmas, the source of a story's suspense, and the "proairetic" code charts sequences, the units that provide the linear armature for the other codes. Rather than isolating the "two sequential codes" (30) in a formal realm, the way some structuralists did, Barthes relates them to some of the founding notions of Western culture. The hermeneutic code is what gives the West its conception of truth: "Expectation thus becomes the basic condition for truth: truth, these narratives tell us, is what is *at the end* of expectation" (76). The proairetic code also functions "by and through the authority of the great models" (82). Both codes organize and are organized in turn by larger cultural patterns.

Although all five codes venture out of the text, Barthes does not value them equally. He characterizes the two sequential codes as decidedly retrograde. They are aligned with the old, the so-called classic text, which is less capable of producing multiple readings. Their very status as the building blocks of narrative excluded them from the explosive dissemination that characterizes the rest of the text. The linear and teleological orientations of these codes make them suspect. Here is Barthes's formulation: "of the five codes, only three establish permutable, reversible connections, outside the constraint of time (the semic, cultural, and symbolic codes); the other two impose their terms according to an irreversible order (the hermenueutic and proairetic codes). The classic text . . . is a multivalent but incompletely reversible system. What blocks its reversibility is just what limits the plural nature of the classic text" (30). Narrative is the villain that blocks the full plurality of the text.

This theme was repeated throughout the seventies in the writing of numerous other critics. It eventually became the basis of a consistent, although simplistic, critique of the ideological nature of narrative, a critique found not only in deconstructive writing but in other forms of poststructuralism. In works by Hayden White, J. Hillis Miller, Edward Said, and others, narrative was aligned with a conservative, inegalitarian, or authoritarian politics.

The Politics of Linearity

Hayden White, an historian who throughout his career has written on narrative's relation to modes of factual representation, tirelessly demonstrates that storytelling is a fundamental way of understanding reality. Beginning with *Metahistory* (1973) and continuing in numerous influential essays, he has argued that narratives (and particularly historical narratives) "emplot" reality by drawing on one of four masterplots, each of which can be coordinated with one of four mastertropes. The title of his latest collection of essays, *The Content of the Form* (1987), identifies the assumption he shares with the other writers in this chapter: that the formal conventions of narrative convey a message that is independent of the specific content of a story. In one of his most frequently cited essays, "The Value of Narrativity in the Representation of Reality" (1980), White's basic thesis was given a more overtly political inflection. Here he proposed not merely that narrative structures understanding but that it is implicated in the development of the modern legal state.

> We cannot but be struck by the frequency with which narrativity, whether of the fictional or the factual sort, presupposes the existence of a legal system against or on behalf of which the typical agents of a narrative account militate. And this raises the suspicion that narrative in general, from the folktale to the novel, from the annals to the fully realized "history," has to do with the topics of law, legality, legitimacy, or, more generally, *authority*. (17)

It is not just that the topics of law and authority appear in narrative as an important subject matter; it is that narrative is implicated *formally* in the emergence and maintenance of authority. The structure of narrative gives a shape, a moral coherence, to the events that have led up to the establishment of the current order. "Insofar as historical stories can be completed, can be given narrative closure, can be shown to have had a *plot* all along, they give to reality the odor of the *ideal*" ("Value" 24). Historical stories accomplish this feat by drawing on narrative's most venerable characteristic, the power of making events, which may be arbitrary or contingent, seem to possess "coherence, integrity, fullness, and closure" (27). In the process, narrative "makes the real desirable, makes the real into an object of desire" (24).[9]

White's theory sees the power of narrative as the power of exciting and fulfilling a desire. This perspective is not so far removed from that of Morrison. For all Milkman knew, the gold was real when his father first tried to persuade him to steal it. Narrative, however, made the real desirable. When Milkman told Guitar the story, the events that had appeared to have so little relevance to his life suddenly became full of significance. They took on a coherence, an integrity, and a fullness, which made them valuable to him, desirable in a way that mere bullion evidently was not. As I remarked earlier, Milkman's new desire is derivative. For Hayden White, the desire that narrative creates is always suspect. "The notion that sequences of real events possess the formal attributes of the stories we tell about imaginary events could only have its origin in wishes, daydreams, reveries" (27). Narrative teaches us that only those events that have the shape of a good story possess value and meaning, or the value of meaning.

J. Hillis Miller, one of the best-known exponents of deconstructive literary criticism and a writer who has spent much of his career exploring the question of narrative, advanced an argument in the mid-seventies that resembled White's in several respects. In an essay titled "Narrative and History" (1974), he outlined the traditional assumptions about narrative that have been shared by history and the novel. These assumptions

> include the notions of origin and end ("archeology" and "teleology"); of unity and totality or "totalization"; of underlying "reason" or "ground"; of selfhood, consciousness, or "human na-

ture"; of the homogeneity, linearity, and continuity of time; of
necessary progress; of "fate," "destiny," or "Providence"; of causality; of gradually emerging "meaning"; of representation and
truth. (459–60)

All of these assumptions are features of Barthes's two sequential
codes, and they are what lead White to associate narrative with
authority. Again, in Miller, one finds that these assumptions are
regarded as a species of mystification. Such naive beliefs about
history arise when readers take fictional structures, which are created by and only exist in narrative, as literal descriptions of reality.
Miller differed from Barthes and White by locating the error exclusively in a mistake about language: "the fundamental linguistic
error of taking a figure of speech literally" (464). The assumptions
listed above depend upon mistaking a part for the whole, forgetting
the figurative status of the metonomy that is narrative. Miller's
deconstruction consisted of showing how even a masterpiece of
realistic fiction such as *Middlemarch* subverts the system of assumptions upon which it depends. At crucial moments, "the novel,
so to speak, pulls the rug out from under itself and deprives itself
of that solid ground without which, if Henry James is right, it is
'nowhere'" (467).

Miller's conception of deconstruction was not merely negative,
however. Side by side with the naive assumptions generated by
narrative, *Middlemarch* asserts an alternative system of ideas.
These different assumptions depend upon textual relations very
similar to the "permutable, reversible connections" established by
Barthes's other three codes. Miller wrote:

> The concepts of origin, end, and continuity are replaced by the
> categories of repetition, of difference, of discontinuity, of open-
> ness, and of the free and contradictory struggle of individual
> human energies, each seen as a center of interpretation, which
> means misinterpretation, of the whole. (467)

These categories — of repetition, difference, discontinuity, openness, and interpretation — all have special significance for Miller.
For the moment, it is important to emphasize that Miller believed
both sets of assumptions were evoked by every narrative text. This
attention to subversion signals one of his differences from White

and one of his affinities with Barthes. Like the latter, who traced both the sequential and the reversible codes in *Sarrasine*, Miller found the traditional notions of origin, end, unity, selfhood, linearity, progress, Providence, causality, meaning, and truth in the narrative, "along with [their] subversion" (470).

Miller's technique in this essay, which has come to be called "double reading," represents deconstruction's greatest contribution to narrative studies. In the seven interpretations of English novels that make up *Fiction and Repetition* (1982), Miller gives extended examples of this technique at work, and in even more recent works on ethics in literature, such as *The Ethics of Reading* (1987) and *Versions of Pygmalion* (1990), he continues to explore many of the same concerns. Again Miller asserts both the relation between narrative and authority and the subversion of that relation: "There is a peculiar and unexpected relation between the affirmation of universal moral law and storytelling[,] . . . even if that storytelling in one way or another puts in question or subverts the moral law" (*Ethics* 2).

Another example of the importance of double reading to the development of a deconstructive approach to narrative was Cynthia Chase's article, "The Decomposition of the Elephants: Double-Reading *Daniel Deronda*" (1978). This well-known article offered a deconstruction of George Eliot's novel and, "by implication, of story in general" (216), through the procedure of locating self-contradictory aspects of the text. These contradictions ranged from a single comic sentence by a minor character, to a crucial episode in the Deronda plot, to the rival conceptions of language invoked by the text. Jonathan Culler generalized Chase's argument (along with two other examples of double reading) into a critique of a fundamental narratological distinction—that between story and discourse. In accordance with the method of double reading, Culler found two logics at work in narrative: "These two logics cannot be brought together in harmonious synthesis; each works by the exclusion of the other; each depends on a hierarchical relation between story and discourse which the other inverts" (*Pursuit* 175).

Adversaries of deconstruction have asked how double reading differs from the process of analyzing ambiguity in a work of literature, a process that the New Critics made common. There are at least three important differences. First, double reading reveals a contradiction that exists in every text and that is involuntary, uncontrolled by the author's craft or intention. Second, it locates the place where a text calls into question the very principle upon which the text depends for its order and meaning. As Paul de Man puts it, one cannot say "that the poem simply has two meanings that exist side by side. The two readings have to engage each other in direct confrontation, for the one reading is precisely the error denounced by the other" (12). Third, this conflict is not resolved at a higher level of analysis into a harmonious or balanced whole. Instead of looking for the way in which the literary object achieves unity, double reading shows the way in which fundamental linguistic conditions dictate that every text is internally fissured.

In double reading, as in most deconstructive criticism from the seventies, the analysis of power was merely oblique. Miller, for example, implied that the "metaphysical" notions evoked by narrative were connected with the social and political orders. In his most recent books, he makes this relationship the center of his inquiry, but he still views the connection as an unchanging feature of language, textuality, and reading. As double reading was elaborated in the seventies, it did not involve an historical account of how narrative intersected with specific social or political formations.

Edward Said's long, difficult book *Beginnings: Intention and Method* (1975) did much to promote the ideas of French poststructuralism in the United States, though it carefully discriminated its more Foucauldian perspective from the deconstructive views on intertextuality found in Derrida. In subsequent works Said has become one of the foremost advocates of a committed political criticism. The essays collected in *The World, the Text, and the Critic* (1983) offered one version of what I have just said deconstruction lacked, an explicitly historical theory of the relation between text and politics. *Orientalism* (1978) put this theory in practice and seemed to modify some of the conclusions about narrative reached in *Beginnings*. It is worth attending to the narrative theory developed in *Beginnings*, however, both because of its relation to the deconstructive strategy of double reading and because of its continuing influence on the field of narrative studies.

In *Beginnings* Said repeatedly contrasted the writing of twentieth-century modernists with that of earlier authors, especially nineteenth-century realistic novelists. This contrast established once again a hierarchy in which the later, permutable structures were privileged at the expense of the earlier, narrative forms. Like Miller, Said phrased his account in terms of one set of assumptions replacing another:

> The series being replaced is the set of relationships linked together by familial analogy: father and son, the image, the process of genesis, a story. In their place stands: the brother, discontinuous concepts, paragenesis, construction. The first of these series is dynastic, bound to sources and origins, mimetic. The relationships holding in the second series are complementarity and adjacency; instead of a source we have the intentional beginning, instead of a story a construction. (66)

A number of these terms had special meanings for Said, but the general drift of his argument should be clear. Narrative was seen as one of several structures (others included the family and the image) that bound one inflexibly within a continuous line of development. Narrative established a dynastic rather than an egalitarian relationship among its terms, and it supported a mimetic view of representation in which words imitated rather than displaced their objects.

Said's view of the novel in *Beginnings* can be characterized as deconstructive because of his insistence on the role of self-contradiction in the formation of the genre. From the beginning—as a condition *of* its beginning—the novel was shaped by a contradiction between "authority" and what he calls "molestation" (an unfortunate term, as I shall show). As a central concept in Said's book, authority acquires complex, suggestive meanings, but the kinds of relations it is said to have with narrative are indicated by the above quotation. Both authority and narrative are grounded in notions of a generative beginning, a source that can control its issue and maintain the continuity of its course. Narrative creates authority, but at the same time one must have authority to begin to narrate. Molestation, by contrast, is a term for whatever undermines those notions that give a narrative authority. "Molestation, then, is a consciousness of one's duplicity, one's confinement to a fictive, scriptive realm, whether one is a character or a novelist" (84).

As a secular genre, the novel is haunted by the inevitability of molestation, of the way molestation inhabits authority from the very beginning. Each of the three special conditions that Said thought characterized the institution of the novel involves some kind of awareness that the authority of narrative is constructed by discourse itself (see 88–93). This awareness did not discredit the novel for Said; rather, it was something of a badge of honor, displayed surreptitiously by the more courageous nineteenth-century texts but worn openly on the jacket sleeve of modernist fictions. Perhaps the chief way the institution of the novel reveals its awareness of the conditions that have made it possible—its awareness, that is, of the constructed nature of authority—is by challenging or replacing narrative. Challenging narrative represents an advance in knowledge, a contribution—made by the novel itself, as a speculative instrument of intelligence—to the development of Western rationality.

Unlike some deconstructive critics, Said did not stop with pointing out narrative's role in constructing authority. He went on to argue that even a constructed authority retains a valid intentionality, a power (demystified, deconstructed, yet still effective) to initiate projects in the real world. This additional step was important. It represented an attempt to find a place for agency in writing without returning to the notion of an individual creative subject. Said was interested in event as well as structure, social change as well as system; and these interests accounted for his insistence that beginnings produce both a break with the past and a direction for new work. Texts must retain authority if they are to make a difference, do something that matters in the world, but this authority must not be dependent on mystified notions of the autonomous self, the individual's originary genius: "authority cannot reside simply in the speaker's anterior privilege" (*Beginnings* 23). Said maintained that "beginning is a consciously intentional, productive activity" (372), even though his deconstructions showed that nothing grounds consciousness, intentionality, production, or act. Further, he maintained that a "beginning intends meaning" (373), even in the kind of text that has repudiated narrative in favor of "discontinuity," "adjacency," "nonlinear development," "complementarity," "orders of dispersion," and "nonnarratable units of knowledge" (282, 373).

Said's project may be seen as an early attempt to define what, in the next section, I shall call the "subject of deconstruction." My phrase suggests that there is a position of agency—a subject that acts—despite one's awareness that such a position or subject is socially constructed rather than natural or God-given. The problem with Said's formulation of this idea in *Beginnings*, however, lay in his belief that this position must be nonnarrative.[10] A demystified notion of intentionality may be conveyed by discontinuity and dispersion, but there is no reason why it may not also be conveyed by narrative. After all, the association of the fully psychologized, autonomous self with the protagonist of a narrative is a relatively recent invention. In prior historical periods—above all, in oral-narrative societies—the subject of narrative was often a transindividual construction, as Said's own discussion of Homer showed (56-8). My discussion in Chapter 4 of the pragmatics of micronarratives in contemporary society will suggest that in many situations the subject of narrative is once again becoming an intersubjective construction, a position dependent on the relations among three very different figures: narrator, addressee, and referent.

Some of the difficulties created by Said's desire to avoid narrative are betrayed by the way he used the word "molestation." It seems out of touch with the politics of sexual relations in 1975 to choose "molestation" to describe a writer's sense of "confinement to a fictive, scriptive realm" (84). The molested woman or child was (and remains) one of the crucial subjects of contemporary feminism, a figure in countless stories of sexual harassment, abuse, or assault. Said's abstraction of the word from its social and sexual contexts allowed him to ignore these contexts in assessing the value of narrative.

Related difficulties emerged when Said turned to the thematics of celibacy in the late nineteenth-century novel.[11] Because he associated narrative with fatherhood and generation, what he called its "paternal role—to author, father, procreate a rival reality" (152), he was interested in celibate males, bachelors or men whom he characterized as emasculated or otherwise sexually thwarted. The "rejection of natural paternity" in favor of a "celibate enterprise" (145), Said argued, is a "stage in the narrative's developing consciousness of its (by now) peculiarly unnatural aims" (146), those of revealing the socially constructed status of its own authority. Today one is troubled by the association of a sexual choice of celibacy with emasculation and male sterility. Further, one wonders why he focused solely on male celibates if he only wanted an alternative to paternity. Surely motherhood represents a major alternative, one more pervasive yet just as ambivalent about the status of authority—a point Margaret Homans's *Bearing the Word* (1986) has brilliantly demonstrated. If not mothers, then why not other marginal figures, ranging from sexually active gay men, lesbians, adulteresses (see Tanner), to the angels, demons, and whores that Nina Auerbach discusses in *Woman and the Demon* (1982), to less clearly gender-marked figures such as orphans, working-class protagonists, members of racial or ethnic minorities, or even the religious nonconformists so prominent in English novels? Many of these figures registered their uneasiness with authority *through* narrative rather than in opposition to narrative, in part because of their historical exclusion from narrative. Expanding his investigation to include other marginalized peoples (as he does in *Orientalism*) might have helped Said to see (in *Beginnings*) that narrative is equally able to confirm the bourgeois subject, disperse that subject, or reconstruct it in a postcritical formation.

Despite their differences, Barthes, White, Miller, Chase, Culler, and Said shared in the seventies a common evaluative stance toward narrative. This uniformity of position leads one to suspect that something was being overlooked. The either/or structure of so many models is troubling. One wonders if a new issue was being made to conform to preexisting modes of thought. Everywhere one heard that narrative supports old-fashioned conceptions of unity, selfhood, linearity, and truth, whereas the disruption of narrative is, in and of itself, politically liberating. The opposition sounded suspiciously like the way critics of the novel used to talk about the change from nineteenth-century realism to the modernist perspective. Barthes and Said correlated this opposition with the historical shift to modernism. White, Miller, Chase, and Culler viewed the distinction as timeless. Yet in all the valued terms were those usually associated with modernist literature and philosophy. Techniques of fragmentation, reversal, repetition; relationships that escape or overturn notions of beginning and end, continuity, and totality; conceptions of the text as an open-ended network rather than as a closed (narrative) structure; methods that emphasize the reader as a center of interpretation or that view meaning as necessarily indeterminate; and nonrepresentational assumptions about language — these are the characteristics of literature that were seen as questioning the established order.

This consensus about narrative was most effectively challenged at the time by critics on the left. Gerald Graff, for example, objected to the assumption that literary experimentalism has an intrinsically liberating effect. In *Literature against Itself* (1979), he argued instead that strategies of fragmentation and decentering contributed to the marginalization of literature and literary studies. Drawing on a Marxist critique of capitalism, he maintained that postindustrial society turns all the revolutionary energies of avant-garde art into another product for consumption. His thesis had (and continues to have) great explanatory power. He clearly identified an important problem in the contemporary literary scene. His solution, however, was less promising. He advocated a return to realism and a faith in the referential powers of language. His proposal did not generate much enthusiasm, for it depended upon the contention that a traditional notion of representation would give critics a more authentic voice in contemporary debates. For all Graff's polemical vigor, he presented few convincing reasons why this should be the case. It was not clear, for example, why the voice of a traditional critic would not be turned into an item for consumption by a jaded society any more than would the voice of the experimentalist. (It is not surprising, therefore, that his most recent work, *Beyond the Culture Wars* [1992], has abandoned this earlier solution for the more constructive proposal of "teaching the conflicts.")

Although Graff's positive proposals did little to displace deconstruction and other versions of poststructuralism, his diagnosis of "the new moralism" (22), which assigns literary practices to fixed places in a hierarchy, can hardly be denied. Further, the dichotomy that makes narrative authoritarian and disjunction revolutionary can be questioned on its own terms. One way of proceeding with such a critique would be to suggest that the habit of mind that elevates experimental literary techniques over traditional narrative forms is in direct contradiction with virtually every tenet of poststructuralism. Only a teleological view of the history of literary forms can justify the suggestion that one set of assumptions about literature is more sophisticated than another. Even if, like Miller, one believes that both sets of assumptions have always coexisted in every text, one still cannot assert the superiority of either set without forgetting that the choice between them is supposed to be "undecidable." Look again at the rhetoric of Miller's essay. "It is no accident that *Middlemarch* has been so consistently misread as affirming the metaphysical system of history it in fact so elaborately deconstructs" (470). What but a critical narrative that relies on notions of "progress," of "origin and end," and of "gradually emerging 'meaning'" could have authorized Miller to declare that one interpretation of the novel is a "misreading" and that another is "in fact" correct? If a poststructuralist approach to the question of narrative and politics was to be useful, it had to evolve a way of thinking about the issue that did not merely invert the established hierarchy of values.

Perhaps it was inevitable that critics constructed narratives even when they meant to call narrative into question. But this story about the complicity of stories with authoritarianism left out too much. It left out history, for example. An historical account of the manifold ways narrative has actually been used would turn up as many instances of rebellion as of complicity. It left out practice. As I will show in later chapters, telling stories may be a subversive activity even when the content of the stories remains trapped within the terms of a dominant ideology. It left out difference, the difference of minority perspectives. The pragmatics of storytelling may have different values for different communities within the same society. For women and men who are excluded from the dominant discourse, the politics of linearity often changes. Taking into account alternative subject positions changes deconstruction's view of narrative by the paradoxical means of being true to the narrative implicit in deconstruction.

Deconstruction in the Nineties

Near the end of E. L. Doctorow's novel *Billy Bathgate* (1989), the eponymous hero and narrator finds a stash of money hidden away by his former boss, the notorious gangster Dutch Schultz. Unlike Milkman's sack of gold, the crisp large-denomination bills and the bundles of Treasury certificates were located exactly where Billy had deduced he would find them. The money's discovery is one of several revelations that brings the narrative to a satisfying close; another is the discovery that Billy, a boy who had long sought a substitute for the father who abandoned him, is now a father himself. This latter event he declares the "fount of all my memory" and the guarantee of the "truth" (321) of what he has just related. The events that culminate this narrative, resolving the story's deepest conflicts and fulfilling the narrator's innermost dreams, seem to confirm everything the deconstructive critics said above about narrative's complicity with traditional notions of origin and end; unity, selfhood, and truth; and the dynastic relations of father and son.

The terms in which Billy describes his money, however, reveal him to be as conscious as Morrison that the value of his discovery is constructed by a (shopworn) cultural code: "it was like pirate swag, monument to an ancient lust, and I had the same feelings looking at it that I get from old portraits or the recordings of dead though still fervent singers" (321). On the same page, Billy shows himself to be equally aware of the intricate ways his identity has been constructed by traditional, even hackneyed stories: internalized stories of orphanhood, criminality, romance, and redemption that structured his experiences as he had them and that join seamlessly in the autobiographical fabric he weaves. Reflecting on the power of symbols to construct reality, a power he had first learned about from the genius who ran Dutch Schultz's numbers game, Billy writes:

> I will confess that I have many times since my investiture sought to toss all the numbers up in the air and let them fall back into letters, so that a new book would emerge, in a new language of being. It was . . . the perverse proposition of a numbers man, to throw them away and all their imagery, the cuneiform, the hieroglyphic, the calculus. . . . But I have done it and done it and always it falls into the same Billy Bathgate I made of myself and must seemingly always be. (321)

Billy is a genuine pragmatist in that he does not enshrine either his skepticism or his faith as the last word about reality. And he has a keen historical sense about his stories, which is hardly surprising in the narrator of a Doctorow novel. He recognizes that his identity is partial, socially constructed, and historically contingent but regards this insight as an opportunity and a challenge. Rather than view the skeptical moment as an end in itself—a cause for anxiety or even Nietzschean joy—he looks around to see what must be done next. Like Morrison's novel, *Billy Bathgate* incorporates the critical moment of deconstruction in a larger pattern of action. This situating of the deconstructive critique within some other activity is emblematic of the way in which literary critics have come to use deconstruction in the nineties.

When deconstruction was first introduced to the United States in the late sixties, literary critics began to employ it for the analysis of works of literature, just as they had previously employed the techniques of New Criticism, archetypal criticism, psychoanalysis, and structuralism. It did not take long for purists within deconstructive circles to indict this practice as politically conservative, a means of ςoopting the radical potential of Continental deconstruction by incorporating it into the existing institution of academic literary criticism. At the very moment when right-wing commentators were worrying that deconstruction would destroy established values, left-wing commentators were worrying that "American" or "Yale" deconstruction would blunt the movement's revolutionary edge. Both wings in this controversy turned out to be correct, although not quite in the ways they feared. On the one hand, literary deconstruction, even in its tamest academic forms, clearly has helped overturn some of the assumptions that sustained the traditional canon; but just as clearly, it has not been responsible for the enormous outcry, heard from all quarters, for expanding cultural boundaries. The agents of this change lie elsewhere, among new social movements and among forms of identity politics that take only incidental (or instrumental) notice of disputes within literary theory. On the other hand, the form in which U.S. academic literary critics institutionalized deconstruction clearly did blunt its edge, but in retrospect it has become apparent that this edge was never designed to cut through the web of social, political, and economic ties that radical critics hoped to sever.

How is it possible that deconstruction has unsettled crucial assumptions of the status quo while becoming institutionalized within the literature departments of U.S. research universities? The answer returns us to the altered relations between intellectuals and power in a postindustrial order. When deconstruction became an available technique of literary criticism, it also became a "practice" or "tactic," to return to terms drawn from Bourdieu and de Certeau. The most radical contention of Continental deconstruction was that it could not be reduced to a practice; its critical edge, its terrible purity, if you will, depended upon its always being a new encounter with uncertainty, a fresh engagement with the limits of metaphysics. In the work of Derrida, and in some philosophical circles, such as that of the French researchers, Jean-Luc Nancy and Philippe Lacoue-Labarthe,[12] or those of the U.S. scholars John Sallis, Charles Scott, and Rudolphe Gasché, a theoretical purity is sustained. In U.S. literary circles, however, deconstructive theory has long since given way to applications. The simplest measure of this situation is that today it would be difficult to publish an article that merely deconstructed a literary text for the sole purpose of demonstrating (once again) that meaning is indeterminate. New historicists and traditional critics alike have taken this fact to mean that deconstruction has "ended"; but it has ended as a theoretical movement only because its procedures have become so transparent, so fully available, that it is now possible to speak of deconstruction as a "practice of everyday life" in literature departments.

As a practice within specific institutions, deconstruction exhibits the political effectiveness that it never possessed as rarified theory. I take it as established—by Lentricchia (*Criticism*), Paul Smith (41–55), Nancy Fraser (69–92), and a host of others—that the "formalism" or "abstraction" of the deconstructive critique of metaphysics made it remote from actual political conflicts and sites of resistance. As a practice, however, it is situated within those conflicts; its targets are historically specified; the range of its blindness and insight is circumscribed by the local site of its application. Considering deconstruction as a practice makes double reading, for example, an available tactic, a procedure that may be employed in particular political struggles. And this is how it has been employed by a large, diverse group of younger U.S. scholars, many of whom are politically committed to "Third World" struggles, feminism, lesbian and gay rights, minority causes, and other issues. This engaged use of deconstruction represents an example of Foucault's "specific intellectual" in action. Nancy Fraser has defined more precisely than Foucault the relationship of academic radicals to the various groups in which they participate: "In relation to our academic disciplines, we function as the oppositional wing of an expert public. In relation to extra-academic social movements, on the other hand, we function as the expert wing of an oppositional public" (11). In either case, the practice of deconstruction becomes political not because of any intrinsic qualities but because of its deployment at the site of a specific historical conflict.

The movement of Gayatri Chakravorty Spivak away from philosophical theory in a deconstructive mode toward an oppositional practice of deconstruction aimed at imperialism is a good illustration of what I mean. Spivak's translation of Derrida's *Of Grammatology* in 1976 played a crucial role in the spread of deconstruction within U.S. English departments, just as her lengthy "Translator's Preface," with its rigorous consideration of Derrida's roots in the texts of Hegel, Heidegger, Nietzsche, Husserl, and Freud, served as an introduction to the way in which theoretically inclined English professors were going to have to learn to talk in the succeeding decade. By the mid-eighties, however, at the very moment when many U.S. critics had begun to master the discourse, Spivak began calling for a redirection of deconstruction toward new issues. In "Three Women's Texts and a Critique of Imperialism" (1985) she influentially spoke of the need to bracket or "ignore the lessons of deconstruction" in order to "strategically take shelter in an essentialism" (244); and in "Imperialism and Sexual Difference" (1986), she advocated using the "resources of deconstruction" to develop a "strategy rather than a theory of reading that might be a critique of imperialism" (521). It is important to recognize that Spivak did not renounce deconstructive methods, nor did she temper her difficult, transgressive style of writing. In one of her latest pieces, "Acting Bits/Identity Talk" (1992), she continues to deconstruct notions such as identity and origin, but only in order to reclaim, as agency, a person's insistence on the mark of origin, the mark of identity. Her text weaves together citations from several of her recent public lectures; stories of the occasions of those talks, which prompt her to reflect on the staging of her own "identity"; and commentaries on the autobiography of an Algerian Muslim woman, Assia Djebar, on a Lebanese-Canadian artist, Jamelie Hassan, on an artist from Tijuana-San Diego, Guillermo Gómez Peña, on Morrison's *Beloved*, on Derrida's *Glas*, on a film by the Bengali filmmaker Gautam Ghosh, and on a novel by Kamalkumar Majumdar on which the film was based. Her practice, it is fair to say, has had much to do with the prominence of deconstructive procedures in some parts of the fields of postcolonial and subaltern studies.

Within the Yale school of deconstruction—the very group accused of compromising deconstruction's radical potential— Barbara Johnson's increasing commitment to a political use of deconstruction is another illustration of the phenomenon I am describing. In 1987 Johnson introduced her second collection of essays, *A World of Difference*, with a statement of how they differed from those collected in her earlier book: "They all attempt, in one way or another, to transfer the analysis of difference (as pursued in such studies as my earlier book, *The Critical Difference* [1980]) out of the realm of linguistic universality or deconstructive allegory and into contexts in which difference is very much at issue in the 'real world'" (2). In several essays in her later book, she poses deconstruction as a stage or moment encompassed by a larger political project. The deconstructive moment may be necessary, Johnson now writes, but it should not be the final word, the endpoint or goal of criticism.[13] Discussing the concept of the writerly text found in Barthes and other poststructuralist critics, she says: "If writerliness cannot be set up as an *ultimate* value without neutralizing itself, it nevertheless seems to stand as the unbypassable site of the *pen*ultimate—the place where a new passage through otherness can be opened up, if and only if one is attempting to follow an imperative not to stop there" (*World* 31).

A third illustration is to be found in the "return to the subject" among many feminists today, some of whom remain quite sympathetic to poststructuralism.[14] Nancy Miller, for example, in one of her now-famous responses to Barthes's and Foucault's claims about the death of the author, writes: "Only the subject who is both self-possessed and possesses access to the library of the already read has the luxury of flirting with the escape from identity . . . promised by an aesthetics of the decentered (decapitated, really) body" (83; see also 75, 106). But Miller does not argue for a return to the unitary authorial self found in much biographical criticism; instead, she looks for ways to integrate deconstructive insights with the needs of a "specifically feminist" (102) theory and practice. Significantly, many of her problems with the poststructural critique

of the subject focus on the way it forecloses the question of agency
(80, 106). But, again, her notion of agency does not depend on an
old-fashioned vision of the author as originary genius, as authorita-
tive and authorizing self behind the text; instead, she works toward
a conception of agency that reminds one of Said's ungrounded,
transindividual notion of intention discussed above. What makes
Miller's version of agency more attractive than the version Said
outlined in *Beginnings* is her emphasis on practice. Her models of
the socially constructed, positional subject generally involve more
than one figure, and these figures are generally engaged in communal, embodied activities—weaving (80), a square dance, the "ritual
of a minuet" (103)—that leave room for "hesitation" (103), improvisation, unauthorized creativity, spontaneous grace—the unfor-
mulated moves, in short, of practice rather than theory. The subject of these activities is often transindividual, the collective or
collaborative subject common both to traditional women's practices and to contemporary social movements. In fact, Miller's own
formulations profit from the collaborative work of many women,
feminists who have never been afraid of the word "practice" (if
anything, U.S. feminists have more often shied away from the
word "theory").[15]

Equally important as these feminist returns to the subject is the
engaged use of deconstruction in the work of some gay, lesbian,
and antihomophobic critics. Eve Kosofsky Sedgwick, for example,
makes her strategic invocations of the method very clear in *Epistemology of the Closet* (1990): "One main strand of argument in this
book is deconstructive, in a fairly specific sense. The analytic move
it makes is to demonstrate that categories presented in a culture as
symmetrical binary oppositions—heterosexual/homosexual, in this
case—actually subsist in a more unsettled and dynamic tacit relation" (9–10). The analytic move, in other words, is double reading,
but she quickly distinguishes her practice from (1) universal, ahistorical assumptions about the undecidability of language, (2) the
simplistic politics of linearity characteristic of earlier deconstructive thinking about narrative, and (3) a "fetishized" celebration
of difference per se, which so empties difference of "its possible
embodiments that its most thoroughgoing practitioners are the last
people to whom one would now look for help in thinking about
particular differences" (23). Other critics engaged in queer theory

highlight their simultaneous appropriation and displacement of deconstruction in similar fashion (see, among others, Butler, *Gender*; Edelman; Epstein and Straub; Fuss, *Essentially*, 13–21; and Treichler).

A final illustration comes from legal scholars involved in the movement called Critical Race Theory, as well as from some feminists in the Critical Legal Studies movement. I turn to these scholars of the law for two reasons: (1) radical legal theorists have never had much ambivalence about integrating deconstructive ideas into a larger political practice. In truth, the culture of legal scholarship has traditionally been unembarrassed about borrowing methods from diverse sources, sometimes without worrying about whether or not the methods were consistent with one another. Historically, the focus of legal writing has been on the issue at hand, on settling the thorny problem of doctrine, on proposing a new remedy for a pressing injustice. (2) Critical Race Theorists have made issues of narrative central to their deconstructive practice. They have turned to narrative, I believe, for some of the same reasons Nancy Miller turns to communal activities such as weaving—because a focus on narrative allows one to investigate issues of voice, subjectivity, group allegiance, and social agency without falling back into essentializing paradigms. If narrative is openly acknowledged as helping to construct each of those positions—voice, subject, group, and agency—then the partial, intersubjective nature of these terms can never be in doubt.[16]

The subtitle of a moving, story-filled article by an African-American law professor, Patricia J. Williams, captures exactly the point I am trying to make about the use of deconstruction within a larger social agenda—in this case, the continuing struggle for civil rights by African-Americans. Her article, "Alchemical Notes: Reconstructing Ideals from Deconstructed Rights," addresses the tendency in Critical Legal Studies to attack liberal rights theory from a radical and deconstructive perspective. The core of her argument resembles Nancy Miller's position in some ways; Williams argues that African-Americans who historically have been dispossessed of all rights do not perceive rights rhetoric as a source of alienating autonomy. "Only those who have it can play with not having it," as Miller said (75). The special circumstances of racial oppression in the United States, however, leads Williams to present arguments that Miller did not make. Williams suggests that African-Americans have reinvented rights, given "them life where there was none before" (430). This "alchemical" process involves creativity, motherhood, and production—as well as deconstruction and critique—and it is fostered by telling stories that have too long gone untold.

Mari Matsuda is another Critical Race Theorist who hopes to sustain a complementary relationship between the deconstructive energies of Critical Legal Studies and the constructive energies of civil rights activism. For her, too, consciousness of narrative plays a double role: it assists in both the critical and the reconstructive phases of her project. By telling what she calls "stories from the bottom" (2322), she shows that official histories, enshrined in law, are themselves partial accounts, founded on silences and exclusions; at the same time, she helps to build new forms of community.[17] A third member of this movement, Richard Delgado, effectively sums up their sense of narrative's double task: it possesses a critical function, at odds with the authoritarian portrait drawn by deconstructive critics in the seventies, and a productive function, what in the first chapter I called a positive form of cultural power. Delgado writes:

> stories build consensus, a common culture of shared understandings, and deeper, more vital ethics. Counterstories, which challenge the received wisdom, do that as well. . . . But stories and counterstories can serve an equally important destructive function. They can show that what we believe is ridiculous, self-serving, or cruel. . . . stories can shatter complacency and challenge the status quo.[18] (2414–5)

The important work being done with deconstruction by critics engaged in a range of political projects, both inside and outside the discipline of literary criticism—postcolonial studies, feminism, lesbian and gay studies, Critical Race Theory, and other oppositional criticisms not considered here[19]—illustrates the way this theoretical movement has been put to the service of social action. Once readers thought that the story of deconstruction would be that of dedicated theorists pursuing their uncompromising project within the bounds of an austere formalism. Today many people think otherwise. The practice of deconstruction has come to displace the very theoretical enterprise that gave birth to its procedures. Who is the subject of this new story? It is not the resolute theorist but the committed tactician. The subject of deconstruction is the critic who decenters deconstruction by putting it in practice.

I began this chapter by commenting on an episode from Toni Morrison's novel *Song of Solomon*. Like similar passages from Doctorow's novel, this episode seemed to confirm many of the indictments of narrative proposed by deconstructive critics in the seventies. By exposing the link between storytelling and ideology, Morrison uncovered the role that narrative plays in sustaining existing patterns of subjectivity. At the end of the novel, however, the power of narrative brings Milkman into a community, educates him to the importance of his past, and makes him willing to sacrifice himself for a different future. Milkman eventually becomes sensitive to the powers of narrative, although he must learn about them from the mouths of people more marginal than himself—from Pilate's songs, from old men's tales, from children's riddles. Milkman discovers that narrative possesses the power, for him at least, to reorder reality itself. His final act, the leap from a rock onto the wings of the air, occurs because of his knowledge of the stories that have governed his life, the tales of his ancestor who could fly.

For Morrison and Doctorow, the critical and the productive potentials of narrative are both inescapable, but for them, as for many "outsider" critics, the productive capacity may be the most vital. It is easy enough for deconstructive theorists to say that narrative's concern with origins and ends, with teleology, with selfhood and meaning is baneful. But for an African-American woman writing in the United States during the seventies, narrative's social function may be entirely different, both more critical and more creative than some critics have let themselves imagine. There are many ways to read literary texts, only one of which involves examining their political power. But if one wants to focus on this dimension, then one must situate one's conclusions within a specific historical context. For it is the particular (and varied) locations of cultural activities within society that give them their power today.

In the next chapter, I consider psychoanalytic models of narrative. Like deconstruction, psychoanalytic narrative theory strives to overcome the static models or structuralism, and it attempts to reach beyond formalist concepts of textuality by discussing the ways in which stories position readers as desiring subjects. By looking at some of the theories of desire that have become pervasive in narrative studies, I explore whether psychoanalysis provides a more useful account of narrative's power.

3

Theories of Desire

In Philip Roth's *The Professor of Desire* (1977) the protagonist, who is planning a lecture for a course he calls Desire 341, suggests that his students try not to think of literature in terms of plot, character, structure, or form; that they try to forget the critical terms that they have learned with such difficulty, words like symbol, epiphany, and persona; and that they try instead to talk about novels in the language that they would use with their grocer or their lover. Roth's character hopes that the students' familiarity with erotic impulses will help them "locate these books in the world of experience" rather than in a "manageable netherworld of narrative devices" (183). The unstated assumption is that desire itself is a language that all men and women speak. To be knowable, longings must conform to some conceptual model, but at least it is a model that has been proved on the pulse. Rather than refer to narrative devices, one can point to the complexities of actual experience, to the subtle structures of desire. The dream, in Roth's version, is to find "a more *referential* relationship" (183) to literature. The dream, in more general terms, is to use the exploration of desire as a way to move beyond formalism and thus to draw connections between literature and life.

The hope of moving beyond formalism is one of two things that unites an otherwise diverse group of literary theorists who have begun to explore the role of desire in narrative. Peter Brooks, for example, in *Reading for the Plot*, says in more than one place that his interest in desire "derives from my dissatisfaction with the various formalisms that have dominated critical thinking about narrative" (47). Leo Bersani sees desire as establishing a crucial link between social and literary structures. Teresa de Lauretis faults structuralist models for their inability to disclose the ways in which narrative operates, through the desires it excites and fulfills, to construct the social world as a system of sexual differences. Other names could be added, both within and outside the field of narrative theory—Nancy Armstrong, Roland Barthes, Georges Bataille, Jessica Benjamin, Gilles Deleuze and Félix Guattari, René Girard, Luce Irigaray, Fredric Jameson, Peggy Kamuf, Linda Kauffman, Julia Kristeva, Jacques Lacan, Jean Laplanche, Catharine A. MacKinnon, and Eve Kosofsky Sedgwick—for desire has become one of the master tropes of contemporary criticism.

The second thing that unites these figures is an emphasis on violence. Bersani is the most insistent. In a complex series of arguments, he maintains that "desire is intrinsically violent" (*Future* 13) and that there is a "complicity between narrativity and violence" (*Forms* v). He begins his book *A Future for Astyanax* with "two scenes of erotic violence" (3), one from Racine and the other from a contemporary pornographic novel, *L'Image*, by the pseudonymous "Jean de Berg." The latter scene, a sadistic dream involving the mutilation and murder with triangular stilettos of two naked women, becomes an emblem for Bersani of the activity of desiring at its most intense. De Lauretis also equates narrative with violence, although her attitude toward this violence is very different from Bersani's. She begins her essay "Desire in Narrative" with an inquiry into the "*structural* connection between sadism and narrative" (104). Brooks places less emphasis on violence, but even he perceives a connection between deviance, transgression, and the kind of desire that he calls "narratable" (85).

With these two similarities, however, the common ground staked out by an interest in the topic of desire comes to an end. In truth, the word "desire" appears to have no single, stable meaning in contemporary criticism. The term names a range of concepts, running from Brooks's usage, which is essentialist in character, to that of Lacan, Laplanche, and Bersani, which represents a more structuralist orientation. Brooks sees desire as a creative force, aligned with Eros or the life instinct, an energy that fuels one's most basic projects toward the world, including that of narrative. Bersani sees desire as determined by a lack that lies at its origin, the absence of any possible object of satisfaction; less an energy than the displacement of energy, it is inherently insatiable, condemned to a restless search for an absent object. Teresa de Lauretis, whose vision of desire is closer to Bersani's end of the spectrum than to Brooks's, attempts to historicize and gender the concept. This attempt introduces important qualifications into the structural model, qualifications that may call the model itself into question.

If the word desire designates no single idea or model of human behavior, then why attempt to bring these diverse thinkers into dialogue with one another? The exercise will clarify the complex, often contradictory notions that are sometimes confused under the same term. Opposed views, such as those of Brooks and Bersani, compete for control of a term whose privileged status lends a glamor to the arguments that successfully employ it. The term is popular because it provides a way of discussing both the individual pleasure of a literary text and the social regulation of that pleasure. In psychoanalytic-oriented discourses, it functions much the way the power/knowledge problematic functions in Foucault. In fact, desire and power can be seen as contemporary rephrasings of an older way of talking about the *function* of literature—the idea that literature must please and instruct. What this new vocabulary adds, however, is an emphasis on the way in which both pleasure and knowledge are socially constructed. Hence it represents another aspect of the analysis of narrative's power in contemporary society.

All three narrative theorists take sexual desire as their paradigm. This choice follows its own economy of pleasure, as critical texts promising instruction compound their interest by capitalizing on readers' fascination with all matters pertaining to sexuality. For obvious reasons, psychoanalytic critics are oriented toward the sexual model. One might expect some theorists, however, to represent desire in other than sexual terms—as craving for money, power, knowledge, or God—but narrative theorists almost never stray from the sexual paradigm. This chapter retains the emphasis on sexual desire for three reasons. First, the sexual example has the advantage of allowing us to compare a cultural product—the literary text—with an apparently natural process, sexuality. Second, sexuality provides us with a limit case with which to test de Lauretis's attempt to historicize desire. Sexuality is more often regarded as a universal, unchanging aspect of human character than is, say, the desire for material possessions. It might be easier to see the longing for consumer goods in an historical perspective; Marxists, for example, relate changes in what people desire to the evolution of capitalism.[1] Restricting examples to the realm of sexuality, however, puts the burden of proof squarely on the shoulders of anyone attempting to develop an historical model of desire.

Third, the restriction to sexual desire both reflects the idea's provenance in contemporary North American fiction and brings out its disturbing connections with violence.[2] Throughout the *Professor of Desire*, Roth's protagonist looks back to a period in his early twenties when he was at the pinnacle of his libidinal career. His fondest memories of this time are of acts of sadism, domination, and bondage. In one memory he is standing over a blindfolded woman, whipping her between her legs; in another, she is kneeling before him as he ejaculates on her face and hair; in yet another, she helps him bind a woman over a chair and have sex with her from behind. Numerous other novels strive for a referential relationship with life by focusing on the violence of sexual desires. Lois Gould's *A Sea Change* (1976), which features rape with a pistol barrel; Jerzy Kosinski's *Blind Date* (1977), in which the hero perfects a method of assaulting women without being seen; John Irving's *The World According to Garp* (1978), a book preoccupied with mutilation and rape; Margaret Atwood's *Bodily Harm* (1982), which uses violent pornography as a metaphor for contemporary politics; Andrea Dworkin's *Ice and Fire* (1986), where the heroine teaches her too-innocent husband "how to tie knots, how to use rope, scarves, how to bite breasts" (101) — these are but a few examples from recent years.

This last book, written by a feminist who is known for her stand against rape and pornography, has surprising resemblances to Roth's novel. Both are first-person narratives about Jews who live for a time in Europe, where they are initiated into the joys of sadomasochism. Both stories are *künstlerromanen* or tales of a writer's education. Both narratives move from early childhood memories, through youthful experimentation with sex, to a crisis of confidence, followed by a gradual recovery, which requires the characters to embrace a life of diminished sexual desire but allows them to become successful writers. The lives of both these characters—feminist and would-be roué—follow a similar course, one apparently beyond their control.[3]

Dworkin's novel, however, is more self-conscious about the way the desire that shapes her narrative is itself shaped by the narratives of her society. In the first chapter, the narrator describes a game that she and the neighborhood children played in the evenings when there were no adults in sight. They called the game "Witch," and the object of it was for the boys to catch one of the girls and put her in a cage that they hoisted up on a telephone pole. But there was a trick: the boys decided among themselves ahead of time which girl they were going to catch, so the girls on the street were put in the ambivalent position of both wanting and not wanting to be the one singled out. "Sometimes they would tie your hands behind you and sometimes they would put tape over your mouth. . . . You weren't supposed to want to be the witch but if you were a girl and running there was nothing else to want because the game was for the boys to chase you" (11). The way in which the narrator's desire is both engaged and disabled in the same gesture prepares her for (and helps us to understand) that later period when she will take the lead in teaching her husband how to tie her down and abuse her.

Before turning to some exemplary theorists of desire, I want to pose two questions that will guide the inquiry. Are there connections between the interest displayed by critics in moving beyond formalism and their preoccupation with violence? Does the violence of the world commit a psychoanalytic criticism that wants to connect literature with life to a meditation on violence?

The World According to Brooks

Peter Brooks might well answer these questions in the negative. His goal in challenging formalism is to establish narrative as a valuable mental tool, a way of knowing. He wants to restore a cognitive dimension to our sense of narrative, to show how it is a "specific mode of human understanding" (7). For that reason, he describes narrative as a process or operation rather than a structure and talks of the many ways people "need plotting" (35), of the different kinds of experience that cannot be comprehended without narrative. In particular, those meanings that must be "construed over and through time" (35) or those processes that can only be understood at their end, by hindsight, are dependent on narrative. These meanings arise at different stages in the reading process: the former is experienced in the middle of a story, the latter only at the end. Brooks relates these two stages to the operations of metonymy, which is the organizing principle of narrative middles, and of metaphor, which is his name for the figure that governs totalizing interpretations at the end of a story.

Brooks invokes metaphor and metonymy in order to defend his notion of narrative understanding from attack by what he views as the most all-encompassing of formalisms, deconstruction. As discussed in the prior chapter, J. Hillis Miller, Cynthia Chase, and Jonathan Culler developed closely related theories of narrative that challenged narrative's impulse to totalization by revealing a crucial moment in every narrative that undoes its logical claim to coherence and meaning. Although Brooks is ready to concede the fictive status of totalizing interpretations, he does not believe that this concession undermines the value of the conclusions to which narrative leads. Drawing on Frank Kermode's theory of endings, he claims that the benefaction of meaning at the end remains valuable, despite the indeterminacy that undoes fixed meaning, as long as one acknowledges the fictiveness of all totalizing interpretations. This is a halfhearted way to defend narrative understanding and not much of a way to move beyond formalism either, since understanding is still trapped within an entirely fictive realm.[4] Brooks is more persuasive and original when he turns to the other means by which narrative creates understanding. The middle of narratives, Brooks claims, has a value that is neither expunged nor superseded by the summing up of the end. He returns to this idea frequently: "If at the end of a narrative we can suspend time in a moment when past and present hold together in a metaphor . . . that moment does not abolish the movement, the slidings, the mistakes, and partial recognitions of the middle" (92). Middles are where one works through the sorts of issues that can only be posed as sequences; and the sequential reasoning of middles is different in kind from the unifying, synthesizing reason of the end.

For Brooks, the cognitive dimension of narrative is complexly related to the question of desire. The latter is defined as a force, a blind and uncomprehending pressure, rather than as a mode of understanding. Nevertheless, without the pressure of desire, one would not have the dynamic movement that is essential to narrative understanding. In the first step of an analogy that will become the governing principle of his entire book, Brooks compares desire to a "motor." Desire is the motive force of narrative, a self-contained motor that propels the plot. He justifies this analogy by referring to the nineteenth-century novel's fascination with motors and to Freud's use of the same analogy to explain the force or pressure of an instinct. In subsequent arguments, Brooks extends the analogy until he can maintain that the text of a narrative is a dynamic system analogous in all its parts to Freud's dynamic model of the psyche. Brooks is able to find narrative principles that correspond to Freud's concepts of Eros, the death instinct, the repetition compulsion, working through conflict, and transference.

In Freud's dynamic model, mental life is governed by the conflict between forces or drives. There are two basic sets of drives: the sexual instinct, which he calls "libido" or (late in his career) "Eros," and the death instinct. Desire is a function of the first set, and Brooks compares narrative desire to Freud's notion of Eros in several places (37, 47, 106). Like Eros, the desire that a narrative awakens is free-floating, mobile, subject to no law, and likely to seek immediate discharge until something binds it in place. Repetition serves this binding function, linking moments in a text by similarity rather than mere contiguity. It creates the delays and digressions that are so necessary to the suspense of a good plot and that augment, by postponing, the pleasures of the end. Repetition, however, also introduces the specter of the death instinct, because, for Freud, the repetition compulsion is the chief sign of a repressed drive that strives toward the completion of death. According to Freud, both the life and the death instincts are conservative in nature, striving toward the restoration of a state that existed before life began, so both instincts can be said to aim toward death, but the life instinct strives to follow its own dilatory path. The danger that arises, in narrative as in life, is that the path will be cut short, that the story will come to an untimely end. Thus the instincts, which share an ultimate aim, are in conflict over the means of reaching that aim. Brooks concludes that the desire in narrative, the force that sets a story in motion, is a longing for the end, for the conclusion of both narrative and desire, but the conclusion must come in its own way, must be the destined, the devoutly prepared consummation. Brooks summarizes the analogy between narrative and the psyche as follows: "We emerge . . . with a dynamic model that structures ends (death, quiescence, nonnarratability) against beginnings (Eros, stimulation into tension, the desire of narrative) in a manner that necessitates the middle as detour, as struggle toward the end under the compulsion of imposed delay, as arabesque in the dilatory space of the text" (107–8).

Let me pause to ask why Brooks and others find this kind of analogy attractive. What does one do with the assertion that narrative is "like" the psyche, other than admit that the parallel is intellectually interesting? Brooks is not arguing that one side of the analogy generates the other, that the form of the psyche creates or determines the form of narrative, because he does not want to engage in a genetic mode of psychoanalytic criticism. Like many theorists today, he is suspicious of causal models. Hence Brooks turns to a critical analogy that juxtaposes two formal patterns — one located within a literary text, the other within a thoroughly textualized social world — without giving priority to either. But such a procedure presents problems, especially for a criticism that aims to move beyond formalism. What is gained by juxtaposing two patterns if neither is conceded to be fundamental and hence explanatory of the other? There is a heuristic benefit, to be sure; what one perceives in one place may become newly perceptible in another domain. Nonetheless, these mirrored perceptions cannot move one outside of formalism, unless one concedes superior authority to one image rather than the other.

John Irving's novel *The World According to Garp* can illustrate both the value and the limits of Brooks's psychoanalytic model. In accordance with Brooks's theory, the novel begins and ends in quiescence. Its opening chapter recounts how Garp's mother, a woman who, in her son's words, "never once felt sexual desire" (162), impregnated herself through intercourse with a dying, semiconscious man. An epilogue, "Life After Garp," carries each of the characters to the death that has already claimed the protagonist, and its final sentence reads, "But in the world according to Garp, we are all terminal cases" (437). Between the calm, considered act that engenders the story and the final tranquility of death that concludes the tale lies a middle in which the violence of desire seems undeniable. There are three brutal sexual assaults in the novel, and rape is a topic in more than a dozen other places. Desire seems to provoke murder or bodily mutilation—characters lose their tongues, penises, ears, and eyes.

"'Life,' Garp wrote, 'is sadly *not* structured like a good old-fashioned novel'" (418), but everything in the book proves him wrong. Irving links literature with life by paralleling Garp's biography with the events of a story embedded in the novel. Following a terrible accident that kills one of his children and maims the other, Garp writes a novel about a father who causes his child's death and later his own murder. Ultimately, Garp too is murdered, an event that "underlined everything Garp had ever written about how the world works" (414). The causes of his murder go back to events in his childhood, and his death is connected with all the desires that have shaped and informed his life. Garp's life is structured like a good old-fashioned novel, Irving suggests, because the structure of narrative is the same as the structure of desire. Both propel us toward the same violent end.

The connection between violence and desire in Irving's novel makes us consider whether Brooks has sanitized the analogy he presents, smoothed over some of the potentially disturbing consequences of comparing narrative with the psyche. Irving's novel, in effect, deconstructs the theory it seemed to confirm. If narrative is fueled by desire, and desire, according to both Irving and Brooks, leads only to death, then Brooks's own theory should prompt him to attend more carefully to the dark, uncomprehending elements in narrative and less to its cognitive dimension. Brooks bases his dynamic model of narrative on the tension between the life and death instincts, but should one really talk of the death instinct in such soothing, recuperative tones? Brooks speaks of the end of narrative suspending time in a metaphor that bestows meaning on all the turbulent struggles that have gone before, but this celebration of the power of human understanding ignores the pessimism of the late Freud, from whom this model of narrative is derived.

There are other problems with Brooks's presentation of the psychoanalytic analogy. Throughout most of his book, he views desire as a drive and speaks of the "drive of desire" in narrative (111).

Occasionally, however, he thinks of desire as the displacement of a drive, a modified form of a more basic force in the psyche. As Brooks puts it in one place, "the aims and imaginings of desire . . . move us from the realm of basic drives to highly elaborated fictions" (105). This second way of thinking of desire, which he derives from the work of Jacques Lacan, is useful in explaining the inability of desire ever to achieve satisfaction. Lacan views desire as a "derangement of instinct," no other derangement "than that of being caught in the rails—eternally stretching forth towards the *desire for something else*—of metonymy" (167). In this formulation, desire is a continuous sliding or displacement set in motion by a drive but not reducible to it. Desire originates in a gap, the gap between what Lacan calls "need"—such as the need for food— and "demand," the appeal to the Other for satisfaction. Thus desire is not itself a force; it borrows its restless energy from the pressure of the drives that set it in motion.

The consequences of this distinction for Brooks's theory are great. Lacanian desire cannot be the motor force of narrative, as Brooks would have it, but only the metonymical deployment of some other, prior force. To be consistent, Brooks should either drop his occasional references to Lacan or cease to speak of desire as a drive. If he does the former, however, he will have lost the only justification he provides for thinking of desire as inherently insatiable. As a drive, at least some desires could be satisfied by appropriate objects. On the other hand, if he ceases to speak of desire as a drive, then the source of that "textual energy" he wants to identify in narrative will remain a mystery.

The other theorists considered in this chapter never waver on this issue. For them, as for Lacan, desire is always displaced and deferred. It can never be satisfied by an object, for the displacement is founded on an originary absence. Brooks's willingness to consider desire as a force in its own right, a positive energy or drive, separates him both from Lacan (whom he mistakenly invokes) and from most other theorists of desire in narrative.

A final difficulty arises from the universal character of Brooks's analogy. His model of desire, and hence of narrative, is based almost entirely on a male sexual paradigm. Brooks speaks of "the arousal that creates the narratable as a condition of tumescence" (103), the danger of "premature discharge" (109), and of delay as a "forepleasure" that precedes the "gratification of discharge" (102-3) at the end of the story.[5] This neglect of sexual difference has been criticized by feminists in regard to other narrative theorists. De Lauretis indicts similar figurative language in Robert Scholes for leaving out "those of us who know no art of delaying climax or, reading, feel no incipient tumescence" (108). Jessica Benjamin goes further, suggesting that the problematic of desire itself leads to a concern with male structures—in psychoanalytic theory and, I might add, in narrative studies ("Desire," 83-4). In another article, Benjamin historicizes such apparently universal structures as male desire by connecting them with the increasing rationalization of society since the Englightenment ("Rational Violence," 43-7, 63-6). Her work draws on Max Weber and the Frankfurt school of critical theorists in condemning a mode of thought and desire that differentiates experience, emphasizing polarity and opposition rather than mutuality and interdependence, in order to dominate the external world. Benjamin's work leads one to think again about Brooks's claim for the cognitive power of narrative, at least insofar as that power is dependent upon the pressure toward a "gratifying discharge" at the end of reading. Perhaps one pays too high a price for the rationality of a structure that appears to comprehend all struggles.

The Mobile Home of Desire

Jerzy Kosinski has written a number of novels that connect sexual desire with the most brutal forms of violence. In the late sixties his novels were praised for their political vision. *The Painted Bird* (1965) and *Steps*, which won the National Book Award in 1968, were seen as indictments of the totalitarian structures that govern both politics and sexuality. By the end of the next decade, however, his continuing preoccupation with sexual violence, combined with an attenuated political concern, made one wonder what the justification was for depicting such graphic scenes. In novels such as *Blind Date* (1977) and *Passion Play* (1979), Kosinski's characters celebrate the liberating potential of sexual violence in settings that create only the sketchiest of political contexts. *Passion Play* is the story of an itinerant polo player, Fabian, banned from every major polo organization for savage play and unethical conduct, who travels around the country in his mobile home looking for pick-up games and part-time work as a coach. His enforced restlessness is presented as a metaphor for the intrinsically restless character of sexual desire, since his mobile existence both facilitates and corresponds to his insatiable demand for sexual variety. The novel suggests that desire can have no fixed home, that it is always restless, always on the move.

This idea obtains a literal embodiment in Fabian's sexual encounters with a hermaphrodite, a man treated with hormones to increase his biological "femininity" but who still retains his male genitals. Their sex allows Fabian to experiment with every possible sexual position: "at her mouth and breast, he was a boy necking with a girl; entwined with her, entering her, he was a man taking his woman; arousing her with his hand, he was a boy at play with a man; straddling her as she lay helpless beneath him, he was a man toying with a boy; inert, pinioned by her, he was a man at the mercy of a boy" (119). The mobility of their sexual play liberates desire, until it becomes "a fluent stream between them" (119), a movement unbounded by the structures that customarily shape and control desire, including those of gender itself. Despite the appearance of freedom, however, the movement of desire keeps falling into the same abusive patterns. Fabian binds one woman with the bit and harness from his tackle room, drawing blood with his spurs and the blows of his hand; his harsh treatment of another woman leads her to kill herself; he has intercourse with a third woman in the middle of a circle of spectators while her husband is murdered outside; he attempts to buy a female child from a white slavery ring; and he habitually seeks out young girls — still minors — in order to "imprint" his will on them, in the hope that they will then be slaves of his future sexual designs.

If Kosinski's recent novels lead us to ask if there is a link between the mobility of desire and a sadistic, ultimately misogynistic violence, the work of Leo Bersani can perhaps provide an answer. In a series of critical books written since the mid-seventies, he has striven to define the relationship between violence and what he calls "mobile desire." He is interested in a "radical psychic mobility," which he views as liberating, even though it can involve "brutally dehumanizing activities" (*Future* x–xi).

In a book from the mid-eighties, *The Forms of Violence: Narrative in Assyrian Art and Modern Culture*,[6] Bersani argues a thesis diametrically opposed to Brooks's. Bersani maintains not that desire propels narrative but that narrative contains, directs, and subdues desire. Like Brooks, he views narrative as one of culture's principal ways of organizing experience, but he sees this power as largely pernicious.[7] He criticizes the "sense-making orders of narrative" (89) for being rigidly linear, goal-oriented, single-minded, and intrinsically hierarchical; for promoting passivity in the reader and encouraging us to isolate and immobilize privileged scenes; for being congenial both to violence and to a "frictional," linear mode of sex that results in "explosive climax" (109). As these comments suggest, Bersani is above all an ethical critic, and his prose is laden with value judgments. He tends to reduce the world to opposed groups, sorting all phenomena into positive and negative categories. Narrative ranks high on his list of negatives, as do realistic art and the concept of a stable, unified self. On the positive side, he puts mobile desire, nonmimetic strategies of art, and a discontinuous or "shattered" self.

The evils of narrative, realism, and a unified self are all interrelated. According to Bersani, narrative is "intimately linked" (41) to the mimetic impulse and to the creation of realistic art generally, because of the way it organizes the people and events it depicts. Narrative creates hierarchies by assigning characters to major and minor roles and by foregrounding certain experiences while relegating others to the background. Thus narrative has something fundamental to do with perspective. This argument extends to the realm of the visual arts several criticisms of the novel he made in an earlier book, *A Future for Astyanax: Character and Desire in Literature*. There, in a chapter titled "Realism and the Fear of Desire," he focused on the way "form in realistic fiction serves the cause of significant, coherently structured character" (55). In both works he maintains that there is a "complicity" among the organizing structures of narrative, realism, and a unified personality.

Narrative and mimesis, in particular, are related to Western culture's fascination with violence. They are violent both in themselves—because of the way they impose order on experience—and as modes of depicting the violence one encounters in life. Bersani illustrates and indicts the former by comparing narrative with the

type of military march featured in the *Triumph of the Will* by Leni
Riefenstahl. He maintains that the analogy between narrative and
the military march suggests that readers and spectators enjoy a
narrative not because of anything in the story but because of the
"security of being passively carried along by an unfolding order"
(*Forms* 87).

As modes of depicting violence, narrative and mimesis are troubling because they emphasize the violent act as the significant moment in a work and thus invite a "pleasurable identification with its
enactment" (52). This privileging of the violent moment encourages
what he calls a "mimetic excitement" (52), a way of relating to
experience that always contains a "sexually induced fascination
with violence" (38). Narrative, it turns out, creates the perfect conditions for this excitement, and so narrative is implicated in the
excitement or sexual fascination that is always found in a "mimetic
relation to violence" (52). Bersani illustrates this contention by discussing the Marquis de Sade's *120 Days of Sodom*, which Bersani
views not as an anomaly in Western culture but as a paradigm of
the way mimesis eroticizes experience. Sade's work reveals narrative itself to be erotic, but the eroticism is of a particular, limited
type. Narrative sexuality is characterized by a linear movement
toward explosive climaxes, a movement aided by the "isolation and
imprisonment of the object of desire" (40) and crowned by a violent
act. "The ideal climax in Sade is murder" (41), Bersani writes, and
he implies that the same is true of all narratives.

The benefits of mobile desire, nonmimetic art, and a shattered
self are equally interrelated. Desire, for Bersani, is "always on the
move," an "unending process of displacements and substitutions"
(66). Narrative and mimesis tend to pin desire down, restrict its
mobility, and so Bersani celebrates "nonmimetic desire" (vii) and
"denarrativizing" (9), "counternarrative" (9), "nonnarrative" (14),
and "antinarrative" (46) strategies of representation. All the latter
tend to disrupt the self, and he looks to their potentially shattering
power for a renovation not simply of identity but of politics and
sexuality as well. The renovation of sexual behavior is worked out
in the most detail. Nonnarrative and nonmimetic art teaches an
"interstitial" form of sensuality, which in contrast with the frictional, "straight-line" sexuality of narrative, glories in the pleasures
of "mobile nontouching" (108–9). "Intermittent touch shatters the

body's wholeness and produces pleasures dependent on disseminated, unstructured bodily surfaces" (108).

All this disruption and self-shattering necessarily involves a measure of violence. Hence Bersani is forced to distinguish between two different kinds of violence. Western humanism, through its reliance on narrative and mimesis, has defined violence in a way that may have unintentionally promoted a destructive fascination with it (v). The violence of self-shattering desire, on the other hand, is "curiously mild and pacific" (125), both because it is contained within the bounds of consciousness and because the very restlessness of desire prevents it from ever centering destructively on an actual object. "Intrinsically, desire is perhaps a form of violence — of psychic disruptiveness or self-shattering — *without a place*, and which therefore never succeeds in taking place" (125). This amounts to saying that sexual violence is safe as long as it remains in the realm of desire — or in art. Given a place among real men and women, it can become physically destructive. But Bersani wants to have it both ways. When he discusses interstitial sensuality, he insists that he is referring to actual sexual contact. What happens to the destructive element, the "brutally dehumanizing" aspect of mobile desire, when it is directed toward actual men and women? The trail of dead, bruised, degraded, and enslaved women left by Kosinski's hero indicates one answer; the image of two naked women, mutilated and murdered with triangular stilettos, that opens Bersani's *A Future for Astyanax* provides another answer, which begins to look much the same.

There is perhaps a deeper contradiction in Bersani's argument for "pacific" violence. This mode of violence seems more like a source of control and domination over the terrors of an unruly world than of self-shattering and liberation. Confining violence to a protected aesthetic realm resembles the ritual process in which violence is limited to a sacred victim who has been set apart from the rest of the community. The purpose of isolating the victim is to protect the community from the destructive contagion of violence even as the ceremony indulges in violence. Although René Girard and others argue that all communities need a mechanism for purging violence, this process reinforces rather than disrupts the social order, strengthening the bonds that shape and control the life of the community. Jessica Benjamin argues that violence functions the same way in the lives of individuals. Ordinary violence inspires fear, she writes, "because it represents loss of control," but ritual violence, which takes place in a special, confined space, has the intention of "asserting the self-boundary of control" ("Rational Violence" 50, 54).

Although Bersani's argument about a liberating form of violence appears dubious, there remains his advocacy of nonnarrative and antinarrative strategies of representation. Is it true that these disruptive modes of writing are the only—or even the best—approaches to self-renovation? Andrea Dworkin's *Ice and Fire* offers at least one counterexample. The novel is highly experimental and employs a number of nonnarrative devices, including a fragmentary structure, frequent time shifts, and a central chapter in which the narrative disappears into a litany that circles around a single painful thought: "Coitus is punishment." But the novel does not suggest that these disruptive techniques are a source of liberation; quite the reverse. The most fragmented or denarrativizing moments of the book accompany episodes of crushing oppression. When an editor tells the narrator that he will publish her book in return for sexual favors, she can hardly continue writing, her self is so effectively "shattered." When she tries to negotiate and can scarcely speak, the editor takes her halting, fragmented style in an ideologically determined way: "in his world the breathy pauses mean fuck me, the misery in my voice means fuck me, the desperate self-effacement means fuck me" (162).

In Dworkin's novel, it is not disruption but narrative that holds out hope of liberation. If fragmentation is the sign of oppression, the shapely contours of the *künstlerroman* pattern convey a qualified promise. This work does not gloss over the compromises the main character must face. Like Roth's protagonist, she must renounce desire (the "fire" of the title) to bring her narrative to a successful close ("ice"). But this renunciation is a price worth paying when the (narrative) reward is a chance to be treated as a human being. Dworkin's narrator experiments with something that might resemble Bersani's interstitial sensuality; she has a loving relationship with a figure she calls simply "the boy," a surrogate for her lost brother. Their relationship creates anything but a straight-line sexuality that relies on explosive climaxes: "We were like women together on that narrow piece of foam rubber . . . like one massive, perpetually knotted and moving creature, the same intense orgasms, no drifting separateness of the mind or fragmented fetishizing of the body" (152). But this interlude does not further her successful development. It is a period of regression when the character retreats from the destructive world to a narcissistic state where boundaries have not yet been rigidly drawn. This regressive state is merely one final thing that she must learn to renounce. Closure depends on a single-minded, goal-oriented concentration, true enough, but when the alternative is degradation and exclusion from any position of power, linearity begins to look like a reasonable choice.

Both narrative and mimesis are strategies for placing us within an historically constructed world. As Hayden White, Paul Ricoeur, and others have demonstrated, the very concept of history is dependent upon narrative. Narrative locates the subject in a network of connections that makes the world intelligible and gives actions a context. Thus it should be no surprise that Bersani couples his attack on narrative and mimesis with a warning about historical criticism. He wants to safeguard his topic from "the domesticating effects of historical interpretation," because he feels that associating the disruptions of this art with any historical rupture would glamorize them "as the signs of a great historical crisis" (viii). The self-shattering of which he writes must be seen as a timeless technique, a recurrent, ahistorical resource for the renovation of the psyche. Bersani is right, but not in the way he intends: desire without narrative is desire outside of history. It is cut off from intelligibility, and it is severed from consequences as well. Without a narrative of origins and ends, actions and consequences, desire is isolated from its effects. Such a rootless, mobile conception of desire insulates the violent fantasies of Bersani and Kosinski from the way their representations degrade actual men and women — chiefly women.

Psychoanalysis and Desire

I began this chapter by saying that Brooks and Bersani represent two poles of contemporary thinking about desire, one humanist and essentialist, the other structuralist and largely "posthumanist."

These positions might also be associated with the twin utopian visions that psychoanalysis has produced: the therapeutic and the apocalyptic. Brooks's conception of desire enables him to believe in the beneficial agency of sublimation, to trust that by disciplining desire people can create an enduring civilization. Bersani's conception aligns him with a group of psychoanalytic visionaries — Norman O. Brown and Deleuze and Guattari are his closest precursors — who look to the polymorphous perversity of desire to overturn the very structures of society.

Despite their differences, these opposed models of desire have one great thing in common. They both view desire as ahistorical, a timeless phenomenon, which has taken the same shape in all people, places, nations, and cultures. This congruence might at first seem surprising. One would expect the posthumanist vision of desire to represent it as historically differentiated, since this view sees desire as socially constructed. But such is not the case. The societies that construct desire somehow always end up constructing it according to the same model. The problem may be fundamental to a psychoanalytic approach to the topic and may require an extensive project of historicizing psychoanalysis.[8] Even when psychoanalysis casts desire as a social phenomenon, the discussion still has recourse to invariant models — principally the Oedipus complex. These models are indeed social, but they are not historical. As a way of connecting the text to the world, psychoanalysis attempts to challenge formalism, but the connections it draws are to stable, synchronic patterns, not to history. The dream of moving beyond formalism, through the study of desire, has so far remained just a dream.

Teresa de Lauretis seems at first to present an answer to this problem. She frames the argument of her essay "Desire in Narrative" as an attack on ahistoricism. She complains that recent work on narrative theory, in spite of its shift away from structuralism, still ends up "dehistoricizing the subject and thus universalizing the narrative process" (105–6). Her complaint is directed at narrative theory, however, not at psychoanalysis, and she herself ends up dehistoricizing the subject by accepting a unitary notion of desire, eternally ensnared in the toils of Oedipus. This acceptance of desire as inescapably the same ultimately limits her argument.

Like both Brooks and Bersani, de Lauretis sees narrative as a fundamental way of making sense of the world. The work of narrative, for her, is not cognitive, as it is for Brooks, or repressive, as it is for Bersani. The work is one of producing distinctions, and the chief distinction it produces is that of gender. Narrative organizes the world by mapping sexual difference into every text and hence into culture. It accomplishes this immense task by reconstructing the diversity of human experience into a two-character drama in which man is cast in the role of subject and woman in the role of object. She shows that the structuralist studies of myths and fairytales by Propp, Lotman, and Lévi-Strauss always represent the mythical hero as male, no matter what the gender of the textual figure, "because the obstacle, whatever its personification, is morphologically female and indeed, simply, the womb" (119). Hence she concludes that the mythical subject "is constructed as human being and as male"; female is what resists the subject: "she (it) is an element of plot-space, a topos, a resistance, matrix and matter" (119).

Perhaps the most interesting part of her theory is its account of how narrative gets readers to accept this two-character drama. Rather than generalize about a vague "complicity" between social and narrative structures, she attempts to talk explicitly about the specific mechanisms through which narrative achieves social domination. She argues that the structure of narrative offers readers a limited set of "positions" within the plot space. To receive pleasure from the act of reading, each reader must assume the "positionalities of meaning and desire" (106) made available by the text. For the period that one assumes those positions, one's subjectivity is "engaged in the cogs of narrative and indeed constituted in the relation of narrative, meaning, and desire" (106). The pleasure of the text comes only at a price. That price is one's participation in a circumscribed network of relations, a network that must be described in ideological, not just structural, terms.

To explain how readers are led to assume those positions, de Lauretis turns to the concept of identification. This notion forms a nice bridge between aesthetic and psychological processes, for it is fundamental both to the activity of reading and to the creation of the self. In identification, a person internalizes the image of another, setting up that image as an ideal model. According to both Freud and Lacan, the act of identifying with someone—with the other—is crucial to the formation of the self. Their paradoxical conclusion is that subjectivity is derivative of the other, one's "private" or "unique" self dependent upon a prior social relation. The identifications involved in reading also have a social dimension. The fact that narratives must appeal to us not only as individuals but also as members of social groups suggests that "patterns or possibilities of identification" (136) for every reader must be built into the text. This leads de Lauretis to ask what kinds of identification are available for women if they are always constructed by narrative as obstacle and other.

A too-simple analysis might answer "none." But de Lauretis argues that "we cannot assume identification to be single or simple" (141). Women are caught up in narrative by a "twofold process of identification" (144), a relation both with the desiring subject (or hero) and with the object of desire (woman/obstacle). De Lauretis makes her argument in the course of discussing identification in cinema, but she intends her analysis to apply to all modes of narration. Women, she insists, are capable of identifying with various characters at various times and of alternating between entirely different kinds of identifications. In support of the latter contention she cites Freud's belief that a tendency to waver between masculine and feminine identifications is an essential characteristic of female sexuality. This allows her to give an optimistic conclusion to her tale. If women are capable of oscillating between opposed modes of desire, then it should be possible for the artist to provoke that oscillation, call attention to it, and uncover the contradictions that structure woman's place in narrative. "This would entail a continued and sustained work with and against narrative, in order to represent not just the power of female desire but its duplicity and ambivalence. . . . The real task is to enact the contradiction of female desire, and of women as social subjects, in the terms of narrative" (156).

This optimistic conclusion, however, is still inscribed within the eternal conditions of Oedipus. De Lauretis gives the last words of her essay to Muriel Rukeyser's ironic retelling of the Oedipus story, and de Lauretis's own last sentence concerns the same topic. "The most exciting work in cinema and in feminism today . . . is narrative and Oedipal with a vengeance, for it seeks to stress the duplicity of that scenario and the specific contradiction of the female subject in it, the contradiction by which historical women must work with and against Oedipus" (157). In effect, historical women are required to work with and against an ahistorical conception of desire. If de Lauretis wants to end the habit of "dehistoricizing the subject," then she must bring herself to interrogate desire too; she must ask if there are historical conditions that govern both desire and narrative.

A scene in Sue Miller's novel *The Good Mother* (1986) raises many of the issues that concern de Lauretis. Anna, a recently divorced mother of a three-year-old girl, is engaged in an affair with an artist named Leo. In the early stages of this affair, it is he who initiates her into a new realm of sexuality, helping her to discover a different kind of appetite. This narrative of discovery reproduces many aspects of traditional gender relations. Anna learns to be active, an apparently desiring subject, rather than the passive object of men's desire, but at some level she recognizes that her desire is not her own, that she is still enmeshed in a system controlled by others. In one area, however, she believes she really is the leader, the one who breaks new ground, and this area is, not surprisingly, the realm of motherhood. The way Leo always follows her lead in matters concerning her child is a "fatal part of his sweetness" (122), fatal because it both cedes to her a position of subjectivity and seduces her into believing that this position gives her the freedom to exercise her subjectivity as she wishes. She discovers, however, that even this position, the privileged site of motherhood, is circumscribed by complex social bonds.

One night her daughter comes into her bedroom while she and Leo are making love. She is up on her hands and knees because he has entered her from behind, but she is able to lower herself onto her side to make room for her daughter without dislodging her lover. Without knowing why, Anna keeps moving slowly, gently, in a sexual rhythm while holding her daughter in the curve of her arms. She talks soothingly to her child, stilling her fears and lulling her toward sleep. She has no desire for orgasm but feels completely fulfilled by this different form of erotic activity. The novel suggests that she has a uniquely female experience, discovers for herself a female mode of desire. "I can remember feeling a sense of completion, as though I had everything I wanted held close, held inside me; as though I had finally found a way to have everything. We seemed fused, the three of us, all the boundaries between us dissolved; and I felt the medium for that. In my sleepiness I thought of myself as simply a *way* for Leo and Molly and me to be together, as *clear*, translucent" (124).

Anna may have felt that the incident was an innocent one, but she soon discovers that she is not the only one whose interpretation counts, that she, in fact, is regarded as the least competent judge of the character of her actions. In the eyes of society, what she has done is a form of child abuse, and her estranged husband uses this incident, with a few others, to take her child away. Her recent experience of independence had led her to believe that traditional roles were breaking down, that she could explore new possibilities of being, but the courts were there to remind her that sex was sex. The novel is too complex to state unambiguously that the incident was innocent, but it at least raises the possibility that the title of the book is not ironic. Again, historical women are required to work with and against an ahistorical conception of desire, a conception that says Anna's feeling of completion can be read only in salacious terms.

Historicizing Desire

What would it mean to think of desire as historical? Few theorists have entertained such a proposition, so the task of sketching an historical theory of desire is a formidable one. Perhaps it is impossible. Perhaps desire *is* a constant, a mechanism so fundamental to human nature that no conceivable social conditions could alter its outlines. Anthropology, however, has found few such constants, and the question of whether the Oedipus complex itself is universal has occasioned a long debate within that discipline (Geertz, *Interpretation* 42). Can one be sure that the desires of the artists who painted on the cave walls at Lascaux fell into the same patterns as one's own? If desire is trapped in the economy of the sign, as Lacan maintains, then one has only to imagine the different attitude toward symbolism that Lévi-Strauss attributes to the savage mind for desire itself to be different too. What of the audience who listened to oral, formulaic poetry? What of readers who saw themselves as links in the great Chain of Being, who thought they lived in a desiring universe, a world in which the sun was not a ball of gas but the searching eye of God? The hypothesis that desire is historical, I suggest, is at least as reasonable as the alternative and therefore deserves consideration.

When pressed, some people might be willing to accept a weaker version of this hypothesis, one that says desire is constant but the manifestations of desire in social forms change over time. This weaker hypothesis, however, does not advance the question at all, for the analyst cannot separate desire from its manifestations. One cannot know anything about desire independent of its embodiment in social and historical forms. In psychoanalysis, need is a constant by definition; it is instinctual and always possesses a somatic component. Need is necessarily related to one of the biological conditions for life. If a human being were discovered somewhere who did not require food for continued existence, then eating could no longer be called a need. Desire, on the other hand, is what happens to need when it enters history, language, culture, and society. Desire names the way in which individuals transform their needs under the pressure of the particular social conditions of their time and place.

Despite this distinction, psychoanalysis still regards the form of desire as universal. Consequently, one must look outside psychoanalysis if one hopes to formulate an historical conception of desire. Recent developments in the field of history provide us with a model of the kind of inquiry that is needed. The *Annales* school of historians, particularly in their turn toward the study of collective *mentalites*, has focused attention on all aspects of the private life. Lucien Febvre, cofounder of the journal *Annales*, was one of the first to propose the study of the "whole system of sentiments within a given society in a given period" ("Sensibility" 20). Writing in 1941, he complained that no one had investigated the history of love, death, pity, cruelty, joy, hate, or fear. His essay "Sensibility and History: How to Reconstitute the Emotional Life of the Past" indicated the kinds of sources – in documents on moral conduct, in the representations of art and literature, and in the vocabulary of an age – that were to be used with such success by later scholars such as Philippe Ariès, Georges Duby, and Paul Veyne. The fruits of their labors can most easily be seen in the five volumes of *A History of Private Life*, which surveys changes in private experience, including the life of the emotions, from pagan Rome to the contemporary era.

Other forms of inquiry can also aid this project. Investigations into the history of sexuality by Foucault, John Boswell, Peter Brown, Arnold I. Davidson, John D'Emilio, Estelle Friedman, Peter Gay, David M. Halperin, Thomas Laqueur, Jeffrey Weeks, and the contributors to Ariès and Béjin's *Western Sexuality* are important, as are feminist challenges to prevailing models of sexuality by Monique Plaza, Susan Estrich, Catharine A. MacKinnon, and others. The burgeoning literature on the history of marriage and the family by Lawrence Stone, Edward Shorter, and other historians also sheds light on changing patterns of intimacy. For a different approach to the problem of linking innate characteristics to changes in social structures, one could turn to the sociology of perception, to the studies of odor by Alain Corbin or of sight by Michael Baxandall and Norman Bryson. Finally, Norbert Elias's pioneering study of the civilizing process, which traces alterations in the feelings of shame and delicacy to specific historical changes, could provide another model for this project.

Without doubt, the most important development along these lines in recent years has been the emergence in the academy of lesbian and gay studies, sometimes called "queer theory." De Lauretis, in "Sexual Indifference and Lesbian Representation" (1988), works toward "defining an autonomous form of female sexuality and desire" (170) in exactly the historical terms that were missing from her earlier work on narrative. Both Valerie Traub, whose article on the movie *Black Widow* won the 1990 Crompton-Noll award from the Lesbian and Gay Caucus of the Modern Language Association, and Judith Roof, whose *A Lure of Knowledge: Lesbian Sexuality and Theory* (1991) treats films, novels, and psychoanalytic narratives, bring an historical dimension to the analysis of lesbian desire in contemporary culture. "What *is* a 'lesbian' desire?" Traub asks. "I hope to have shown that such questions can only be answered meaningfully in historically contingent terms" (324). Roof, moreover, calls for complicating the relationship between narrative and desire: "If desire is shaped differently according to gender and sexual orientation, then it may differ in respect to other criteria as well. As the terms multiply, so do the operations of desire. . . . We need to recognize the multiple shapes of desire that drive and shape narrative" (118).

Leo Bersani, too, has become a prominent contributor to the development of queer theory. In "Is the Rectum a Grave?" (1988), he situates his advocacy of mobile desire in the context of one form of gay sexual behavior, which is threatened by the public's homophobic response to the AIDS epidemic. There are limits, however, to this critic's willingness to historicize desire, and these limits require further analysis. His indictment of media representations of gay men in the eighties as "dangerously promiscuous" is compelling, and it effectively locates his advocacy of mobile desire as a specific form of resistance to a heterosexual culture, which works to enforce its values (and its fears masquerading as values) on anyone perceived as "deviant." As a response to homophobic characterizations of some gay sexual practices, his theory has a validity that it does not possess as a universal claim about all desire and all narrative. Bersani remains uncompromising in his insistence on the violence of desire; he believes the "inestimable value of sex" to lie in its character as "anticommunal, antiegalitarian, antinurturing, antiloving" (215), and he continues to celebrate a "more radical disintegration and humiliation of the self" through sex (217). But when he turns from a consideration of the politics of gay culture in the United States to a discussion of Catherine MacKinnon and Andrea Dworkin's treatment of violence against women, the problems with his universalizing model of desire surface once again. He does not object to their analysis of sexuality as violence, but he adamantly opposes their "pastoralizing, redemptive intentions" to stop that violence. "They have given us the reasons why pornography must be multiplied and not abandoned, and, more profoundly, the reasons for defending, for cherishing the very sex they find so hateful" ("Rectum" 215). What may be part of a strategic political practice for some gay men can at the same time be a brutal, dehumanizing means of enforcing the oppression of women.[9]

For valuable counterexamples from the field of gay studies to Bersani's treatment of desire and narrative, one should turn to the works of Eve Kosofsky Sedgwick and D. A. Miller. The former's influential book, *Between Men: English Literature and Male Ho-*

mosocial Desire (1985), played a large role in legitimizing the topic of sexuality in literary theory through its treatment of heterosexuality as structurally connected with homophobia. Indeed, Sedgwick's next book, *Epistemology of the Closet* (1990), argued that issues of "homo/heterosexual definition" have a "primary importance for all modern Western identity and social organization (and not merely for homosexual identity and culture)" (11). From the first pages of *Between Men* she marks her difference from a universalizing psychoanalytic approach: "it is clear that there is not some ahistorical *Stoff* of sexuality, some sexual charge that can be simply added to a social relationship to 'sexualize' it in a constant and predictable direction, or that splits off from it unchanged" (6). The characteristic conclusion of her analysis in this book is that the social or political effect of homosexuality "varies . . . for different groups in different political circumstances" (*Between* 6), just as the characteristic opening point of analysis in her next book is "*not to know* how far its insights and projects are generalizable" (*Epistemology* 12). The most productive aspect of both books for narrative theorists is her insistence on an historical approach to the intersection of sexuality and genre. Unlike Bersani, whose evaluation of mimetic representation remains unchanged whether it appears in ancient Assyrian art, Victorian novels, or twentieth-century pornography, Sedgwick traces the way in which the emergence of a particular narrative genre—the gothic—both responds to and helps constitute an historically specific mode of knowledge that is charged with desire and its repressions: the "closet."

D. A. Miller's essays on the nineteenth-century English novel, collected in *The Novel and the Police* (1988), attend with equal care to the political work performed at different historical periods by narrative genres and subgenres, including the realistic novel, police novel, detective novel, sensation novel, fictional autobiography, and more.[10] His reading of Wilkie Collins's *The Woman in White*, for example, reveals one kind of sexual shattering of the self to be a generic feature of the sensation novel, which arose at a particular historical moment to perform particular cultural work. Miller examines what he calls the "primal scene" of the novel, a touch on the hero's shoulder by the woman in white, which figuratively "unmans" the hero, making him feel like a woman, as if the touch "were a violation . . . and what was violated were a gender identification" (*"Cage"* 111). This "sensation," however, is not an antinarrative shattering, but a narrative effect specific to the sub-genre to which it gave a name: "The specificity of the sensation novel in nineteenth-century fiction is that it renders the liberal subject the subject of a *body*, whose fear and desire of violation displaces, reworks, and exceeds his constitutive fantasy of intact privacy" (117).

Experiences that render men "the subject of a *body*" are one of the many interests of *The Body and Its Dangers* (1990), a moving collection of short stories by Allen Barnett. The book portrays—vividly and powerfully—a range of gay, lesbian, and heterosexual relations, but its depiction of anal intercourse between men is particularly relevant to some of the issues I have been discussing. In three different stories Barnett's male characters describe sexual "sensations" that shatter the self, but this phenomenon has a very different meaning for a man in the 1980s than it did in 1860, when *The Woman in White* was published. The first two scenes record, from different perspectives, a single sexual encounter between strangers from a time before HIV infection had been discovered, although the reader's response to these scenes is inevitably influenced by an awareness of how the dangers of such encounters will change in the course of a few years. Barnett describes a "fear and desire of violation" that reworks and exceeds his character's "constitutive fantasy of intact privacy": "Gordon thought it should hurt, but it didn't, not after a bit; he felt himself dissolve to the point where he was most his body and least his mind. Father Creighton wanted confession, but better than that must be this, Gordon thought, penetration" (31). Or in the second account of the event: "Gordon felt as if he were opening up into nothing at all . . . but it scared him that what distinguished his inside from his outside had dissolved. . . . He wanted the feeling to stop, and he didn't" (165).

Gordon is self-identified as a gay man, and Collins's hero is not, is in fact phobically concerned to recover the "secure" sense of himself as a heterosexual male that he lost when he was shattered by the woman in white's touch. But these differences are specifiable too, as differences in the social and political positions of subjects. A third scene in Barnett's collection, however, registers the transformations of history, not merely from Collins's time but from the years before AIDS. In the long, sensitive story "The *Times* as It Knows Us," the reader learns on the first page that one of the characters has died from AIDS, and the language used by his lover to describe the shattering experience of their lovemaking is crucially different: "You ceased to exist. All else fell away. You had brought him, and he you, to that point where you are most your mind and most your body. His prostate pulsed against your fingers like a heart in a cave, *mind, body, body, mind,* over and over" (106). Why does being the "subject of a *body*" receive so much emphasis here on *mind*? The clue lies in the title of this story, which refers to the cruel ironies that arise from the lag between the *New York Times*'s coverage of the AIDS epidemic and the actual lives and deaths of a group of gay men.[11] But the title also refers to time, the time of history, the time of differences, the time necessary for grieving. The need for such a sense of time, which depends on memory as well as forgetting, on continuity as well as self-shattering, may have contributed to the change in the way the experience of lovemaking is described. The story ends: "You let go of people, the living and the dead, and return to your self. . . . The stretch of time and the vortex that it spins around, thinning and thickening like taffy, holds these pleasures, these grace notes, these connections to others, to what it is humanly possible to do" (116–17).

What do these historical models of desire suggest for the study of narrative? To view desire as historical requires that one not merely say that the way desire is invested in narrative changes but that the economy of desire changes too. One would have to turn to historians for evidence of specific practices of desire in specific historical periods, and one would have to relate those practices to observed changes in narrative. Alterations in narrative would include changes in formal features, such as genres and conventions, but they could not be restricted to such features. They would also have to include alterations in the social function of narrative, because the way literary forms are used by a culture is an important determinant of their nature—and is just as variable as literary structure. One could not take for granted, either, that changes in the organization of desire influenced changes in narrative, for the influence could just as easily have flowed in the other direction. Thus one would be forced to engage in a twofold, reciprocal analysis. Both desire and narrative would be seen as variable social phenomena, either one of which might influence the behavior of the other at a particular historical moment, or more likely still, each of which might work simultaneously on the other in a mutually enriching exchange. The job might then be to determine not only the nature of the exchange but also the place, the particular locus in the social world, where the negotiations between narrative and desire are carried out.

In the next chapter I shall emphasize the importance of attending to such particular sites when dealing with contemporary writing by minorities. The focus will be on the cultural work of narrative in communities rather than in individuals. This new aspect of the topic will illuminate the role cultural forms such as narrative play in the political struggles of marginalized groups in today's society.

4

The Narrative Turn
in Minority Writing

In Louise Erdrich's novel *Tracks* (1988), an old Chippewa known as Nanapush tells of using stories to hold off his own death: "During the year of sickness, when I was the last one left, I saved myself by starting a story. . . . I got well by talking. Death could not get a word in edgewise, grew discouraged, and traveled on" (46). Perhaps because he is the last of his people to follow the old ways, Nanapush is the only character in Erdrich's three interrelated novels to make explicit claims about the power of narrative. Later in the text he tells of saving his granddaughter, who has almost frozen to death, by telling her stories through an entire night: "Once I had you I did not dare break the string between us and kept on moving my lips, holding you motionless with talking" (167).

Only Nanapush dwells on the power of stories, but all of Erdrich's novels rely on this strength, rely on the sinuous thread of narrative to weave the lives of her people into one seamless fabric. Part of the pleasure of reading *Love Medicine* (1984), her first published novel, is slowly piecing together how its many characters are related. *The Beet Queen* (1986) focuses on fewer people, but the theme of connections emerges even more insistently in the imagery that organizes the text. The figure of the web shows up repeatedly, in the "spider web of thick dead vines" that holds one character as in a hammock (154); in the silky nest a spider weaves in a baby's hair, a "complicated house," too beautiful to destroy (176);

in the red maze a woman has kn𝗂𝗍𝗍ed into a sweater, a "tangle of pathways" without an exit (277); and in the thread of flight, a thread that links three generations of people who have hardly known one another (335). Consequently, when Nanapush talks about the mysterious patterns that stories reveal, the reader is prepared to understand: "There is a story to it the way there is a story to all, never visible while it is happening. Only after, when an old man sits dreaming and talking in his chair, the design springs clear" (*Tracks* 34).

The theme of storytelling in Erdrich's fiction raises questions about narrative not only among minority writers,[1] but also among contemporary novelists generally. Why has storytelling—particularly oral, folk, or traditional storytelling—become a prominent topic in current fiction? How does the *theme* of storytelling relate to the increased acceptability of the *technique* of narrative in today's writing? Since the mid-seventies, novelists have increasingly employed conventional narrative forms, which had seemed passé during the heyday of metafiction, language games, and self-reflexive experiments in the sixties. One has only to name a few novels by well-known contemporary writers in which narrative figures not only as a primary technical resource but also as part of the theme—John Irving's *The World According to Garp* (1978), John Gardner's *Freddy's Book* (1980), Anne Tyler's *Dinner at the Homesick Restaurant* (1982), Philip Roth's *The Counterlife* (1986), Cynthia Ozick's *The Messiah of Stockholm* (1987), John Barth's *Tidewater Tales* (1987), Paul Auster's *Moon Palace* (1989), and Brad Leithauser's *Hence* (1989)—to see how widespread the phenomenon has become.[2] These novels, however, can hardly be called old-fashioned. By insisting on the importance of narrative even as they experiment with structure, style, and point of view, many novelists today challenge commonplace assumptions about the difference between narrative and experimental works.

Leslie Marmon Silko's *Ceremony* (1977), for example, mixes accounts of Tayo, a "half-breed" living on a reservation in the years following World War Two, with the poetry and myths of the Laguna Pueblo people; jumps back and forth among at least four different time periods; and combines powerful social criticism—of race relations, of white people's attitudes toward nature and technology, of nuclear arms—with traditional Indian beliefs. It

engages in serious technical experimentation yet begins by instruct-
ing us in narrative's power:

> I will tell you something about stories,
>   [he said]
> They aren't just entertainment.
>   Don't be fooled.
> They are all we have, you see,
>   all we have to fight off
>   illness and death.   (2)

As the book opens, Tayo is suffering mentally and physically
from the ravages of the war. Tayo's world is suffering too: there
have been six years of drought on the reservation. Tayo fears that
his words have caused this drought, the curse he put on the rain
while he struggled to carry his wounded cousin-brother,[3] Rocky,
on a terrible march through the jungle when they were prisoners of
war. By the end of the novel, the drought has broken, the rains
have come, and Tayo has recovered as well. The turning point in
this process is a ceremony of healing, which brings to consciousness
things Tayo has already begun to intuit: that his story has been
going on for a long time, that everything he has done is part of
a larger pattern. This ritual story both restores Tayo to a larger
community and implicates the reader in Silko's vision. For if all
are one, as tribalism[4] maintains and ritual dramatizes, then the
reader too is part of the larger pattern. The climax of the novel
takes place in an abandoned uranium mine,[5] a place that reinforces
the non-Laguna Pueblo reader's sense that everyone is part of
Tayo's struggle—either as supporter or antagonist—a struggle, finally, to save the world from annihilation.

Among other Native American writings one sees the prominence
of narrative in James Welch's myth-filled historical novel, *Fools
Crow* (1986), which constitutes a profound opening to narrative
revelations from the spare, lyrical techniques of his first novel,
Winter in the Blood (1974); in Michael Dorris's *A Yellow Raft in
Blue Water* (1987), with its three generations of narrators; and in
the legends of N. Scott Momaday's *The Ancient Child* (1989). But
Native American fiction represents only one aspect of the recent
interest in storytelling among minority writers. One could equally
point to the use of traditional oral tales—called *cuentos*—in the
work of the Chicano novelist Rudolpho Anaya.[6] Or one could

point to the flamboyant figure of the storyteller in Maxine Hong Kingston's *Tripmaster Monkey: His Fake Book* (1989); the alternating narrators of Amy Tan's *The Joy Luck Club* (1989); and the "American story" (1) of Gish Jen's *Typical American* (1991). Some of the most direct treatments of the theme of storytelling in recent years, however, have taken place in the African-American novel.[7]

Alice Walker's *Meridian* (1976) memorializes a slave named Louvinie, who had her tongue cut out as punishment for scaring a white child to death with her tales. She learned the gift of storytelling from her parents in Africa, who could discover the identity of murderers by entangling them in a detailed retelling of the crime (42-3). The contemporary heroine of Gayl Jones's *Corregidora* (1975) is haunted by the fierce imperative to "make generations" so that the story of her grandmother and great-grandmother's abuse by the same man will not go untold. David Bradley dedicates *The Chaneysville Incident* (1981) to the storytellers and historians in his life, and the novel climaxes in a night-long retelling of an historical narrative, the story of a group of escaped slaves driven to kill their children and themselves rather than be recaptured. At the beginning of the novel, the narrator's memory of an old man's stories is what sets him searching for the truth of the past (48-9); and at the end of the novel, another old man's tale gives the slaves strength to commit suicide (428). More often, stories provide the strength to live rather than to die. Both Toni Cade Bambara's *The Salt Eaters* (1980) and Audre Lorde's *Zami* (1982) feature moments when telling stories literally keeps characters alive.[8] John Edgar Wideman's *Reuben* (1987) focuses on an unlicensed lawyer who solves problems simply by listening to his clients tell their stories, and Ernest J. Gaines uses the voices of multiple narrators in *A Gathering of Old Men* (1983) to bring home the truth of the observation that one of the old men makes to the white sheriff: "You don't see what we don't see. . . . You had to be here to don't see it now. You just can't come down here every now and then. You had to live here seventy-seven years to don't see it now" (89). Finally, the novelist Toni Morrison has often spoken of the importance of storytelling to her art and to the lives of the people she writes about: "People *crave* narration. . . . That's the way they learn things. That's the way human beings organize their human knowledge — fairy tales, myths. All narration" (quoted in Mason 565).

Despite the prominence of narrative in contemporary fiction of all kinds, I have chosen to focus on writers of color in this chapter because the non-Euro-American heritage on which they often draw makes the theme of storytelling particularly visible.[9] This theme, in turn, helps to make explicit some of the special uses to which the technique of narrative is being put today. The narrative turn in fiction is related to the emphasis in our society on local political struggles. The tactical value of narrative in politics is by no means restricted to minority writers or minority causes, but the frequently collective nature of a minority group's struggle against dominant culture highlights the altered political function of narrative today.[10]

The Politics of Contemporary Fiction

When the narrative turn among white establishment writers first began to attract the attention of literary critics, it was quickly dismissed as a symptom of political reaction, paralleling the turn to the right among the U.S. electorate. Writing in 1982, Larry McCaffery noticed that "experimentalism *per se* . . . is not nearly as important to writers today as it was a decade ago" and attributed this trend to the "conservativism of our times" (261). Such diagnoses have become a commonplace of book review sections and literary quarterlies during the decade. Many commentators cannot resist drawing a parallel between what they see as the complacent social attitudes of the Reagan and Bush eras and the turn to more accessible narrative conventions. The very success of recent narrative works in attracting a wider readership than the metafiction of the sixties ever earned has been taken as evidence that some of our most serious novelists have made a compromise with the times. John Gardner's notorious call in 1978 for a return to "moral fiction" certainly reinforced the impression that interest in narrative went hand in hand with conservative social views.

This impression could not be further from the truth. The narrative turn does not represent a return to old-fashioned values. In fact, the very dichotomy between daring experiments and safe traditional works seems anachronistic, an opposition that more accurately describes the high modernist rebellion against nineteenth-century literature at the beginning of this century than the flexible, ad hoc arrangements of contemporary writing. Far from seeming a secure prop of the establishment, narrative is often viewed by novelists today as an oppositional technique because of its association with unauthorized forms of knowledge, what Foucault has called "subjugated" and Morrison "discredited" knowledge ("Interview" 428). Scorned by official culture, narrative is one of the "naive knowledges, located low down on the hierarchy, beneath the required level of cognition or scientificity" (Foucault, *Power* 82), and it can be all the more attractive to iconoclasts for that reason. Certainly, much of its attraction for radicals in other fields, such as history, anthropology, psychoanalysis, and the law, lies in the way it violates the discursive norms of their disciplines. In literature, narrative cannot have the same iconoclastic force, but its association with unauthorized knowledge can be and often is emphasized by drawing on oral forms — folktales, myths, legends, oral histories; by exploring less privileged written genres — diaries, letters, criminal confessions, slave narratives; by identifying the contemporary text with archaic symbolic modes — rituals, dreams, magic; and by writing about traditional activities — vernacular arts, recipes, folklore, quilting and other crafts, native music and dance.[11] The rich mixture of traditional narrative forms and contemporary political concerns found in minority writing represents the most important force transforming the North American novel in the eighties and nineties and has made this period one of the most exciting of the century for literature.[12]

Today the writing of social radicals often finds its best outlet in highly conventional forms. The difficulty of understanding this paradox is a source of confusion for one of the main characters in Walker's *Meridian*. The heroine, a young black activist, confesses to years of frustration with watching her mother's generation sublimate its anger through religion, singing the old hymns about salvation in heaven instead of rising up to demand justice on earth. Meridian "had always thought of the black church as mainly a reactionary power" (199). It is only when she witnesses a service on the anniversary of a young man's death by clubbing that she realizes that revolutionary sentiments can be stirred up by the most venerable observances. She suddenly could hear the congregation pleading: "let us weave your story and your son's life and death into what we already know — into the songs, the sermons. . . . The music, the form of worship that has always sustained us, the kind of ritual you share with us, these are the ways to transformation that we know" (199–200).

I emphasize the subversive uses of narrative in order to dispel a widespread assumption about the political complacency of contemporary fiction, but there is a more specific point to be made about the current revival of narrative. From both their practice and their explicit statements, one gathers that many novelists today believe that the act of telling a story can be empowering. This belief seems to be shared not only by the minority writers mentioned above but also by numerous white novelists. Minority writers and feminists have made the question of empowerment a major theme of their criticism, but that is no reason to deny that narrative can be empowering in other contexts as well. Focusing on writers from minority communities casts in greater relief the political dimension of narrative's capacity, but it is not meant to suggest that this capacity is unavailable or unexploited by writers from other segments of the population. In fact, the increased division of society into local communities, which is characteristic of advanced capitalism, makes this capacity more important to all groups, including economic and social elites that formerly may have relied on other forms of power. But that is another story.

Most minority writers record the reality of domination from above, to return to the definitions of power developed in Chapter 1. From the nineteenth century on, resistance to this domination has reflected a gamut of responses, ranging from liberal advocacy of civil rights to violent rebellion. The first African-American narratives, for example, were addressed to a white ruling class and aimed to impress this readership with the humanity of African-Americans, who were as deserving of freedom and respect as their readers. Although phrased in the pervasive American idiom of autonomy and often following the deeply individualistic pattern of spiritual conversion narratives, this literature sometimes had recourse to the language of civic republicanism when attempting to describe the benefits that would accrue to society at large if black people were given the same rights as white people. Thus this literature made room for positive as well as negative views of power. In his *Narrative*, Frederick Douglass was careful to celebrate freedom's "responsibilities" as well as its "rights," and his break with the Garrisonians came in part because of his defense of the Union and his support of electoral politics (see Andrews 128, 214). In the early twentieth century, the republican note was sounded more loudly by writers such as Booker T. Washington, who in *Up from Slavery* emphasized his strong sense of public responsibility and civic virtue. This strain in African-American writing has sometimes been criticized for its assimilationist ideals, but the dream of a just public realm, which values the equal participation of all people, is a vision of power that continues down through the speeches of Martin Luther King and Jessie Jackson.

This vision, like other African-American models of a free society, is integrally related to narrative modes, to the development of what has been called "free storytelling" (Andrews xi). The ability to tell a free story is as empowering as any image of freedom contained within it. The contemporary novelist Charles Johnson would seem to agree, for in *Oxherding Tale* (1982), his extraordinarily free reworking of the slave narrative genre, he presents the liberation of his storytelling technique, "the manumission of first-person viewpoint" (152), as being just as important as the freeing of his main character. The vision of rebuilding and conserving a shared world, which ends the novel, depends on the narrator's being able to pen the final words of his text: "This is my tale" (176).

More common in contemporary minority discourse is the use of narrative to exploit, in positive ways, what Foucault calls "disciplinary" modes of power. De Certeau, it should be recalled, terms this use "tactical," and he identifies four ways stories help people to escape disciplinary control. First, stories preserve the memory of successful tactics, ruses that can be used in daily life. They are "living museums of these tactics, the benchmarks of an apprenticeship" (23), and their very status as unsystematic, "naive" discourse allows them to perform this service, because they flourish beyond or beneath the regulatory mechanisms of science or truth. The once-upon-a-time of fairytales and legends signals the creation of "a space outside of and isolated from daily competition" (23), a less serious space, which nevertheless insinuates itself into official discourse—even into scientific writing—in the form of case histories, analogies, interviews, and so on. Second, stories preserve tactics not only in their content but also in their structure. The tricks and turns of narratives encode "moves," demonstrate native procedures, that perhaps could not be taught directly. In thrall to a story's charm, one is moved in ways for which one cannot entirely account, made to practice procedures without being able to formulate exactly what has been learned. By showing rather than telling, narrative may escape the processes that recuperate or coopt more explicit forms of knowledge. "Narration does indeed have a content, but it also belongs to the art of making a *coup*. . . . Its discourse is characterized more by a way of *exercising itself* than by the thing it indicates. And one must grasp a sense other than what is said. It produces effects, not objects" (79).

This aspect of stories — their trickiness, the canniness of a vernacular mode — is very important to minority writers in the United States, who may draw on oral traditions shaped in part by the necessity of concealing the meaning of one's utterance from those in control. Henry Louis Gates has demonstrated the centrality, through more than three centuries, of trickster figures like Esu-Elegbara and the "Signifying Monkey," which turn up in Africa as well as in all "New World African-informed cultures" (4). A similar trickster, the "tripmaster monkey," is the improvisational genius behind the manic narratives of Maxine Hong Kingston's latest work. Riddles, deceptive stories, and dreams that say more than the dreamer knows are common techniques of Coyote, the trickster figure in much Native American literature (see Vizenor).

Third, the temporality of narrative offers an alternative to the spatializing procedures of most disciplines. Temporal devices, which are basic to narrative, make an impression of their own. As one moves through a story, false leads, flashbacks, digressions, and reversals create effects that may be at odds with the official message that a work conveys. Whereas the meaning of a narrative can always be recovered by the organizing grids of disciplines, the process of reading or hearing narrative cannot be so easily systematized. Finally, narrative possesses a performative dimension; it enacts as well as means. Just as the ritual process can have a transformative effect on its participants, so stories can change the person who becomes caught up in their charm. This transformative capacity is another aspect of narrative that figures prominently in writing by minorities. Silko emphasizes this principle by beginning *Ceremony* with the Laguna myth in which "grandmother spider" creates the world by spinning out a tale.[13] African-American novelists frequently claim this power for their narratives: Walker dedicates *The Color Purple* (1982) to the Spirit; Morrison opens both *Sula* (1974) and *Song of Solomon* (1977) with allusions to ritual; other writers make healers, voodoo figures, or conjure women the presiding spirits of their novels — Bambara's *The Salt Eaters*, Ntozake Shange's *Sassafrass, Cypress and Indigo* (1982), Paule Marshall's, *Praisesong for the Widow* (1983), Gloria Naylor's *Mama Day* (1988), and Randall Kenan's *A Visitation of Spirits* (1989).

The conjunction between minority practice and some contemporary theories of power helps to clarify why narrative can be a source of empowerment for many oppressed or marginalized peoples. This conjunction, however, raises its own set of difficulties. How does a particular verbal structure possess power, either to raise up or to oppress? Is the power *in* a form of discourse or does it reside in the way that form is used? What relation, if any, exists between the kinds of power narrative possesses today and the organization of contemporary society?

Narrative Communities

Near the end of Toni Morrison's *Song of Solomon*, the protagonist Milkman travels to a small town in Pennsylvania where his father had lived as a boy. Milkman remains there for four days, during which he receives visits from every old man in the area who had known his forefathers, and from some who had only heard about them. They all speak of Milkman's family with awe and affection. For the first time, Milkman finds himself feeling some tenderness for the father he had always resented. As the old men talk, Milkman begins to realize that there is something he can do for them, a service he can perform; he can continue the story: "That's why Milkman began to talk about his father, the boy they knew, the son of the fabulous Macon Dead. He bragged a little and they came alive. How many houses his father owned (they grinned); the new car every two years (they laughed); and when he told them how his father tried to buy the Erie Lackawanna (it sounded better that way), they hooted with joy" (236).

Storytelling educates Milkman in the virtues of community, in the importance of an organic link to the past and to the lives of those who surround him. It teaches him to respect the very people he had taken advantage of and abused—his family. A few pages later, Milkman will hear another story about his family's past, this time in a song chanted by children in a circle, and the experience will complete his transformation. Through the power of narrative he will have found his place in a community that he can call his own. It is a place for which he is willing to die.

The proliferation of such local narrative communities, according to Jean-François Lyotard, is a defining feature of contemporary Western societies. In the course of the twentieth century, Lyotard argues in *The Postmodern Condition*, one has seen the decline of the grand metanarratives, especially the narratives of scientific progress and political freedom that, since the time of the American and French revolutions, had legitimated modernity. By means of these inspiring stories, modern science was able to establish itself as the reigning paradigm of truth and the modern state was able to achieve unity. But now the grand narrative, as a genre, has lost its credibility; people are suspicious of tales that claim to be true for everyone everywhere and at all times. In place of a few metanarratives, there have arisen countless micronarratives, which offer "immediate legitimation" (23) to diverse, often conflicting enterprises and groups. Rather than promoting consensus, these micronarratives enable a splintering of the social world; rather than confirming a monological conception of truth (rational, scientific in its orientation), they offer an alternative model of knowledge.

This alternative, which Lyotard calls "narrative knowledge" (18), is perfectly suited to the needs of contemporary, postmodern society. It includes not just verifiable statements about reality but also notions of competence, images of how to do things, how to live, how to care for one another, how to be happy. The question of usefulness must be considered in any judgment about its value. Does it teach something that matters to one's existence in the particular historical conditions one inhabits? Does it convey some accepted belief, some habit or custom, some technical procedure or knack that one needs to know in order to succeed? This form of knowledge is local, contingent, and ephemeral; it is tolerant of "error," of everyday lore and "old wives' tales," as long as the results are satisfactory.

Lyotard's contention that this kind of knowledge is peculiarly suited to the demands of living in a postmodern world provides another reason to look carefully at the relation between narrative and empowerment. Lyotard's view of narrative practices parallels that of de Certeau in two respects. For both writers, narrative's temporality and its ability to record successful tactics are major reasons why it figures prominently in contemporary society. Lyotard's interest in legitimation prompts him to add two further reasons. First, stories, unlike scientific knowledge, lend themselves to a multiplicity of "language games" (20). If "there are many different language games—a heterogeneity of elements"—then monolithic institutions have trouble maintaining control over society. Micronarratives, distributed among discrete language games, only legitimate ad hoc arrangements, "only give rise to institutions in patches—local determinism" (xxiv). Second, stories position both the speaker and the listener within a pragmatics of communication or "speech act" situation (21). In both cases, postmodern legitimation is oriented toward the local. The notion of multiple language games, adapted from Wittgenstein, preserves the integrity of differing perspectives, and the notion of "speech acts," adapted from Searle, locates the narrative subject and the addressee within a specific community of discourse.

Lyotard's localism fits in nicely with other accounts of contemporary society—with Foucault's "specific intellectual," engaged in local struggles; with Cover's conflicting normative communities, created and sustained in large part by the "jurisgenerative" capacity of narratives; with the vision of our country as a Babel of competing cultures, common to many critics on both the left and right; and with Daniel Bell's discussion of the "participation revolution," in which "many more groups now seek to establish their social rights—their claims on society—through the political order" (*Post-Industrial* 365, 364). Not every aspect of Lyotard, however, is as convincing as his treatment of the connection between micronarratives and today's society. His account of "postmodern science" oddly exalts a few areas of contemporary research—the theory of *fracta*, catastrophes, and chaos—into an account of all contemporary science and then uses it as proof that even science "is theorizing its own evolution as discontinuous, catastrophic, nonrectifiable, and paradoxical" (60). His faith in "paralogy," the pursuit of instabilities and paradoxes in every realm, merely privileges the disruption of order for its own sake. One needs to distinguish Lyotard's acute descriptions of advanced capitalist societies from what has been called the "anarchist" and "irrationalist" strains in his thinking.[14]

Even if we restrict ourselves to the "sociological" vein in Lyotard, we are still confronted by the other questions posed earlier. How does a cultural form such as narrative possess power? The first point to be made is that nothing *in* narrative gives it a determined relation to a particular social order. This assertion goes against the conventional wisdom of much contemporary narrative theory of the sort examined in Chapter 2. In its support, however, one should note that Lyotard nowhere distinguishes the formal properties of micronarratives from those of metanarratives. Although the two legitimize entirely different social orders, there is no difference in their structure. Both are characterized by all the common attributes of stories: a beginning, middle, and end; a hero that acts as the subject of the narrative; obstacles that impede the hero's progress; a mimetic or representational dimension; and a teleological organization of the whole.

If nothing in their formal character as narrative enables them to authorize conflicting forms of society, then perhaps the difference lies in how they are used, when and where they come into play, who is employing them, and for what ends. I had this conclusion in mind when I drew attention to the way minority communities could turn conventional forms to their own uses. Another good example is the revisionist use of slave history in contemporary novels by African Americans, a large body of works that Bernard Bell has named "neoslave narrative[s]" (289). These novels often tell the story of slavery not merely to document an oppressive institution but also to uncover the forms of agency that persisted within it. In a groundbreaking article on this subject, Deborah McDowell writes: "Contemporary Afro-American writers who tell a story of slavery are increasingly aiming . . . to reposition the stress points of that story with a heavy accent on particular acts of agency within an oppressive and degrading system" (160). It is not the facts of slavery that change in these accounts, but who is telling the story and why, a point made forcefully in Paule Marshall's latest novel, *Daughters* (1991).

It goes against the grain of much twentieth-century thinking to assert that conditions outside of a text—the conditions of its production and reception—should be considered in assessing a work of literature. But this idea in no way returns one to a nineteenth-century aesthetics of expression. For it is not the individual author and reader that count here but the social unit that these figures help to constitute. Lyotard implies as much when he draws an analogy between traditional, oral storytelling and the pragmatics of micronarratives. In oral literature the narrative locates all relevant participants—the storyteller, the hero, and the listeners—within a community that the telling itself helps to bring into existence.[15] A "collectivity that takes narrative as its key form of competence"— traditional communities and, I am arguing, many groups in advanced capitalism, particularly those that are characterized as minorities—"finds the raw material for its social bond not only in the meaning of the narratives it recounts, but also in the act of reciting them. . . . In a sense, the people are only that which actualizes the narratives" (22-3).

In *Just Gaming*, a work published in the same year as *The Postmodern Condition* (1979), Lyotard explains in more detail how traditional narratives achieve this effect. In oral societies the person who tells a story does not create it but passes it on; the narrator has heard the story being told, has been its recipient or addressee before becoming its speaker. As a result, the narrator is not an autonomous subject; the storyteller already is constituted by the relation between two poles, that of narrator and of addressee. But there is a third position, that of referent, and every traditional storyteller implicitly occupies that position too, because the story always concerns the life of the tribe (its myths, legends, genealogy, achievements, tragedies, etc.) from which the storyteller's identity is derived. Thus the pragmatics of traditional narrative creates interdependence, an intersubjectivity that exists not only among but also within every member of the community. Further, it obligates one to pass on what one has heard. Not to "relay" a story is to isolate oneself. Having heard a story, one "is bound to retell it, because, to refuse to retell it would mean that [one] does not want to share" in the life of the community; "as soon as I have been spoken to as well as spoken of (in the sense that I have a name, etc.) I have to speak" (*Just* 35).[16]

According to Lyotard, written narratives operate within the same pragmatics in a postmodern society, particularly in groups with a highly developed sense of shared concerns. This point returns to a topic that I addressed in Chapter 1, the changing nature of culture today. In the contemporary United States, whatever interdependence exists between author and audience obviously cannot be a function of a traditional oral community. But that does not mean that such bonds of relation have vanished. There are writers today—more than one might guess, and not in minority communities alone—who are decisively shaped by their relations with an audience and a heritage. This interdependence stems not from traditional communities, as I have said; or from the modern ideal of a great writer speaking to a general public, a situation that has also largely disappeared in the United States; but from the emerging conditions of a postmodern society. In particular, this relation depends upon the erosion of distinctions between "high" and "low" culture and the breakdown of disciplinary boundaries. Hortense Spillers describes the way postmodern arrangements for the dissemination of knowledge both constitute and empower a particular group of writers and readers:

> The American academy, despite itself, is one of the enabling postulates of black women's literary community simply because it is not only a source of income for certain individual writers, but also a point of dissemination and inquiry for their work. . . . The room of one's own explodes its four walls to embrace the classroom, the library, and the various mechanisms of institutional and media life, including conferences, the lecture platform, the television talk show, the publishing house, the "best seller," and collections of critical essays. (249–50)

Although this new social formation is particularly visible in a minority feminist community, where literary interests intersect directly with sexual, racial, and political issues of urgent concern to society, similar arrangements help to constitute writers and audiences in all sectors of the culture. If such local communities perceive themselves as trivialized and neglected—the way, for example, many white male poets do today—that is not because an audience for their work has vanished. More volumes of poetry are published in the United States today than ever before (see Wallace). It is because the audience for poetry has changed, has become local and specific, has become a part of a "poetry community" (an oft-heard phrase in literary quarterlies). Some poets and critics do not like this change, but they should cease railing against the supposed dereliction of other contemporary poets. The change is part of a far larger shift in social, economic, and cultural conditions, and it presents opportunities as well as difficulties for everyone.[17]

This contemporary context, as much as the urge to recover a communal past, may explain the frequent references to oral story-telling in minority fiction. This is not to deny the existence of oral practices in contemporary life — in the tribalism that Silko describes or in the storytelling Morrison celebrates; rather, it is to assert that the power of these practices stems both from social conditions in the present and from the revival of forms from the past.

For both reasons, then, minority writers frequently make the pragmatics of traditional narrative a theme in their fiction. Silko describes a medicine man who speaks "as if nothing the old man said were his own but all had been said before and he was only there to repeat it" (35); by the end of the novel, the reader understands that the protagonist's story is meant to have the same status — does in fact have that status for the tribal council that first hears it. The secularized hero of Kingston's *Tripmaster Monkey*, a graduate of Berkeley, given to quoting Rilke, Yeats, and Whitman, still believes that passing on the traditional stories he has heard will have the same effect: "We make our place," the narrator proclaims. "We make theater, we make community" (261). The prologue to Gloria Naylor's *Mama Day* recounts a parable about a college-educated black man, doing ethnographical research on the island where he was born, who had forgotten how to listen and, hence, had no idea how to tell a story correctly. Morrison comments explicitly on the way the oral tradition affects her written works: "The point was to tell the same story again and again. . . . People who are listening comment on it and make it up, too, as it goes along. In the same way when a preacher delivers a sermon he really expects his congregation to listen, participate, approve, disapprove, and interject almost as much as he does" ("Interview" 421). In her fiction, she continues, "What you hear is what you remember. That oral quality is deliberate. . . . The open-ended quality that is sometimes a problematic in the novel form reminds me of the uses to which stories are put in the black community.

The stories are constantly being retold, constantly being imagined within a framework" (427).

It would be easy to dismiss such sentiments as naive, mere nostalgia for a non-Western sense of community, which has long since become impractical in the contemporary United States. Habermas levels similar charges at postmodern thinking, including the ideas of Lyotard, because he perceives them as participating in a neoconservative attempt to escape modernity and to undo the emancipatory project of the Enlightenment.[18] Does the interest of both minority writers and postmodern theorists in the intense communal bonds characteristic of traditional societies reveal them as mystified? Not at all. Those who reject this form of community as unrealistic tend to ignore the pragmatic dimension of narrative. They focus only on the magical or folkloric content of the narratives and not on the act of storytelling itself. For better or for worse, there is nothing mystified about the claim that telling stories can create community.

Silko, Kingston, Naylor, Morrison, and numerous other minority writers are authorized as narrators in part by their prior status as listeners. This is another way of saying that they are able to speak of black experiences, say, because they are members of black communities. This notion is often phrased in negative terms, as the assertion that white writers are incapable of capturing what it is like to be African-American. The distress that such statements produce among members of the dominant culture—and the protest that whites have written sensitive works about blacks—misses the point. The argument does not concern the capability (or incapability) of an individual but the dynamics of social bonds. It has nothing to do with sensitivity, imaginative power, negative capability, or the gift of empathizing with the other. It has to do with the pragmatic situation of the writer. Regardless of its content, a work by a white writer cannot function at this moment in time in the same way as a work by a black writer. It cannot create the same kind of community for African-Americans because it does not issue from the same pragmatic situation. To speak from a position of marginality is to engage listeners in a different social relation from that of the dominant culture.

With this account of narrative's pragmatic role in forming communities, I hope to have provided another insight into the contemporary power of narrative. It should be clear by now that narrative can assist in forging social bonds. Its power, in this area, is urgent and inescapable. We are exposed to it from earliest childhood, and it continues to work on us throughout our lives, helping to shape every community of which we are a part—families, professional associations, ethnic groups, social movements, regional identifications, national allegiances, and countless more. This notion of bonds returns us to one of the passages from Erdrich's *Tracks* with which I began: "Once I had you," Nanapush said to his granddaughter, "I did not dare break the string between us and kept on moving my lips" (167). The event he is remembering makes a claim about the power of words to heal. As part of the content of a novel, Nanapush's ability to keep his granddaughter from dying of hypothermia by telling her stories can be assessed in physiological, psychological, or shamanistic terms—or perhaps in some combination of all three. But the content of this episode is not the only thing that matters. There is also the pragmatic dimension, the exchange between someone telling a story and someone listening to it. By speaking about their past, Nanapush forms a relationship in the present, a bond that had not existed prior to their exchange. More important than the event he recounts is the act of recounting itself. By moving his lips, Nanapush not only heals an individual; he creates a community.

5

Rituals of Change:
Ethnography on the Border

¡Ay! To make love in Spanish, in a manner as intricate and devout as la Alhambra. To have a lover sigh *mi vida, mi preciosa, mi chiquitita*, and whisper things in that language crooned to babies, that language murmured by grandmothers, those words that smelled like your house, like flour tortillas, and the inside of your daddy's hat, like everyone talking in the kitchen at the same time, or sleeping with the windows open, like sneaking cashews from the crumpled quarter-pound bag Mama always hid in her lingerie drawer after she went shopping with Daddy at the Sears. . . . How could I think of making love in English again? English with its starched *r*'s and *g*'s. English with its crisp linen syllables. English crunchy as apples, resilient and stiff as sailcloth.

SANDRA CISNEROS, *Woman Hollering Creek* (1991)

Such reflections trouble Lupe, the narrator of *"Bien* Pretty," a Chicana artist whose U.S. education left her Spanish "sounding like the subtitles to a Buñuel film" (153). The stories in Sandra Cisneros's new collection capture the joys and pains and sorrows of living in two cultures (at least two), in a style that often flits between languages in the same sentence. Her work fleshes out the latest abstraction, "multiculturalism." It embodies the wonderful, vertiginous, at times terrifying truth that many people in this nation live in more than one culture.

This chapter will focus on texts that provide multicultural analyses of U.S. society. Multicultural study has received much of its impetus from changes within the field of anthropology. Consequently, this chapter will work back and forth between literary representations of this heterogeneous nation and anthropological theory. Part of the point of this exchange will be to show that both discourses are equally "theoretical." Multiculturalism embodies many of the themes I have stressed so far: the importance of interdisciplinary perspectives; the notion of cultures as sites of political conflict and power; the belief that popular practices can have meanings and effects that differ from official accounts; the need to attend to the viewpoints of marginalized, minority, or oppressed communities; and the value of combining local analysis with a sense of global relations and geopolitical structures.

Although every part of the United States is affected by the presence of cultural diversity, the mixture of rival heritages is particularly dramatic wherever borders are found—at the edge of the nation and within the country too, in its large cities especially. For this reason, I concentrate on texts that deal with what have been called "border zones" within society. These works are not written exclusively by members of minority communities or authors with mixed heritages. For many writers—"Anglos" included—the border has come to symbolize the plural, syncretic, sometimes conflictual nature of the nation as a whole. "In fact," the poet Gloria Anzaldúa argues, "the Borderlands are physically present wherever two or more cultures edge each other, where people of different races occupy the same territory, where under, lower, middle and upper classes touch" (ix). The anthropologist Renato Rosaldo agrees:

> More often than we usually care to think, our everyday lives are crisscrossed by border zones, pockets, and eruptions of all kinds. Social borders frequently become salient around such lines as sexual orientation, gender, class, race, ethnicity, nationality, age, politics, dress, food, or taste. . . . Such borderlands should be regarded not as analytically empty transitional zones but as sites of creative cultural production that require investigation. (*Culture* 207–8)[1]

Texts that investigate such border zones are inevitably political. Because this commitment sometimes results in cultural praxis rather than issue-oriented protest, some commentators have missed its political urgency, contributing to the myth of the eighties as an apolitical or even conservative period for literature.[2] The last fifteen years or so, however, have produced an impressive body of political fiction concerning borderlands.

This fiction reveals its affinity with contemporary anthropology in the prominence of ritual. Ritual figures both as content and as a structural principle in many of these novels, which is hardly surprising considering the importance of ritual in giving societies their distinctive characters. Nothing dramatizes the contrast of cultures in a border zone more effectively than attending to rival rites and forms. Moreover, these novels make an implicit claim about their own power when they demonstrate the social importance of ritual. If a cultural form such as ritual possesses the power to influence society, then perhaps literature does too. This analogy diminishes the gap between common or everyday cultural practices and "high" cultural forms, but much of the latest anthropology does the same thing. Contemporary writers—let the word encompass both novelists and ethnographers—view cultural forms of all kinds, "low" and "high," as sites of struggle, places where meanings are negotiated, where traditions are modified, constructed, or combined.

The novels discussed in the next section concentrate on the ritual of sacrifice. All of these novels are set on the periphery—some in the "Third World," which serves as a geographical as well as a political periphery—others in a marginal zone within U.S. society. In each case, a novel shows how society attempts to contain violence by symbolically excluding it, pretending that it exists only on the margins, not at the center of culture. This symbolic process, by means of which a dominant group expels the violence that threatens it, and in doing so reaffirms itself as a community, is modeled on what René Girard has called the "scapegoat mechanism." And each of the novels contains vivid images of sacrifice—images that effectively organize its narrative.

Violence on the Periphery

The category of sacrifice is best known in literary circles from the work of René Girard, but in recent years there has been burgeoning interest among anthropologists, historians of religion, classicists, and literary critics in the bloody practice of ritual killing. In 1972, two massive and influential, although highly speculative, studies independently proposed that sacrifice lay at the origin of all societies and that it continues to play an important role in contemporary communities. For both Girard, in *Violence and the Sacred*, and Walter Burkert, in *Homo Necans*, violence is the crucial element in ritual, the core that makes sacrifice, in Girard's words, the foundation of "all the great institutions of mankind, both secular and religious," and even the "working basis of human thought, the process of 'symbolization'" (306). Burkert, too, maintains that "blood and violence lurk fascinatingly" at the heart not only of religion but of civilization as a whole (2). The function of all this slaughter, in both accounts, is to bring us together in a community. "The purpose of the sacrifice," Girard writes, "is to restore harmony to the community, to reinforce the social fabric" (8); Burkert says, "a sense of community arises from collective aggression," and adds, "The closer the bond, the more gruesome the ritual" (35-6).[3]

Since the beginning of this century, anthropologists and sociologists have been looking at the social implications of ritual. Henri Hubert, Marcel Mauss, and Emile Durkheim derived religious beliefs and institutions from ritual rather than vice versa. In spite of this demystifying impulse, they still retained an explanatory role for the category of the sacred.[4] Even though Hubert and Mauss, for example, argued eloquently for viewing sacrifice as a "social function" (101-3), they also insisted that it was a "religious act" (13), involving, at a minimum, the "sacralization and desacralization" of a victim (95), with the goal of "establishing a means of communication between the sacred and the profane worlds" (97). The great change in contemporary explorations of ritual is the disappearance of interest in the sacred per se. Ritual matters solely because of its effect on society, and religious notions, such as the sacred, are viewed as necessary mystifications, illusions needed to keep people from recognizing the violent nature of the social bond. "We should not presuppose that people perform religious acts because they believe," Burkert writes, "but rather that they believe because they have learned to perform religious acts" ("Problem" 156). As a result, Girard, Burkert, and other contemporary theorists connect sacrifice with political issues, not just religious observances. Ritual is significant because of the way it creates and legitimizes political orders.

This shift in scholarly emphasis coincides with the increased interest among novelists in the phenomenon of sacrifice. And for both groups, the same features have come to fascinate: its violence, its social character, and its political consequences. Novelists, like the critics above, turn to ritual not to represent the manifestation of a god or spirit, not to show links between the sacred and profane worlds, not to invoke totemic or animistic beliefs, but to explore one of the most puzzling anomalies of group life: the propensity of communities to engage in acts of collective violence.

Girard explains sacrifice as a social mechanism designed to deflect onto an appropriate scapegoat the internal violence that might otherwise be unleashed on its own members. This mechanism depends on concealing the substitution at work, hiding the displacement of violence onto someone who cannot fight back. Hence the sacrificial victim is always chosen from among people who are outside or on the margins of society: traditionally, prisoners of war, slaves, virgins, or children; in our own day, members of minority groups, women generally, gay men or lesbians, even entire countries located in the "Third World." These are, in Girard's words, "exterior or marginal individuals, incapable of establishing or sharing the social bonds that link the rest of the inhabitants" (*Violence* 12). The victims must come from the periphery, from a zone so marginalized that few in the dominant population will object to their victimization. "Between these victims and the community a crucial social link is missing" (*Violence* 13); if such a link were not missing, the community might find it difficult to unite against them.

The problem with Girard's model lies in its static, ahistorical character.[5] Girard maintains that sacrifice has played the same role in all societies, at all times, and in all places. According to this view, ritual reinforces the status quo by strengthening the existing social ties between individuals. This position is characteristic of functionalist approaches to culture generally. Going all the way back to Durkheim's *The Elementary Forms of the Religious Life* (1915), functionalists have emphasized how ritual reinforces the "social sentiments" (390). Girard and Burkert are quite explicit about this allegiance. The former has never turned away from the vocabulary of "function" and "social efficiency" ("Generative" 94, 121), and the latter has recently composed a defense of the "functional approach," which he admits "has been out of favor for some decades" because of the "automatism of tradition that would result from its premises" ("Problem" 155). This automatism is something both theorists are prepared to accept. Ritual "preserves solidarity among the members of the group" and "society thereby ensures its own stability. . . . Thus ritual, especially religious ritual, is self-perpetuating" ("Problem" 155).

Contemporary North American fiction, however, presents anything but a static vision of ritual. Instead this fiction contributes to what Dominick LaCapra has called the "critical task" of "work[ing] out alternatives" to scapegoating (*Soundings* 24). Sacrifice often reinforces community in these novels, but paradoxically, community just as often becomes an agent of change. This paradox is a feature of contemporary multicultural societies, one with profound ramifications for understanding the politics of both texts and practices. Ritual may have a subversive or even revolutionary tendency when performed in cross-cultural contexts. Does this mean that ritual has an altered function in current societies? Or should one abandon the vocabulary of functionalism altogether and search for a new, more flexible perspective on traditional rites?

Striking dramatizations of the subversive potential of ritual appear in political novels treating a whole spectrum of issues from diverse points of view. One of the most notable examples may be found in Don DeLillo's *The Names* (1982). Set in the Middle East, on the fringes of what one character keeps referring to as the "Empire," the novel features a cult that carries out ritual murders of victims chosen by an alphabetical code. These sacrifices reinforce a sense of order or pattern for the group. The people chosen for death are "victim[s] of some ordering instinct" (115), an instinct that the novel links to ancient Cretan practices of ritual killing. More important, it links this instinct for order to the interest of the United States in maintaining the status quo, the balance of power around the world. The main character is a writer turned risk analyst who files reports for insurance and banking concerns on the prospects of instability in a number of countries throughout the region. The novel underlines the ties that unite the cult's passion for order, the hunger for knowledge that motivates several archaeologists in the book, the attraction of linguistics and language games, corporations' need for information assessment, and the fortunes of empire. "Is this the scientific face of imperialism?" one character asks; and another answers, "Subdue and codify. . . . How many times have we seen it?" (80). Despite all this obsession with order, however, despite the repeated insistence that ritual creates a sense of security, the narrator is changed by his understanding of the cult's practices; his access to what he hopefully calls "a second life" (329) depends upon his new familiarity, his immersion in the alien communities that produce these rites.[6]

Recent novels by African-American women provide different examples of this same phenomenon. In well-known texts, both Gloria Naylor and Toni Morrison portray what Girard would call the scapegoat mechanism within black communities. In Naylor's *The Women of Brewster Place* (1982), a collection of African-American women are brought together only after one of their number has been sacrificed.[7] The victim is a lesbian whom most of the other women have persecuted, in part because she is one of the few figures in this oppressed group more marginal than the others. In Morrison's *Sula* (1974), the title character is herself the scapegoat that unites the group. Once the people of the black community discover that Sula is different from themselves, they come together in rejection of her. "They began to cherish their husbands and wives, protect their children, repair their homes and in general band together against the devil in their midst" (117–18). Despite the cruelty of these scenarios, both novels end with visions of social change, visions that are directly related to the agency of ritual. *The Women of Brewster Place* closes with the dream of women working together to tear down the wall that confines them, and *Sula* records the community's one overt protest against oppression, a riot that occurs after Sula's death when an annual ceremony takes on a new meaning. The role of ritual scapegoating in provoking such communal action becomes an analogy, in both texts, to the role of literature.

Another group of novels can serve as a final example, demonstrating that in multicultural contexts the scapegoat mechanism should not be interpreted solely in terms of its stabilizing effect. This group is the remarkable series of political novels that came out in the last decade focusing on U.S. relations with Latin America and the Caribbean, and with the refugees from those regions. I am thinking of Margaret Atwood's *Bodily Harm* (1982),

Paul Theroux's *The Mosquito Coast* (1982), Harriet Doerr's *Stones for Ibarra* (1984), George Dennison's *Luisa Domic* (1985), stories from both of Bob Shacochis's collections, *Easy in the Islands* (1985) and *The Next New World* (1989), Denis Johnson's *The Stars at Noon* (1986), Douglas Unger's *El Yanqui* (1986), Thomas Sanchez's *Mile Zero* (1989), Robert Boswell's *The Geography of Desire* (1989), John Sayles's *Los Gusanos* (1991), and two of the most highly praised novels of the decade, Robert Stone's *A Flag for Sunrise* (1981) and Russell Banks's *Continental Drift* (1985). Rather than listing the sacrificial motifs in all of these texts, let me turn directly to the last two books.

Russell Banks's *Continental Drift* tells the story of two displaced people: Bob Dubois, a young white furnace repairman who abandons his job in New Hampshire for the lure of a better life in Florida, and Vanise Dorsinville, a black Haitian who, with her baby, is attempting to make her way to Florida too. In the utter futility of both journeys, Banks registers a stinging criticism of North American society—a society that has betrayed the very dream that sustains these characters through hard times:

> When you finally get to America, . . . you get Disney World and land deals and fast-moving high-interest bank loans, and if you don't get the hell out of the way, they'll knock you down, cut you up with a harrow and plow you under, so they can throw some condos up on top of you or maybe a parking lot or maybe an orange grove. (312)

Bob is a man whose hard work has brought him to poverty; who is living in a trailer home that he does not own, with a wife who no longer trusts him and a child who is rapidly becoming emotionally disturbed; a man who has killed a fifteen-year-old black thief in defense of a cash register in the liquor store where he clerks; and who has been tricked by his best friend into buying a quarter interest in a fishing boat that was not his friend's to sell. Bob's troubles come to a head when in his first illegal act—an inept attempt to smuggle Haitians into Florida—he ends up drowning fifteen old men, women, and children, including Vanise's baby. It is a terrible scene, one that horrifies Bob as profoundly as it does the reader. But Bob has no way of making amends. Nothing in his society can expiate his guilt, not even the justice system, which has already let him go. Out of desperation, he turns to the Haitian community, and there, before Vanise and her Voodoo loa, gives up his life. Lacking a material way of making amends, he chooses a symbolic means. He sacrifices himself.

This sacrificial act has no parallel with any other experience in Bob's life. The only equivalent experiences occur in Vanise's story, the Voodoo ceremonies of ritual killing that help her interpret her suffering. These ceremonies are among the most compelling parts of the book. Viewed from within, from Vanise's perspective as participant and believer, these detailed accounts of Voodoo rites do not call to mind the scapegoat mechanism. Similarly, Bob's psychological and religious terms—guilt and expiation, sin and redemption—are rationalizations of scapegoating that obscure some of the social processes involved. But the narrative frames Bob's death and Vanise's sacrifices in larger terms—literally frames them, with italicized chapters at the beginning and end of the novel— which will not let the reader avoid the political meaning of the novel's action. In incantatory prose, "Invocation" and "Envoi" locate the characters at the heart of social patterns that they cannot perceive. "Invocation" begins, "This is an American story of the late twentieth century, and you don't need a muse to tell it"; you need "clear-eyed pity and hot, old-time anger" (1). For much of the novel, the narrator's anger and pity effectively drive home how the dominant sectors of U.S. society profit from the sacrifice of these outcasts and countless others like them. But "Envoi" has a different use for their suffering: "Good cheer and mournfulness over lives other than our own, even wholly invented lives—no, especially wholly invented lives—deprive the world as it is of some of the greed it needs to continue to be itself. Sabotage and subversion, then, are this book's objectives. Go, my book, and help destroy the world as it is" (366).

Robert Stone's *A Flag for Sunrise* is set in two imaginary Central American nations, loosely modeled on El Salvador and Nicaragua before the Sandanista revolution. The world it portrays is rife with ritual sacrifices, some sanctioned by official institutions like the Catholic Church, others implemented by the state and its agents, still others invented by singular, obsessed individuals. The sacrificial images in the novel range from the senseless slaughter of two dogs at sunrise by their drugged-out master and the serial murder of young children by a psychopath who believes he has been chosen by the Lord to atone for the world's sins to intriguing accounts of ancient Maya practices of human sacrifice, meditations on the significance of Christ's passion, and an ecstatic vision by the main female character, who decides that she is the handmaid of the Lord as she is being tortured to death for her political activities.

I want to pause over one sacrifice in the novel: the murder at sunset of Pablo Tabor by Frank Holliwell, a disaffected anthropologist, former employee of the CIA, and the closest thing in the book to a surrogate for the author. Pablo is a Mexican-American, a paranoid drug runner who has deserted from the U.S. Coast Guard. Poor, uneducated, illegitimate son of a prostitute, member of a minority, mentally unbalanced, a ruthless killer, on the run from the law — Pablo is the most marginal figure in a novel filled with misfits and outcasts. Holliwell's motives for killing him are too involved to go into — suffice it to say that they do not seem sufficient to warrant murder, for he has no knowledge of Pablo's past — but immediately after Holliwell has pushed a knife between the other man's ribs and thrown the body overboard at sea, a strange transformation occurs:

> Against his will, Holliwell looked at Pablo's face. He was at a loss now to find the shimmering evil he had seen in it before. . . . It was a brother's face, a son's, one's own. Anybody's face, just another victim of ignorance and fear. Just another one of us, Holliwell thought. (431)

Another one of us, a brother, a son. The recognition of a bond with Pablo would have seemed inconceivable at any other point in the book. But the bloody act of sacrifice creates community in the most unlikely of places. Perhaps the grimmest contention in this grim book is that the peace of white, prosperous North Americans like Holliwell depends upon the existence of outcasts like Pablo. By pretending that the worst aspects of U.S. society — poverty, drugs, crime, insanity, and violence — exist only on its periphery, and by condemning a few to inhabit that peripheral world so that many may dwell secure in their world of affluence, the nation sacrifices a significant proportion of its population as surely as Holliwell sacrificed Pablo. Further, the novel suggests that U.S. involvement in "Third World" nations possesses a similar symbolic meaning, one in which unwanted features of our own society are projected and expelled in order to reinforce a sense of stability at home. One minor character says as much explicitly: "'What I wonder . . . is whether the people down here have to live this way so that we can live the way we do'" (158).[8]

The ancient Maya believed that the entire social order depended upon the institution of human sacrifice. According to anthropologists, the Maya thought that human blood "was sustenance for the gods. . . . The very existence of the universe depended upon the willingness of human beings to sustain the gods with their blood" (Schele and Miller 176, 181). The sun itself, in some Maya legends, could not rise without a daily human sacrifice—a legend that hints at one way to read the title *A Flag for Sunrise*. But the title actually comes from a line by Emily Dickinson, which is quoted in the novel: "Sunrise—Hast Thou a Flag for Me?" (Dickinson, #461; Stone 380), and this reference suggests another reading. Dickinson's poem images death as a transition, a change from one state to another, here figured in terms of a bride's consummation on her wedding night. Rituals—marriages, deaths—bring change; they are about transition, even if for the worse.

On the evidence of these last two texts, as well as of the other novels mentioned above, it seems clear that many contemporary writers view ritual rather differently from Girard. In these accounts, sacrifice tends to implicate the participant in the suffering of the victim rather than to cleanse the community by expelling a scapegoat. Why does this happen? Multicultural perspectives force one to recognize that the sacrificial event can have multiple meanings and variable social effects. By giving the outsider, the marginalized person or community, equal time, novelists and ethnographers dramatize how the fate of the dominant community is tied up with that of others, even with the fate of those it sometimes victimizes. This implicative view of sacrifice, which is becoming increasingly unavoidable in today's world, historicizes and politicizes a model that in Girard's hands is unduly universal.

The Creation of Ritual

Like narrative, the creation of ritual is a complex relational event, one that continuously negotiates boundaries among communities, and among individuals and their communities. This phrase, the "creation of ritual," is meant to capture the diffuse, often hidden way culture possesses power in radically pluralist societies. It signifies both the way ritual is daily reinvented, modified, forged in the fire of social conflict and the way ritual invents, modifies, and forges for itself new social arrangements. To understand this complex cultural practice, we need to explore the new anthropology in more detail. I will focus on the work of Renato Rosaldo, Michael M. J. Fischer, and the historian James Clifford, because their ideas have already begun to affect thinking in other disciplines, but other contributions deserve attention: that of Michael T. Taussig, Johannes Fabian, James Boon, and all the authors in Clifford and Marcus's volume, *Writing Culture* (1986).

As it happens, Rosaldo has commented on Girard's theories in a brief response to the latter's paper "Generative Scapegoating." Rosaldo objects to the "structural functionalism" of Girard's work, then goes on to argue against the unitary and monolithic character of both Girard's and Burkert's models ("Anthropological" 241). His principal point is that Girard draws on an older anthropological vision, the "classic vision" that sees culture as unified and consistent; it "emphasizes shared patterns at the expense of processes of change and internal inconsistencies, conflicts, and contradictions" (*Culture* 28). Classical norms portray ritual as static and timeless, a storehouse of collective wisdom. As I noted earlier, ritual functions, in this model, solely to reduce conflict and stabilize the community.

Rosaldo objects to the classical vision on many accounts. Four of his arguments seem especially pertinent to this chapter's discussion. First, Rosaldo sees ritual as a "busy intersection" (*Culture* 17), a place of foment and change, a site of resistance, revision, and cultural production. By attending to the social position of participants, he discovers that ritual is anything but static. It is dialogic, agonistic, impure, partial, changing, and improvisational. Instead of always reducing conflict, it sometimes becomes a place where grievances are aired, struggles staged. Instead of always stabilizing the community, it sometimes becomes a vehicle of social change. Second, Rosaldo insists that today everyone is a member of multiple communities. Anthropologists can no longer afford to weigh ritual's effect on harmonious, internally consistent patterns: "the fiction of the uniformly shared culture increasingly seems more tenuous than useful" (*Culture* 207). Third, he maintains that ritual should be seen as practice rather than structure. Like Bourdieu and de Certeau, Rosaldo thinks ritual can be a strategy or tactic, one that relies on the flux of temporality to unsettle fixed (spatial) orders. There is "social unpredictability" within the most venerable rituals, an "indeterminacy" or slack that "permits people to develop timing, coordination, and a knack for responding to contingencies" (*Culture* 112). Finally, he argues that the narrative character of practices, including rituals, calls for a narrative response from the analyst. Narrative techniques, such as multiple points of view, may "dialogize" the account, may make room for perspectives other than that of the anthropologist. The resulting "double vision" will not produce a "unified master narrative" (*Culture* 128) but rather partial, context-dependent, sometimes conflicting micronarratives of the sort Lyotard advocates.

If Rosaldo is correct, then one ought to attend to the different ways ritual can affect communities, and even to variations within communities along lines of class, status, gender, sexual orientation, age, health, and other divisions. Ritual may reinforce the status quo, just as functionalists from Durkheim to Girard have claimed. Alternatively, it may be a vital source of political resistance, as is demonstrated by nativistic religious movements, such as those that originated in the colonial Caribbean (see Lanternari; Wilson; Laguerre), or by the liberation theology that flourishes in Latin America today. Finally, it may possess a positive, creative power, one capable of producing new conjunctions among conflicting spheres or of constructing novel modes of being. One frequently sees this last possibility represented in texts and practices situated in the borderland.

Let me turn again to novels of the border, this time to works by writers of color.[9] When one locates texts within specific social and political contexts, one learns more about the forms of creativity ritual may possess. Banks treats Voodoo as a living tradition, and he criticizes one unsympathetic character for viewing the ceremonies as degenerate survivals of once-pure African rites (293). This gesture parallels one of the latest developments within ethnography—best articulated in the work of James Clifford—a tendency to criticize earlier anthropologists for collecting specimens of native cultures, which are valued for their authenticity and purity. I should not be taken as faulting Banks, then, if I note that his perspective on culture clashes along the Florida border emphasizes different issues from the accounts of some Caribbean novelists. For Banks, the "continental drift" from both North and South toward the southern borders of the United States is the issue. For Paule Marshall and Caryl Phillips, black novelists of Caribbean descent, a different pattern claims their attention: the drift both away from and back toward the islands.

Marshall's *Praisesong for the Widow* (1983) tells the story of Avey Johnson, a widow of sixty-four, who has lived all her life in New York City, moving from Harlem to the comfort and security of the suburbs.[10] In the midst of a Caribbean cruise taken with two friends, she jumps ship and joins the pilgrimage of an old man she has just met to the tiny island of Carriacou for an annual ceremony known as the "Beg Pardon" (*Pa'doné mwê*). The novel counterpoints Avey's experiences in the Caribbean with two sets of memories, her girlhood visits to her aunt in South Carolina and her years of marriage to a man driven by the North American dream of upward mobility. Like many black women novelists, Marshall explicitly asserts the power of ritual: rites "both protected [Avey and her husband] and put them in possession of a kind of power" (137). It does not matter whether rituals are formal, established observances or intimate, everyday routines: either is equally efficacious. Moreover, even organized rites contain elements of improvisation. When Avey finds herself able to join in the frenzied dancing of the Carriacou Tramp, it is because she has recognized its similarity to the Ring Shout she had witnessed as a child in Tatem Island, South Carolina. There are differences as well, however; each combines African rites with Christian beliefs in a distinctive fashion. Avey's participation in the Beg Pardon symbolizes her return to an ancestral home and her reincorporation in a long-forgotten community, but it does not prevent growth and change. The ceremony binds her to a community—the novel uses the image of "threads" streaming out of everyone to enter her—yet it speaks of "possibilities and becoming" (249). Finally, Avey's actions are mediated by her age, class, gender, and language. The novel stresses the way each of these factors influences how and when she enters the dance; what it symbolizes to her; and what it means to the other participants.[11]

It is instructive to compare Marshall's vision of Carriacou with that of James Clifford, who uses the Caribbean, at one point in his book *The Predicament of Culture* (1988), as an emblem of contemporary multiculturalism. "Twentieth-century identities no longer presuppose continuous cultures or traditions," Clifford writes. "Everywhere individuals and groups improvise local performances from (re)collected pasts, drawing on foreign media, symbols, and languages" (14). Classical anthropology, which he finds to be steeped in modernist myths of breakdown and cultural decay, view such impure rituals as contaminated survivals. A postmodern ethnography, however, sees everywhere "a more ambiguous 'Caribbean' experience" (15). Like Marshall, Clifford is willing to risk optimism. He concentrates not on the "loss of traditional orders" but on "presents-becoming-futures" and on a "utopian, persistent hope for the reinvention of difference" (15). If for Banks the Caribbean "border zone" prompts a story full of pity and anger, and for Marshall it conjures a tale of "possibilities and becoming," then that is all to the good. Neither story need exclude nor be subordinated to the other. As Clifford puts it, "The Caribbean history . . . is a history of degradation, mimicry, violence, and blocked possibilities. It is also rebellious, syncretic, and creative. This kind of ambiguity keeps the planet's local futures uncertain and open. There is no master narrative that can reconcile the tragic and comic plots of global cultural history" (15).

Caryl Phillips's *A State of Independence* (1986) eschews both tragic and comic plots for one of personal discovery, but the local future it describes is just as bound up with global cultural history. The protagonist, returning after a twenty-year absence in England to his native St. Kitts on the day before it becomes independent, finds that the changes in his home all involve the island's altered geopolitical relationships. As a politician who has profited from the new order tells him: "'Well, what you must realize is that we living State-side now. We living under the eagle and maybe you don't think that is good but your England never do us a damn thing except take, take, take'" (112). A less privileged citizen puts it differently, but the message is the same: "'I guess if you really want to make some money in this country you best butter up your backside with some bendover oil and point your arse towards New York'" (131). At first these global changes seem to have little to do with the narrator's local problems in readjusting: the bitterness of his mother, his guilt over his brother's death, and the awkwardness of encountering the woman he had deserted. Once again, however, one finds that the text itself emphasizes the links between social context and the significance of ritual. The newly created festival of independence takes on a paradoxical meaning for the protagonist as he grows to understand that *his* independence depends upon returning to the place of his birth, resuming his responsibilities to his mother, and renewing his commitment to his old lover.

If we shift our attention to the U.S. border with Latin America, we find a similar variation in the way rituals are created and in the kinds of creativity they possess. Robert Stone employs sacrifice as a metaphor for U.S. intervention in Latin America, although one should construe such a statement broadly, for he is as interested in its effects on his "Yankee" characters as on their southern neighbors, and he considers intervention to include the activities not only of soldiers, ambassadors, and spies but also of missionaries, businessmen, anthropologists, media people, and tourists—no matter how well-intentioned their motives. One of Stone's main characters is an anthropologist, and the novelist probes as effectively as Clifford the ambivalent emotions, ironic stance, and exploitive potential of this figure's classical attitude: participant-observation. Stone's solution even resembles Clifford's; both look to multiple perspectives and dialogic writing strategies to overcome some of the "irreducible violence" of what Clifford terms "ethnographic liberalism" (*Predicament* 79). Valuable as is Stone's vision within its own context, however, it understandably does not address all the concerns about U.S. relations with Latin America that are raised by Chicano and Chicana writers.[12]

Rituals of "return" figure prominently in many Chicano novels, often in conjunction with the legend of Aztlán. The homeland to the north of the Aztecs, Aztlán symbolizes the ancient claim of Mexicans of Indian descent to the southwestern portion of the United States. In Chicano writing the journey northward of people from Latin America represents a centuries-long process of return, which inverts the North American anxiety about an "invasion" of illegal aliens. Gloria Anzaldúa makes the relevant point: "Today we are witnessing *la migración de los pueblos mexicanos*, the return odyssey to the historical/mythological Aztlán. This time, the traffic is from south to north" (11). In Rudolfo Anaya's novel *Heart of Aztlan* (1976), the blind singer Crispín tells one of the "many versions of the legend" (123), the story of how *the people* left their home in what is now the United States to travel south. "'They never forgot the heartland,'" however; "'it called them back, and they returned, a new people, under a new guise. . . . They returned to complete the cycle'" (126). Anaya's portrait of the barrio is full of ceremonies that celebrate the rediscovery of a lost home, rites that fuse the circumstances of the characters' new urban life with traditional practices. These invented rituals, which the novel contrasts with those of the Catholic Church, have a politically subversive rather than a stabilizing effect, leading one character to become a leader in a labor struggle. Thus if legendary tales give the rites both form and content, contemporary political contexts give them power.

Rituals of return need not be associated with Aztlán, however, or celebrate a northward migration. The circular journey, away from a spiritual home and back again, may explore other paths. In Ana Castillo's novel *The Mixquiahuala Letters* (1986), the Chicago-born heroine seeks to return to her "home" in Mexico, a homeland that she consciously chooses, despite repeated experiences of rejection.[13] Another heroine from Chicago, the youthful narrator of Sandra Cisneros's short novel, *The House on Mango Street* (1984), traces a journey away from and back to the home of her childhood, much like that in Caryl Phillips's novel. Once again, factors such as youth, gender, and a working-class background inform her daily (re)creation of ritual and give point to the theme of return that brings the book to a close:

> I like to tell stories. . . . I make a story for my life, for each step my brown shoe takes. . . . I am going to tell you a story about a girl who didn't want to belong. . . . One day I will go away.
>
> Friends and neighbors will say, What happened to that Esperanza? Where did she go with all those books and paper? Why did she march so far away?
>
> They will not know I have gone away to come back. For the ones I left behind. For the ones who cannot out. (101–2)

A second concern, again closely linked to the distinctive social position of Chicanos, influences this literature's attitude toward ritual: the issue of multiculturalism itself. Anzaldúa uses the image of "the new *mestiza*" (the subtitle of her book *Borderlands/La Frontera*) as a symbol of the way in which mixed cultural heritages can result in a "shifting and multiple identity" (ix):

> The new *mestiza* copes by developing a tolerance for contradictions, a tolerance for ambiguity. She learns to be an Indian in Mexican culture, to be Mexican from an Anglo point of view. She learns to juggle cultures. She has a plural personality, she operates in a pluralistic mode—nothing is thrust out, the good the bad and the ugly, nothing rejected, nothing abandoned. (79)

Such juggling, such shifting from one culture to another, one identity to another, governs Anzaldúa's fluid creation of rituals in her poetry. The invented, the mixed, possess power, all of which leads her to value "a hybridization of metaphor" in her writing, "an assemblage, a montage, a beaded work . . . a crazy dance" (66). Often this hybrid mode extends to genre (see Torres; de Lauretis, "Sexual Indifference" 165) or to language itself. The new *mestiza* speaks many languages: "I may switch back and forth from English to Spanish in the same sentence or in the same word" (Anzaldúa 56).[14]

The anthropologist Michael M. J. Fischer takes code switching or "inter-reference" as the characteristic feature of Chicano writing[15] and then proposes this "polyphony of multiple voices (English, Spanish)" as a model for a "more textured, nuanced, and realistic ethnography" (223), one that can record the many voices of the subjects being studied as well as the Western voice of the theorist. His sense that anthropologists can learn from ethnic writers stems from the contemporary awareness within many minority cultures that "ethnicity is something reinvented and reinterpreted in each generation" (195). The process of invention is always relational. Communities define themselves over and against other communities, not simply in the hierarchical opposition of dominant/minority but in a system of multiple relations. As Anzaldúa puts it, "we call ourselves Mexican, referring to race and ancestry; *mestizo* when affirming both our Indian and Spanish (but we hardly ever own our Black ancestry); Chicano when referring to a politically aware people born and/or raised in the U.S.; *Raza* when referring to Chicanos; *tejanos* when we are Chicanos from Texas" (63). Like Clifford and Marshall, Fischer stresses that the continuous reinvention of ritual is "future-oriented" (Fischer 196); it aids in the daily construction of new possibilities, of new social arrangements. Further, he suggests that a sensitivity to cultural inventiveness is an important component of "a wider social ethos of pluralism" (196), a pluralism more radical than that envisioned by liberalism, which is a possibility I shall return to in the conclusion.

A third concern of much recent Chicano writing is self-reflexive: the question of how Chicano ritual is created. No author has explored this topic in more depth than Rolando Hinojosa.[16] His continuing series of novels about the fictional borderland, Belken County, Texas, views cultural inventiveness as both conflict and carnival. As a weapon in the struggle with Anglo culture, the invention of ritual enables the Chicanos of the Valley to adapt to the incursions of a white population possessing the economic and political upper hand.[17] For example, Esteban Echevarría, the oldest contemporary inhabitant of Belken County, the only one who remembers "how it used to be before the Anglos came in herds, before the army, the state government and its rangers, all the bureaucratic paper-work" (*Claros* 128), chooses to die under a mesquite tree that had been planted at his birth. "An enduring tree, just like us," he thinks. "Good idea, that of the Buenrostros, that the second son shall plant a tree at baptisms, weddings, and funerals" (*Claros* 220). As a move in the far longer history of competition among Mexican families in the Valley, however, the invention of ritual can serve a somewhat different purpose. Hinojosa's novels record the constant revision of custom, the subtle changes in established rituals, that can result in the carnivalization of the social order. For example, the daily routines of another old man, don Marcial de Anda, speak volumes to those who know him, tell an ironic tale of how the mild de Andas have come to supplant the Tamez family, once so rowdy and tough, who just fifteen years before could prevent the de Andas from attending their own daughter's wedding with Joaquín Tamez (*Klail* 33).

As the texts I have examined testify, the creation of ritual is one of the most effective ways of exercising power in a multicultural society. The process, however, also reveals how elusive the question of agency becomes in such societies. An individual can clearly influence the development of ritual—not only of private, daily ceremonies of the sort depicted by Cisneros and Hinojosa, but also of communal, organized rites like those described by Marshall and

Anaya. All the same, conscious decisions, planned interventions, are not the most important factors in the creation of ritual. Instead, ritual is most often created by spontaneous, improvisational practices and unformalized moves — what Rosaldo has nicely termed "social grace" (*Culture* 112). And ritual is most creative, in turn, when social unpredictability "allows the emergence of a culturally valued quality of human relations where one can follow impulses, change directions, and coordinate with other people" (*Culture* 112). Such innovation may be individual or collective, but its hallmark is the readjustment, the recoordination, if you will, of an altered individual in an altered community.

Some Implications for Cultural Studies

Let me conclude by indicating how this shift in perspective on ritual might affect future cultural studies. In the last decade, cultural criticism has borrowed heavily from anthropologists not considered here — theorists who share neither the classic vision criticized by Rosaldo, Clifford, and Fischer nor the latter group's multicultural focus. These anthropologists are best represented by Clifford Geertz and Victor Turner, who, despite their differences, have together contributed enormously to revising ideas about the relations between culture and society. Both of these authors have helped literary and social theorists articulate the belief, widespread today, that culture is less like a deep structure to be scientifically catalogued than a textual construct to be interpreted. Culture as text or script has become the banner of much innovative work in new historicism, cultural materialism, feminism, gay and lesbian studies, African-American studies, border studies, and other oppositional criticisms.

Empowering as these models have been, they may prove less useful for multicultural studies than some of the approaches considered in this chapter. Clifford, in an essay called "On Ethnographic Allegory," suggests that critics explore the allegorical aspect of ethnography instead of concentrating on culture-as-text. These two alternatives are not exactly symmetrical — one emphasizes the process of ethnography, the other its object — but that difference is part of the point. Allegory brings out the constructed character of culture as clearly as does the text model, but it focuses on the act of construction rather than on the finished object. It locates conflicts over meaning in a forward-looking practice — of writing, of invention — as well as in the retrospective act of reading. This positioning seems productive because a model of culture that invokes reading still puts the interpreter in a position of authority as the one who construes the text. If critics expand their sense of creative practices to include the sorts of inventions of narrative and ritual examined above, then they may come face-to-face with the active role that the subjects of a culture play in its construction. The subjects of a culture are involved in a continuous inventive process; they participate in the allegorization of their own lives as surely as does any ethnographer.

I mention Clifford's essay not in order to recommend his method as a replacement for the text model but to draw attention to the whole range of approaches considered here, approaches that emphasize things being done rather than what things finally mean. The common denominators of all these approaches are an interest in practice, not theory; movement toward something unknown, not the arrival at a predetermined goal; presents-becoming-futures; uncodified procedures, ad hoc techniques, unrehearsed tactics. Clifford's interest in culture as allegory is just one instance of this reorientation away from the rule-governed models of classic anthropology, on the one hand, and the text models of interpretive anthropology, on the other hand.

I also mention Clifford's essay because, as Clifford says, "Allegory draws special attention to the *narrative* character of cultural representations" (100, italics in original). Viewed as allegorical, the interpreter's representation becomes only one of many possible stories about a society. Just as important are the stories told by the participants themselves. Moreover, even the stories from within a culture must compete with other indigenous tales. The young as well as the old; women as well as men; the poor and homeless as well as the rich and powerful; the disabled as well as the able-bodied — these, and many others, may have distinctive versions to tell. A recognition of allegory shows "ethnography to be a hierarchical structure of powerful stories that translate, encounter, and recontextualize other powerful stories" (121).

It might be objected that viewing culture as a text allows for alternative versions of a society, for the simple reason that many cultural theorists today accept an indeterminate, self-contradictory, or deconstructive notion of the text. Nonetheless, the idea of competing narratives adds something to the analysis that is missing from the notion of cultural contradiction: that is, of course, the temporal dimension of conflict. In Clifford, we once again find a theorist praising narrative for the way it restores the "temporal aspect" to cultural studies (100). The movement of narrative embodies cultural tensions not only in the contrast with rival stories but also in the uncertainty over how the narrative will end. It is the temporal dimension of narrative that makes allegory a tempting model for Clifford. Might any model that highlights this dimension serve other cultural critics as well?

6

Feminism and the Politics of Community

One of the last novels I read while completing this study was Gail Godwin's *Father Melancholy's Daughter* (1991). This moving, intellectually rich narrative has many similarities to a highly praised novel of the late seventies, Mary Gordon's *Final Payments* (1978). Both concern young women who have spent years as their father's primary companion; both explore the influence of religion on the narrators; and both attend to unfashionable topics such as responsibility, tradition, and self-sacrifice.

As it happens, Gordon's novel was one of the first texts that made me think a change was taking place in contemporary women's writing. Feminist novels by white women at the beginning of the seventies had often dramatized their heroines' struggle for independence and fulfillment outside of the home. The battle was for personal liberation, and it involved individual, sometimes lonely combat against the oppressive entanglements of husband and family, as well as the stifling social roles of housewife and mother.[1] Prominent among these books were Lois Gould's *Such Good Friends* (1970), Margaret Atwood's *Surfacing* (1972), Alix Kates Shulman's *Memoirs of an Ex-Prom Queen* (1972), and Erica Jong's *Fear of Flying* (1973). These texts posed the issue of feminism largely in terms of the individual, and they saw the goal of political action as personal freedom. By the end of the decade, however, issues and goals seemed to be shifting. The question of women's relation to one another, to their mothers, to their families, and to their communities began to show up in novel after novel. In some circles at least, the issue of women's connections was supplementing that of women's liberation.

The titles of many of the novels published during this period convey something of the shift in emphasis. Note how often words for "family," "mother," "home," or more generally "a community of women" turn up in this list: Laurie Colwin's *Family Happiness* (1982), Lee Smith's *Family Linen* (1985), Mary Elsie Robertson's *Family Life* (1987), Godwin's *A Southern Family* (1987), Sue Miller's *Family Pictures* (1990), and J. California Cooper's *Family* (1991); Rosellen Brown's *The Autobiography of My Mother* (1976), Godwin's *A Mother and Two Daughters* (1982), Miller's *The Good Mother* (1986), Terry McMillan's *Mama* (1987), Candace Flynt's *Mother Love* (1987), and Gloria Naylor's *Mama Day* (1988); Marilynne Robinson's *Housekeeping* (1980), Joan Silber's *Household Words* (1980), Anne Tyler's *Dinner at the Homesick Restaurant* (1982), Marge Piercy's, *Fly Away Home* (1984), Sandra Cisneros's *The House on Mango Street* (1984), and Vicki Covington's *Gathering Home* (1988); Gordon's *The Company of Women* (1980), Naylor's *The Women of Brewster Place* (1982), and Alice Adams, *Superior Women* (1984). Other novels that I will discuss do not name their topics so clearly on the jacket cover but are equally concerned with issues of family and community.

What should one make of this shift from novels about liberation to novels about connections? First, one should not interpret this change as a sign that the country has entered a "postfeminist" phase, as some have argued. Reading these books would persuade no one that U.S. society has progressed beyond the need for feminist advocacy on equal rights, comparable wages, wife and child abuse, rape, sexual harassment in the workplace, the conflict between family and career, divorce, the feminization of poverty, aging, and a host of other topics. All are resolutely women-centered and often combine their reflections on community with a critique of existing gender relations. Still less should one interpret this change as evidence of a retreat from political involvement or a backlash against the committed fiction of the prior decade. Such charges are a variant of an old story, one that has been used to minimize or dismiss the political dimension of women's writing for more than two centuries. Critics should know by now that arrangements in the domestic sphere have as much bearing as those in the public sphere on the constitution of a just society.

Some have contended that this change signals a conservative turn within parts of the "women's community."[2] Motifs that would support such a view crop up occasionally in this fiction.[3] *Father Melancholy's Daughter*, for example, contains an extended meditation on responsibility and sacrifice that seems to evoke a more traditional (and Christian) account of women's roles. The novel ends with the narrator taking care of two elderly people whom she had once hated and defending herself against an ex-lover's accusation that she is "sacrificing" her life by grabbing at the first "parent figures" she could find (398). This turn of events becomes almost eerie when one recalls that *Final Payments* ended with the same kind of sacrifice: Gordon's narrator gives up everything to take care of an old woman whom she too has long hated.[4] Before one decides how to interpret the ending of either novel, however, one should note that Gordon gives the last sentences of her book to the value of female friendship and that Godwin brings her heroine to a new understanding of her mother's lesbianism.[5] Before one assesses the political implications of these novels, one needs to look carefully at the models of community they provide.

Models of Community

In the decade of the eighties, a vigorous dialogue took place around the concept of community. Stimulated in part by feminist theory and in part by social scientists advocating the revival of the language of civic republicanism, this discussion produced both left- and right-wing versions of what is often called "communitarianism." Advocates of these positions argue that the United States must supplement or replace its obsession with individualism by cultivating a new public language, a discourse of shared understandings and values rather than of personal rights and prerogatives. In two of its most influential formulations—those of Alasdair MacIntyre and Robert Bellah—this language of commonalty can be nurtured only within a tradition of shared narratives and practices, which are national in their character.[6]

I have discussed aspects of this position before: Chapter 1 explored the ways in which the discourse of civic virtue and the common good could contribute to a theory of the positive uses of power; Chapter 4 noted the strain within African-American writing that relies upon communitarian assumptions. Here I need to examine its claims for two further reasons. (1) Communitarian thought represents one of the most sustained contemporary challenges to the discourses of localism and multiculturalism. It is unusual in disputing these discourses directly over the meaning of several of their central terms: "community," "subject," "practice," and "narrative." (2) Communitarianism intersects at a number of points with several strands of contemporary feminist theory, including psychoanalytic and developmental work emphasizing interconnectedness (Nancy Chodorow, Jessica Benjamin, Carol Gilligan), historical and literary research on communities of women (Carroll Smith-Rosenberg, Nina Auerbach), cultural studies of the family and domesticity (Ann Douglas, Jane Tompkins), lesbian perspectives on female friendship (Adrienne Rich, Lillian Faderman, Bonnie Zimmerman), and the reconstruction of women's traditions in popular or folk arts (diaries, letters, quilting, gardening, recipes, etc.).

By offering their own definitions of a national community, communitarian writers implicitly counter theories of local affiliation. Michael Sandel, for example, identifies three major types of theories about community: "instrumental," "sentimental," and "constitutive" models. The instrumental view of community is the sort common to liberalism, "where individuals regard social arrangements as a necessary burden and cooperate only for the sake of pursuing their private ends" (148). The sentimental view goes to the other extreme, positing unrealistic bonds of affection uniting everyone within a group. Only the constitutive model represents a viable alternative to modern individualism. Constitutive visions see identity as shaped in part by one's role in the community. Political theorists should not view the "bounds of the self" as "fixed, individuated in advance and given prior to experience" (183), Sandel concludes, but as implicated in the traditions and practices of a larger collectivity.

This definition of community differs greatly from the local communities, specific networks, and new social movements I have examined. Lyotard's postmodern vision of microcommunities clearly qualifies as constitutive rather than sentimental, but it does not reflect the totalizing impulse in much communitarian thought. The latter embraces the ideal of a single, shared culture and a unified tradition and history. Bellah characterizes many local forms of association negatively as "lifestyle enclaves" (*Habits* 71–5). Even more to the point, he rejects Fredric Jameson's contention that new social groups might represent a basis for radical change: "we would hold that lifestyle enclaves are an even more fragile basis for any effective opposition to the dominant structures of power and legitimacy" ("Idea" 281–2).

The communitarian critique of the subject also stands as an implicit challenge to the related critique found in postmodernism. Both are united in their opposition to the liberal conception of the autonomous self. But there the similarity ends. Whereas Derrida and Barthes see the subject as decentered, dispersed in a virtually infinite network of language, most communitarian writers argue for a "situated" subject, defined by its place in a national heritage and community. In Sandel's account, liberalism presents an ideal of the "unencumbered subject," a model of the self as essentially independent and thus free to exercise genuine choice in issues of state. By contrast, communitarians argue that identities are socially embodied, partly constructed by their place in a tradition and their roles in a community.

Two further terms that are central to multiculturalism play prominent roles in communitarian thought: "practice" and "narrative." MacIntyre, for example, claims that the self initially finds its place, its social embedding, in particular practices, which he defines as any "cooperative human activity" whose goods are "internal to that form of activity" (175). Bellah and his coauthors, who draw their notion of practice from MacIntyre, develop the concept with exemplary clarity: "Practices are shared activities that are not undertaken as means to an end but are ethically good in themselves" (*Habits* 335). This notion descends from Aristotle's concept of practical reasoning, just as does Bourdieu and de Certeau's idea of practice. Additionally, all parties agree that practices differ from other aspects of social life in the way they subordinate or defer instrumental goals. But here again the similarities end. Far from being potentially subversive of official institutions (as they are in their French expositors), Bellah and MacIntyre's practices serve as the hidden armature of society. "A genuine community," Bellah writes, "is constituted by such practices" (*Habits* 335), and MacIntyre contends that practices are intimately related to a society's institutions: "Indeed so intimate is the relationship of practices to institutions . . . that institutions and practices characteristically form a single causal order" (181).

Finally, narrative plays a pivotal role in both discourses. In communitarian thought, narrative influences all levels of social life. At the level of the individual, narrative gives order and intelligibility to one's actions. "To be the subject of a narrative that runs from one's birth to one's death is . . . to be accountable for the actions and experiences which compose a narratable life" (MacIntyre 202). For the society as a whole, narrative provides a framework for understanding both practices and institutions. Among many versions of this idea, Michael Walzer's stands out: "A community's culture is the story its members tell so as to make sense of all the different pieces of their social life" (319). James Boyd White, who has probably devoted more attention to narrative than any other communitarian, summarizes this theme nicely: "One could go further and say that the idea of community itself depends upon both language and story: a community is a group of people who tell a shared story in a shared language" (172).

The prominence of narrative in communitarian writing qualifies this discourse as my final example of the way literary forms and modes of analysis have begun to figure in social and political disciplines. Again, however, its role is different from that observed in earlier chapters. The degree to which communitarians celebrate the teleological and legitimizing dimensions of narrative certainly contrasts with the role marked out for "micronarratives" in Lyotard, "unauthorized" narratives in Foucault, "radically uncontrolled" narratives in Cover, "discredited" narratives in Morrison, "counternarratives" in Critical Race Theory, or "border" narratives in Anzaldúa.

What emerges from this comparison are two opposed models of community: an inclusive, historically stable, unified community based on shared values, common traditions, and respected practices versus partial, contingent affiliations based on openness to revision, political struggle, and the subversive power of counternarratives and unofficial practices.

A similar set of parallels and contrasts exists between communitarian and feminist theories. The importance of community, the need for a situated subject, the value of ordinary practices, and the power of narrative have all been major themes in feminist writing—sometimes individually, sometimes in various combinations. Feminists in the social sciences have not failed to notice the degree to which some of their concerns parallel communitarian ideas. Seyla Benhabib and Drucilla Cornell have traced the relationship between feminist and communitarian theories of the subject (11–13), while Susan Moller Okin has warned feminists who "look on communitarianism as an ally in their struggle against what they see as a masculinist abstraction and emphasis on justice, impartiality, and universality" to be "wary of such alliances" (43).

These issues have provoked controversy within feminist circles too. One of the more devisive debates in the eighties centered on what one writer calls "The Challenge of Conservative Pro-family Feminism" (Stacey). The most loaded words in this debate are "home," "family," and "community," words that also dominate the novel titles listed earlier. Judith Stacey inquires, "Are Feminists Afraid to Leave Home?"; in the same vein, Biddy Martin and Chandra Talpade Mohanty ask, "What's Home Got to Do with It?"; and Iris Marion Young criticizes feminists for adopting "The Ideal of Community."[7] All of these authors refer to the 1982–83 exchange between Jean Bethke Elshtain and Barbara Ehrenreich over the former's article "Feminism, Family, and Community," which seems to have been the immediate cause of the controversy within feminism. Their objections to *feminist* communitarian thought range from its potential racism and exclusionary practices, to its narrowness and safety, to its naive dreams of face-to-face interactions and unalienated modes of experience, to its totalizing tendencies and ideal of unity.

It is important to emphasize two things about this controversy. First, these are radical, not liberal, arguments against the communitarian vision. None of the parties in this debate wants a return to the rhetoric of individualism, and those who use the language of rights call for a revised understanding of that concept. The most recent of these critics advocate not a return to the old liberal agenda but an alternative "politics of difference." Second, even the "pro-family feminists" were not necessarily "conservative." Elshtain, in particular, conceives of family and community in ways that part company with more traditional communitarian ideals.[8]

Martin and Mohanty attempt to avoid communitarian assumptions about the unity of human experience by attending closely to a narrative that highlights differences of race, gender, sexuality, language, region, and class—Minnie Bruce Pratt's autobiography "Identity: Skin Blood Heart." The way that Pratt's work poses the question of "home" captures many of the contrasts that I have been outlining:

> "Being home" refers to the place where one lives within familiar, safe, protected boundaries; "not being home" is a matter of realizing that home was an illusion of coherence and safety based on the exclusion of specific histories of oppression and resistance, the repression of differences even within oneself. (Martin and Mohanty 196)

Pratt's lesbianism, in particular, becomes "that which makes 'home' impossible, which makes her self nonidentical" (202). Her sexuality appears to exclude her from any vision of community modeled on "home."

As a result of such concerns, feminist critics of community have advocated a "politics of difference" or "politics beyond community" (Young 301). If women want to support the notion of a situated subject, Benhabib and Cornell write, they should not give in to a "traditionalism that accepts social roles uncritically" but "view the *renegotiation* of our psychosexual identities . . . as essential to women's and human liberation" (13). If women want to endorse the legitimizing power of their own narratives, Okin says, they should not forget how it feels to be "*subjected to*" the narratives of others, for many stories in "'our' mythology are themselves basic building blocks of male domination" (45). And if women still want to celebrate community, Martin and Mohanty maintain, they should ask what distinguishes feminist justifications for community "from the justifications advanced by women who have joined the Klan for 'family, community, and protection'" (209).

These are stark alternatives. Is it necessary to oppose a communitarian vision by abandoning the ideal of community entirely? Must a "politics of difference" leave behind the notions of home and family? Many novels by women published in the eighties and nineties suggest otherwise. They work with models of community that respect difference and change. Their perspectives often displace the terms of the various oppositions I have outlined: communitarianism versus theories of local community, "pro-family" versus "anti-family" feminism. Their homes have few safe, settled boundaries; their families, few illusions about stability and coherence.

Family Subjects

Near the end of Anne Tyler's *Dinner at the Homesick Restaurant* Beck, a man who had abandoned his wife and three children decades before returns for his wife's funeral. Sitting at dinner with his grown children and grandchildren, he is bemused by this gathering of fourteen boisterous strangers. "'The thing is,' Beck said. He stopped. 'What I mean to say,' he said, 'it looks like this is one of those great big, jolly, noisy, rambling . . . why, *families!*'" (300). The reality, however, is quite different. As his eldest son puts it: "'You think we're some jolly, situation-comedy family when we're in particles, torn apart, torn all over the place, and our mother was a witch'" (301). This comment implies that nothing holds the group together, that the gathering has no common bonds. But Beck's son is wrong too. The entire novel dramatizes the strength of the ties that bind this family together. Nothing seems able to tear them apart, not violence, not sexual betrayal, not misunderstanding, selfishness, or neglect. Time after time, they keep coming back to the Homesick Restaurant, hoping to complete just one dinner without someone leaving in anger. What joins them to one another, the reader discovers, is their pain. Their connection is like a wound that will never heal. "In fact," one character muses, "they probably saw more of each other than happy families did" (157).

Pain as the bond that holds families together shows up in quite a few novels by women: Susan Kenney's *In Another Country* (1984), Bobbie Ann Mason's *In Country* (1985), and Andrea Barrett's *Secret Harmonies* (1989) are three that come to mind. If pain holds families together in these texts, the hold of the family causes pain in other texts. The bond of love is what makes many family members vulnerable. Tyler's novel memorably begins with a mother's fear of losing her children. Jane Smiley echoes Tyler's concern in *Ordinary*

Love and Good Will (1989) when the mother who is waiting for her child's plane to land confesses to "an ancient wave of terror" (8). Janet Kauffman inverts Tyler's concern by focusing on a child's fear of losing her mother in *Collaborators* (1986). The death of a close relative is a major preoccupation in this fiction, and I found it emotionally rending to read such powerful depictions of children's deaths as those that appear in Rosellen Brown's *The Autobiography of My Mother* or Lynne Sharon Schwartz's *Disturbances in the Field* (1983). Too often, however, violence, not love, is the cause of pain. Again, Tyler's novel is a prime example. The eldest son, who called his mother a witch, continues: "'She slammed us against the wall and called us scum and vipers, said she wished us dead, shook us till our teeth rattled, screamed in our faces'" (301). Kenney's novel includes a woman who assaults her grandchild, and husbands who abuse their wives and children appear in novel after novel.

Whatever else these families are, they are not safe and stable, not havens in a heartless world. Feminist criticisms of family and community, however, do not stop with the issue of physical or emotional safety. Far more troubling are questions about the potential for exclusion of those people who do not fit the norm. How does one respond to charges that the ideal of community implicitly denies differences of race, sexuality, class, language, educational level, and more? The family seems particularly vulnerable to such charges, for its boundaries appear to be defined by the institution of heterosexual marriage and by genetic relationship. The novels I have been reading suggest two kinds of answers to this question.

The first lies in the alternative family groupings that turn up in many books. Ellen Foster, the white orphaned child who narrates Kaye Gibbons's novel by that name, tries to define what a family should be while visiting a black household one day:

> I started a list of all that a family should have. Of course there is the mama and the daddy but if one has to be missing then its OK if the one left can count for two. But not just anybody can count for more than his or her self.
>
> While I watched Mavis and her family I thought I would bust open if I did not get one of them for my own self soon. Back then I had not figured out how to go about getting one but I had a feeling it could be got.

I only wanted one white and with a little more money. At least
we can have running water is what I thought. (78-9)

Although this passage assumes a heterosexual norm, it does not
assume the bond of marriage. Ellen's reflections on single parents
are rather astute, here and elsewhere in the novel. Further, the
notion of "getting" a family implies that there may be a degree of
agency involved in constituting this group. One is not simply born
into a family; one works for the privilege of membership. Ellen's
status as an orphan makes her conscious of this possibility, of
course. But many other novels suggest that even close relatives have
to work at creating and maintaining the bond. Finally, problems of
class and race come up explicitly. Wanting a little more money
seems reasonable enough, especially if the person desiring it is wor-
ried about not having indoor plumbing. Wanting a family of the
same race may also be reasonable — opinions vary about the effect
on adopted children of racial difference — but even so, Ellen later
takes back this comment. The conclusion of the novel unmistak-
ably demonstrates that Ellen's definition of a family does not result
in either racial or class exclusiveness. More than anything, Gibbons's novel is a study of ideology, of how its narrator has internalized beliefs about class and race that bear little relation to reality.
The plot culminates in Ellen's successful efforts to make amends
for former slights to her best friend, a poor African-American
girl named Starletta, now that Ellen has been taken into a white,
financially secure foster family.

Ellen Foster is only one text, but similar arguments could be
based on other novels about adoptive families. Rosellen Brown's
Civil Wars (1984) highlights race and class as forcefully as Gibbons's book. Dori Sanders's *Clover* (1990) dramatizes a black girl
gradually accepting a white stepmother. Vicki Covington's *Gathering Home* does not focus on race but does attend to class differences, regional stereotypes, and gay marriage. Tyler's latest novel,
Saint Maybe (1991), weaves single-parenting and class issues into a
single fabric. If one moves beyond novels about adoption, one
encounters other alternative images of the family. Probably the
best-known example is the female-centered family grouping at the
end of Walker's *The Color Purple*; less well known are the same-
gender marriages in Doris Grumbach's *The Ladies* (1984) and Diana McRae's *All the Muscle You Need* (1988).

The image of the extended family found in many novels by women does not challenge the boundaries of heterosexual marriage or blood relationship, but it does include individuals who are sometimes marginalized in U.S. society: the very old and the very young. Portraits of extended families are frequently dismissed as mere nostalgia or as limited to racial, ethnic, or regional subcultures. Thus Erdrich's multigenerational bonds may be viewed as simply a survival of tribal patterns; the extended families in numerous African-American novels may be understood by reference to a distinctive social structure; the prominence of extended clans in novels by southern women may be seen as having a regional basis, as perhaps may Joan Chase's portrait of the midwestern farm family in *During the Reign of the Queen of Persia* (1983). In other cases, the popularity of time-tested generic conventions may be adduced. Thus the multigenerational sagas of the New England rich can be discounted as a fictional formula that has little relation to the actual lives of most people. As a group, however, these novels share an important trait: by focusing on more than one generation, they end up paying attention to children and the elderly, people who are too often ignored in other contexts. Further, these novels often record the special needs of disabled or chronically ill people. Whether this interest in the extended family stems from generic conventions, from nostalgia, or from the social structures of isolated subcultures, its prominence in the texts of women's fiction is noteworthy. This body of writing dignifies the concerns of relatively powerless individuals by the simple means of looking closely at their lives.

The second answer to the question of exclusion lies not in alternative family structures but in relationships within and beyond the traditional family. Within the family, the mother-daughter relationship looms especially large.[9] This attention to the influence of mothering on children—and particularly on the development of the female child—participates in the larger reevaluation of the maternal role in the culture, familiar to feminists from the work of Chodorow, Gilligan, and Kristeva and from subsequent theoretical work such as Margaret Homans's *Bearing the Word* or the essays gathered in Garner, Kahane, and Sprengnether's *The (M)other Tongue*. But how does this theme call into question the structure of the traditional family? To begin with, the intensity of the bond between mothers and daughters often seems to push to the margin other forms of relation and consequently to decenter the traditional image of the patriarchal family. The narrator of Janet Kauffman's *Collaborators* captures the potentially all-consuming character of this bond: "The unreason of my mother, her refusal to face facts, her bodily hauling of God in and out of the room, her coloratura talk about whim, ordinary desire, her goddess talk of the bodies of disembodied men, the power of her denials, her grace, her awkwardness—she is the genie out of the bottle. I don't know how to contain her" (43). This fluid, overwhelming relation can be deeply comforting too. On the last page of Terry McMillan's *Mama*, the black single mother, whose struggle for survival has been the subject of the novel, holds in her arms her grown daughter, who has just come through her own struggle: "Mildred's breasts felt full against her own, and Freda couldn't tell whose were whose. They held each other up. They patted each other's back as if each had fallen and scraped a knee and had no one else to turn to for comfort. It seemed as if they hugged each other for the past and for the future" (260). Sometimes the bond between mother and daughter seems to establish a line of descent outside that of the Father's name. Jayne Anne Phillips conveys this idea in a single sentence in *Machine Dreams* (1984): "But when I knew I had a daughter, I was so thankful—like my own mother had come back to me" (22). Kaye Gibbons's latest novel, *A Cure for Dreams* (1991), embodies the same notion in its point of view: a daughter is writing down her mother's oral narration of her own mother's life.

Focusing on motherhood displaces the traditional image of the family in other ways. The act of giving birth itself has been portrayed as something that can expose the hollowness of established social roles. The narrator of Lynne Sharon Schwartz's terribly sad yet philosophical novel *Disturbances in the Field* reflects on the birth of her first daughter:

> There is an essential and profound strangeness about being a mother that is rarely spoken of, and yet religion does make much of loving others better than one's self, which suggests it does not come naturally. Maternity, though, is considered in the nature of things: that mothers gladly endure pain so that their children may thrive is a useful, sustaining myth. Also something of a cultural joke: the mother as sucker. And between saint and sucker, two sides of one thin coin, is little room to maneuver.

> In childbirth we tunnel through a dark passage to the new and
> strange place, to find there that the myth about mothers is true
> and so is the joke, the corrosive humor. (201)

At the other extreme, the most ordinary aspects of the mother-
daughter relationship can unsettle rather than reinforce roles. The
daughter's fondest memory of her mother in *Father Melancholy's
Daughter* is their subversive weekly game of mocking her father's
parishioners:

> It was ours alone, even Daddy didn't know about our secret war
> of insolence. . . . When [my mother] and I were playing it, she
> seemed more like an older sister leading me willingly into rebel-
> lion against Daddy's Wednesday flock. She wasn't being mali-
> cious—even at six I knew that; she was just letting off some
> steam. And even at six, I knew she had steam to let off. (28)

In many novels the special relation of mothers and daughters
within the family leads seamlessly into a special relationship *beyond* the family: the bond with a larger community of women.
Schwartz's story of family tragedy is also the story of four female
friends.[10] The daughter in *Collaborators* observes with fascination
her mother's lifelong bond with another woman and eventually
grows close to the woman herself. Perhaps the finest moments in
Covington's *Gathering Home* record the grandmother's ties to the
cancer-stricken woman next door who runs the Curl Up and Dye
beauty parlor out of her house. In these texts marriage and family
are not allowed to put a limit on the range of possible relations,
and in particular, are not allowed to exclude a woman-identified
sense of community.

Other novels go further still, portraying women-centered communities as compensating for the inadequacies of traditional families. The most frequently discussed examples of this motif are Marilynne Robinson's *Housekeeping* and Gloria Naylor's *The Women
of Brewster Place*. I would like to end this discussion with a more
recent example, however: Whitney Otto's *How to Make an American Quilt* (1991). This novel tells the stories of eight women in a
quilting circle who meet once a week for more than thirty-five
years. Interpolated between the stories are quilting instructions,
which stitch tips about craft and little-known facts into a patch-
work of metaphor and history. These discursive interludes allow

the novel to reflect, with unusual self-consciousness, on topics such as women's community, art, and heritage. Otto's novel presents the family as a social construct, whose structure, boundaries, and character can change over time. "You want to keep these things in mind: history and family. How they are often inseparable" (12). Differences of race, too, are acknowledged rather than submerged in this community—six are white women, two black: "no one ever made the mistake of saying, 'We don't even notice color; they are just like us.' It was this recognition of their differences that allowed the group to survive" (176). Finally, the novel is able to be critical of the community. The book does not turn the quilting circle into what Sandel would call a "sentimental" community with naive expectations about common goals and cooperative principles. "Sometimes," one of the quilters thinks, "the worst thing about being a woman is having women friends. And the worst part about having women friends is that one must share so many confidences, except the one confidence [she] longs to share, which is the one about not being wild over the idea of women friends" (72). The character also admits, however, that the group nurtures aspects of her life that otherwise would not survive.

I have argued that these novels by women, taken together, constitute a sophisticated discourse about home, family, and community, one that avoids the problems that beset some communitarian thinking. If one extracts the principles of community implicit in these texts, one discovers a vision much closer to the ideal of local affiliation and multiculturalism than to the communitarian philosophy criticized by many feminists. These novels present the family as a partial, contingent structure, vulnerable both to internal and external pressures, yet open to revision. Further, they see the boundaries of home as permeable, subject to renegotiation. They acknowledge that family groupings may be in conflict with other essential forms of association, but they view this conflict, however painful, as a possible source of growth. Conflict may give rise to the kinds of local struggles that have become so prominent a feature of the political landscape today. In the process it may lead to the kinds of unofficial practices, the tactics of everyday life that have always been available to the disempowered or oppressed. It may fuel the new social movements and identity politics that have replaced traditional modes of political expression for many people.

If the old boundaries of home no longer seem secure, then perhaps the country needs more tolerance of diverse arrangements for nurturance and mutual aid.

One thing is clear from looking at these novels by women: homes, families, and communities are products of more creative energy than the official debate always acknowledges. Too much of this creativity is born of desperation. In too many novels, violence, poverty, racism, drug abuse, lack of educational opportunity, and other forms of inequality drive the impulse to create new ways of living together. Yet the creativity remains.

Conclusion:
Literature without
Masterpieces

One of the complicated pleasures of writing a book about contemporary literature is falling further and further behind. When I am tempted to complain about the rising tide of books — the new novels that pile up on the bedside table; the scholarly journals that keep arriving in the mail; the volumes of nonfiction, cultural criticism, and literary theory that threaten to make one's work out-of-date before it reaches the press — I recall the response one often hears to the complaint of growing older: "Think of the alternative." Inevitably, much of what gets published is meretricious — or worse. But much is capable of moving the spirit, exciting the mind, excoriating injustice and oppression, expanding the boundaries of individual experience, and forging bonds with different communities. The last few years have brought new works of fiction that impressively confirm both the vitality and the diversity of our writing. Look at the imaginative strength exerted to understand this diversity — diversity not just of race, gender, and class, as the opponents of "political correctness" would have it, but of so many other characteristics that divide us, and bring us together in new ways, and make us who we are: age, region, education, occupation, abledness, religion, sexuality, ethnicity, family structure, political affiliation, and more. Oscar Hijuelos's *The Mambo Kings Play Songs of Love* (1989), Allan Gurganus's *Oldest Living Confederate Widow*

Tells All (1989), Cynthia Kadohata's *The Floating World* (1989), John Casey's *Spartina* (1989), Katherine Dunn's *Geek Love* (1989), Marita Golden's *Long Distance Life* (1989), David Leavitt's *Equal Affections* (1989), Jessica Hagedorn's *Dogeaters* (1990), John Updike's *Rabbit at Rest* (1990), John Edgar Wideman's *Philadelphia Fire* (1990), Lorrie Moore's *Like Life* (1990), James Welch's *The Indian Lawyer* (1990), Mark Helprin's *A Soldier of the Great War* (1991), Leslie Marmon Silko's *Almanac of the Dead* (1991), Harold Brodkey's *The Runaway Soul* (1991), Norman Rush's *Mating* (1991), Norman Mailer's *Harlot's Ghost* (1991), Richard Price's *Clockers* (1992), Toni Morrison's *Jazz* (1992), Cormac McCarthy's *All the Pretty Horses* (1992) — these are just some of the novels that I did not find a place for in this study. Many of them, it seems to me, would have furthered my argument as well as some of the novels that were discussed.

We live in a great period of writing, certainly the equal of any in the comparatively short history of this nation. Some people are made uncomfortable by talk about "greatness" or by any evaluative terms at all. They perhaps fear that such language leads to an exclusive focus on "masterpieces," which may circumscribe the range of valid cultural experiences and privilege a canon tailored to the interests of a small but dominant group of taste makers. Other people are surprised for the opposite reason when they hear the age praised, since they cannot point to any writer or movement that stands out above the crowd, commanding the entire cultural scene. The two responses may be taken as canceling one another out. The inability of any writer or style to hold sway is a defining characteristic of the times, the result (I have argued) of an increasingly multicultural society, postindustrial economy, and interdisciplinary conception of writing. It is certainly *not* the result of some decline in the imaginative energy of the nation's culture, or of the lack of dedication and talent of writers. If critics of the literary canon have helped readers to see that the very concept of the "masterpiece" is socially constructed, then they need to extend that insight and recognize that today's society is constructing a literature without masterpieces. This does not mean that rich cultural experiences are unavailable. On the contrary, it means that the kinds of experience one would traditionally call "literary" are more diverse and challenging than ever before.

What does a literature without masterpieces mean for this society — for schools, for public debates, for private reading experiences, for civic affiliations, for local politics, for people's varied and changing subject positions? What does a literature without "literature," narrowly conceived, require and make possible? What are the responsibilities of a criticism *in* the present time, a criticism fully implicated in the worlds it describes, a criticism committed to presents-becoming-futures? Implicit answers to such questions occur throughout this book, but I want to formulate a direct response by way of conclusion.

To begin with, taking multiculturalism seriously might lead critics to revise their conception of a pluralist society. The traditional vision of pluralism sees society as a political marketplace where freely associating individuals form interest groups that work to establish a particular agenda as policy for the whole. It assumes that competition among such groups will result in an equitable distribution of social goods and that the political process of give-and-take will eventually end in a harmonious balance of interests. It further assumes that organized groups have coherent, somewhat monolithic desires; that such groups fairly represent all aspects of people's lives and all divisions of society; and that such groups all have equal access, through the democratic process, to the public arena.[1] This vision of pluralism, however, fails to account for people whose interests are not covered by any organized political group; whose desires are contradictory, ill-defined, or socially unacceptable; whose ability to participate in the democratic process is limited by poverty, lack of education, prejudice, and more. Clearly, the balance negotiated under these conditions cannot be described as fair. But is this vision the best possible conception of pluralism for today's society?

William Connolly has advocated a democratic politics based not on the ideal of harmony or concord but on "an ontology of discordance" (*Politics* 11). The problem with both the liberal and civic republican visions, according to Connolly, is their shared insistence on the goal of consensus. Citizens need to preserve an ambiguous relation to public life, one that challenges the system's urge for closure, one that looks for "slack" in the political order. Such a perspective is more tolerant of diversity, more accepting of mystery; it makes room for the liminal, the carnivalesque, the other

(*Politics* 94–6, 107–10). If, in keeping with this book's focus, I recast Connolly's ideas in terms of cultural pluralism, the outlines of a more radical conception of pluralism emerge. Instead of groups of freely associating individuals, conscious of their desires and fully enfranchised to seek them, the groups welcomed by this new pluralism are local, perhaps ill-defined and poorly organized, sometimes ephemeral. They take shape through an everyday practice, a popular procedure or tactic, a narrative pragmatics, a marginalized tradition, or a subjugated knowledge. The forces that bring them together may not produce groups that correspond with any single economic or political interest. These affiliations are cultural and social rather than civic, but they should be eligible for respect just the same, for the communities that embody some people's cherished values and desires are not always those that can currently find a place in the public realm.[2] In today's society, cultural practices and social affiliations inevitably seem to outrun political change; people explore (or find themselves forced into) alternative living arrangements at a pace that far outstrips judicial or legislative efforts to respond to them. A cultural pluralism would acknowledge this fact—acknowledge it not only as a problem but also as an opportunity—and employ such local communities to provide the "slack" that a national order may not possess.

A second consequence of multiculturalism is a transformation in conceptions of the canon. As the evaluative terms used above suggest, a literature without masterpieces does not do away with the concept of canons. But it does call into question the notion of a single, shared canon for all the peoples of this continent. Each of us participates in multiple canons, and these canons vary as widely as the uses to which different texts may be put. There are canons that govern our pleasure reading, canons that shape our understanding of current events, canons that determine what counts as professional expertise, canons of practical information or common sense, canons of intellectual discourse, canons that form around social movements, canons that respond to emerging identity groups. At times these bodies of texts overlap, at times conflict with one another, but one must continually find ways of negotiating among their competing claims.[3] The struggle is often experienced collectively as established or emergent groups attempt to mark out the areas of freedom and commitment that define their lives together. But it is also experienced within the individual, as interests change over time, as different, perhaps only partially congruent aspects of the subject struggle toward speech or listen attentively for voices that will speak to them. Usually the contradictions remain inconsequential. Individuals respond with tiny, automatic adjustments; they coordinate among shifting allegiances through tact or "social grace." The negotiation of such minor contradictions is one of those practices of everyday life that make existence possible.

Sometimes, though, the contradictions are too wrenching to ignore. Sometimes the mixed messages threaten to overwhelm. Then this conflict may become a source of frustration, anger, or despair, as well a powerful means of manipulation or exploitation. One should never forget that the conflict among canons is experienced unequally, that some people are better equipped than others to mediate among rival truth claims. Education, social location, economic status – the entire panoply of what Bourdieu has called "cultural capital" – gives an advantage to some people in making sense of contradictions. But even those who are poorly equipped, even those who cannot read at all, have to deal with a world organized by multiple canons, for we are all subject to numerous bodies of knowledge, which are themselves ordered by implicit and explicit rankings of texts. For minority intellectuals, who may speak on behalf of communities with relatively little cultural capital, negotiating among canons is an urgent concern. But I have tried to suggest that thinking about diversity is a crucial task for all critics, wherever they may be situated. One responsibility of a critic in the present is to identify ways of living in a multicultural society, not to lament uselessly the perceived loss of a single, unified culture.

This last point introduces a third consequence of multiculturalism. The search for ways to live in the present commits the critic to an engaged conception of intellectual work. In both scholarly writing and the popular press, there have been many accounts of the changing role of the intellectual. I have argued that those who bemoan the absorption of this figure into the university indulge in nostalgia for a vanished social organization, and I have cited Nancy Fraser's description of the engaged intellectual, which emphasizes this figure's relationship both to a disciplinary location and to extra-academic social movements. Until recently, most attempts to theorize the new social location of intellectuals focused on "oppositional" critics, usually meaning academics on the left, rarely noting that many intellectuals on the right function as the "expert wing of an oppositional public" too (Fraser 11). For left or right, however, opposition was the role marked out for the political critic. Over the last few years, however, I have noticed an increasing emphasis on the need for committed intellectuals to engage in a double project, one involving both opposition and affirmation. For example, in 1991 Henry Louis Gates urged critics to move beyond "routinized ressentiment in favor of rethinking the larger structures that constrain and enable our agency" ("Good-bye" 725). In *Third World Women and the Politics of Feminism*, published in the same year, Chandra Talpade Mohanty spelled out the twin dimensions of this endeavor, the first a process of dismantling, the second one of rebuilding: "While these projects appear to be contradictory, the one working negatively and the other positively, unless these two tasks are addressed simultaneously, 'third world' feminisms run the risk of marginalization or ghettoization" (51). The second part of the project often involves archival work aimed at recovering alternative practices or countermemories embedded in the works of neglected writers, but it cannot be limited to unreflective salvage operations. Abdul R. JanMohamed and David Lloyd rightly caution: "Unmediated by a theoretical perspective, the mere affirmation of achievement lends itself too easily to selective recuperation into the dominant culture" (7). Further, the rush to affirm neglected traditions may lead to an ahistorical attitude of appreciation or culture collecting and may tempt critics to an increasingly apolitical stance toward intellectual work.[4]

Despite these dangers, many critics have begun to supplement critical or oppositional energies with attempts to recover and theorize the positive dimensions of their cultural heritages. This book has been part of that project. It presents reasons for hope about the answers to at least two questions: whether writing in a multicultural society can possess power and whether this power can be put to constructive use in struggles for freedom and justice. My greatest concern, however, has been that optimism about possible futures might be taken as approval of the status quo. The desire to affirm sources of strength cannot be allowed to become an excuse for complacency. I am well aware that there are more pessimistic ways to assess contemporary culture and that these negative assessments are not restricted to embattled conservatives. On the contrary, the most trenchant critiques of postmodernism have come from writers on the left. The same evidence can be used to construct very different accounts. Paul Bové, writing in 1992, speaks of telling two different stories about today's culture, "a sad story of the defeat of criticism by institutions, of knowledge and seriousness by posture and fashion" or a happier "story of partial success: of reforms in canon formation, critical method, and problems of representation that have occurred since theory helped make it possible to speak of 'difference,' 'subject formation,' 'discourse,' 'the other'" (*Wake* 1). I have gambled that now is the time to tell the story of partial success. At a time when ringing denunciations of cultural diversity have become commonplace in the media, when politicians blame writers, artists, and critics for everything from the decay of "family values" to the violence of inner cities, criticism needs to speak plainly about other ways of viewing the present. Now is the moment to affirm the pleasure and power of writing in this multicultural land of Babel.

Notes

Chapter 1

1. The history of this distinction in Germany and France has been discussed by Elias (1:1–50); in France, by Febvre (219–57); and in England, by Raymond Williams (13–15).

2. In the *Oxford English Dictionary*, early examples of this usage are drawn from Wordsworth (1805) and Arnold ("Culture, the acquainting ourselves with the best that has been known and said in the world" [1876]).

3. For the widespread appeal of this answer to the question of diversity, see Hirsch's description of the activities of the Foundation for Cultural Literacy in his essay "The Primal Scene of Education."

4. Andrew Ross has also noticed this phenomenon, which he characterizes as a "reactionary consensus of left and right, each unswervingly loyal to their respective narratives of decline: charges of post-sixties fragmentation and academification from unreconstructed voices on the left, and warnings of doom and moral degeneracy from the Cassandras of the right" (*No Respect* 211).

5. For challenging discussions of new historicism, see Liu ("Power") and Veeser. The clearest treatment of the difference between new historicism and cultural materialism is Dollimore, "Introduction." The important contributions of the Birmingham School of cultural studies can be seen in the works of Hall and Hebidge.

6. For a fascinating discussion of this development, see Tichi.

7. The modern restriction of the word emerged in part as a response to the tide of popular writing made possible in the eighteenth century by the growth of printing technology, in part as a defense of values that the sweeping changes brought on by urbanization, secularism, and the Industrial Revolution appeared to be threatening. For analyses of this change in

the meaning of the term, see Raymond Williams (46–52), Kernan (*Printing* 7–8; *Imaginary* 3–6, 12–36), and Eagleton (*Literary* 1–16).

8. In a series of articles on the issue of professionalism, Bruce Robbins has qualified Rorty's assertion in ways that I have found useful in thinking about the changing power of culture: "If Rorty is unjustified in conclud-ing . . . that success in interdisciplinary competition is *necessarily* in the public interest—his model here is Adam Smith's invisible hand—his idea that the constellation of disciplines at a given moment will both reflect and help constitute the social order of that moment and that a shift in the first will therefore constitute a shift in the second deserves to be rescued from his free-market assumptions" ("Oppositional" 16–17). Robbins also takes up the topic I discuss in the next paragraph, the fact that "the rise of narrative to authority within literary criticism coincides with, and helps account for, a phase of imperialism in which our discipline has asserted authority over other disciplines" ("Death" 42).

9. Works by the literary critics Fish, Ryan, and Caserio ("Supreme"); the theologian Cornel West; and the anthropologists Marcus and Fischer present a fair sampling of the recent interest in legal theory by scholars who are not lawyers. See also the anthology edited by Levinson and Mail-loux and the new *Yale Journal of Law and the Humanities*. For criticisms of this exchange, see Posner.

10. For a bibliography of Critical Legal Studies current through the winter of 1984, see Kennedy and Klare. The best introductions to this movement are a double-issue of the *Stanford Law Review* (34:1–2 [1984]) and Kelman.

11. For a discussion of contemporary theories of desire and the psycho-analytical assumptions that support many of them, see Chapter 3.

12. In a well-known article, W. B. Gallie maintains that some concepts involve one in irresolvable debates about their proper meaning. Connolly uses Gallie's idea of "essentially contested concepts" to organize his chap-ter, "Forms of Power." Lukes also believes that it is unprofitable to try to settle on one definition of the concept ("Introduction" 4, 17).

13. Both Voltaire and Jouvenel's individualist conceptions of power are quoted by Hannah Arendt: "Power," according to Voltaire, "consists in making others act as I choose"; and Jouvenel writes, "To command and to be obeyed: without that, there is no Power—with it no other attribute is needed" (Arendt 60).

14. For the importance of this movement to legal thought, see the spe-cial issue of the *Yale Law Journal*, "Symposium: The Republican Civic Tradition" (97:8 [1988]), containing articles by Michelman and Sunstein, as well as responses by eleven other scholars. For a more extended discus-sion of civic republicanism generally, see Chapter 6 below.

15. In "Hannah Arendt's Communications Concept of Power," Habermas has effectively criticized Arendt's definition as failing in three ways: (a) it eliminates all strategic elements from politics by terming them violence; (b) it ignores the role of administrative systems; and (c) it neglects the structural violence built into political institutions.

16. In theory, power does have a positive dimension for Foucault because it creates as well as represses. But when Foucault discusses the way in which people respond to power, he phrases matters wholly in terms of resistance. Connolly sees the "exclusion of political affirmation" in Foucault as a denial of part of his own theory, a denial perhaps undertaken for strategic reasons (*Politics* 93). Wolin (198) makes a similar point.

17. For illuminating discussions of the politics of the new social movements, see Aronowitz, Mouffe, and Radhakrishnan.

18. For the increased risks involved for gay men and lesbians since the advent of AIDS, see Crimp (ed.) and Watney. For documentation that not all social attitudes have taken the same "right turn" made in national elections during the Reagan era, see Ferguson and Rogers.

19. Perhaps the most invigorating development in recent years within some social movements has been the call to move away from identity politics toward alliance or coalition politics. Diversity of race, class, and sexual orientation among women, for example, indicates to Donna Haraway that women "cannot affirm the capacity to act on the basis of natural identification, but only on the basis of conscious coalition, of affinity, of political kinship" (156). For sophisticated critiques of identity politics in feminism, see Fuss (*Essentially* 97–112) and Butler (*Gender* 1–6, 142–49).

20. Although Bell uses the word "class" in this passage, he makes clear here and elsewhere that he does not view these groups as forming an "economic interest class" or a "new political class" (*Post-Industrial* 374). Groups in the perhaps misnamed "knowledge class" are bound together not by common economic or political interests but by a shared cultural attitude and a common ethos. For extended discussions of this issue, see Bell's "The New Class: A Muddled Concept" and the other essays collected in the same volume.

21. The large literature on this transformation in post-World War II Western societies includes Bell (*Post-Industrial*), Habermas ("Modernity"), Lyotard (*Postmodern*), Jameson ("Postmodernism"), Berger, and Poster. For my sense of the term "postmodernism," see Clayton ("Genealogy").

22. I prefer Haraway's formulation. If what she calls the "New Industrial Revolution" makes possible alternative modes of resistance, it also creates an "informatics of domination" (161).

23. For essays on the changed status of the contemporary intellectual,

see the collection edited by Robbins and his own writings on this topic ("Oppositional" and "Death"). Gerald Graff has written an important study of changes in the profession of English (*Professing*). Merod's *The Political Responsibility of the Critic* is a challenge to intellectuals to think critically about the authority that stems from their institutional positioning.

Chapter 2

1. Three of the most vigorous attacks on deconstruction as conservative are to be found in Foley, Eagleton (*Literary* 127–50), and Lentricchia (*Criticism*). The case for deconstruction as a vehicle for left-radical causes is made by Ryan (*Politics* 62–81, esp. 71). Culler employs Foucault to argue that the ultimate consequences of any theoretical position are unpredictable (*Framing* 66, 69–82).

2. See the volume *Responses: On Paul de Man's Wartime Journalism*, edited by Hamacher, Hertz, and Keenan; Derrida ("Like"); the responses to Derrida's essay published in *Critical Inquiry* 15/4 (1989): 765–873; and Schwarz (105–41).

3. For an introduction to Critical Legal Studies, see Chapter 1. The Critical Race Theory movement is discussed at the end of this chapter.

4. For the claim that deconstruction, correctly understood, can be part of feminist political action, see Cornell and the essays by Joan W. Scott and Mary Poovey collected by Newton and Hoffman; but, for counterarguments, see Leslie Wahl Rabine in the same collection. For a positive assessment of deconstruction's value to African-American studies, see Gates (*Signifying*; *Figures*; "What's") and Baker ("Dubious"). For arguments against this position, see Barbara Christian (in Newton and Hoffman) and Joyce ("Black" and "Who").

5. See Ryan (*Marxism*). Works by Marxists that object to deconstruction include those mentioned in Note 1 above, as well as Eagleton ("Capitalism").

6. This work's reception in the United States continues to evolve in revealing ways. In this chapter I trace two stories about Barthes: how he moved from being the representative of structuralism to poststructuralism in the seventies, and then how, in the eighties, this poststructuralist Barthes came to be seen by some feminists and other oppositional critics as representative of the problems involved in an ahistorical celebration of difference. In the nineties, though, a third story has emerged. The poststructuralist Barthes is being reevaluated again, this time by gay male critics, who emphasize the importance of seeing his attempts to theorize the plurality

of desire in the context of his own homosexuality. Jonathan Dollimore writes: "Cultural context makes the crucial difference: the appropriation of the romantic, the utopian, and the polymorphous for what has hitherto been marginal, and both demonized and repressed by the centre, and internalized as such at the margins, has quite different effects and implications from, say, a more general (post/modern?) theory that 'anything goes anywhere'" (*Sexual* 330–1). For a more extended discussion of this issue, see D. A. Miller's new book on Barthes. I shall discuss some examples of gay and lesbian theories of narrative in Chapter 3.

7. Elsewhere in "The Struggle with the Angel" Barthes states, "My work on Balzac's story *Sarrasine* [i.e., *S/Z*] belongs more to textual than to structural analysis" (137n1).

8. The two preceding paragraphs are adapted from a discussion of Kristeva in Clayton and Rothstein ("Figures").

9. Robbins notices White's distrust of the authority conferred on and by stories: "Within literary studies, narrative is everywhere spoken against, and precisely because it is taken to embody authority" ("Death" 42). Robbins traces the origins of this distrust to the profession's contest "over how to relate professional expertise to public interest" (39). My discussion of the politics of linearity in deconstruction can be seen as complementing his thesis.

10. In his later *Orientalism* Said seems to admit as much. He constrasts the static, conservative character of panoptic visions of the Orient with the temporal, open, and partial perspectives introduced by narrative:

> Narrative asserts the power of men to be born, develop, and die, the tendency of institutions and actualities to change, the likelihood that modernity and contemporaneity will finally overtake "classical" civilizations; above all, it asserts that the domination of reality by vision is no more than a will to power, a will to truth and interpretation, and not an objective condition of history. Narrative, in short, introduces an opposing point of view, perspective, consciousness to the unitary web of vision. (240)

11. My attention was first drawn to this problem by the members of my narrative theory seminar at the University of Wisconsin–Madison in 1985. I would like to thank everyone in that excellent group and especially Doris Dungey, Carol Franko, Christine Loflin, and Elizabeth Zanichkowsky.

12. For an illuminating account of the activities of this circle in the early eighties, see Fraser (69–92).

13. For a similar argument that deconstruction should be seen "as perpetually a media or means rather than end," see Liu ("Local" 82).

14. In addition to Nancy Miller, whose work is discussed below, other feminists who have contributed to this trend include Cheryl Walker, Paul

Smith, and Susan Stanford Friedman ("Weavings"). It should be emphasized that the return to the subject is not limited to feminists. José David Saldívar, for example, views the "Making of the Chicano-Chicana Subject, 1969–1982" as crucial to defining a "Chicano poetics."

15. For a good example of the feminist case for practice rather than theory, see Kolodny. Alice Walker's "In Search of Our Mothers' Gardens" and Jane Marcus's "Still Practice A/Wrested Alphabet: Towards a Feminist Aesthetic" are two other eloquent expositions of the idea that female agency may be found in the ways of making the familiar world that are passed down from one generation to another.

16. Ryan puts a similar point well: "If the violated were to speak, then there would be many voices, not one. . . . Stories of counter power would require a sense of the tentativeness of other perspectives, of history as a frequently violent field of contingencies, of narrative itself as a fragile and constant exercise in self-construction" ("Social," 1778).

17. Cornel West, who has written frequently about Critical Legal Studies, makes a similar argument. Progressive lawyers, he argues, should be "guided by a deep historical sensibility. This sensibility not only deconstructs the contradictory character of past and present legal decisions (or demystifies the power relations operative in such decisions), but also concocts powerful and enabling narratives that demonstrate how these decisions constitute the kind of society in which we live and how people resist and try to transform it" (1802).

18. For clarity's sake, I have rearranged the order of this quote. The last sentence actually precedes the others in Delgado's text.

19. In Chicano studies, which I take up in Chapter 5, deconstruction (particularly "Yale" deconstruction) figures prominently in the work of some critics. See Chabram (130–3).

Chapter 3

1. See Adrian Forty, *Objects of Desire*, a social history of consumer products.

2. Goodheart has noted the centrality of discourse about desire not only in theory but also in the "languages of fiction" (441).

3. There are differences between the two novels, which should not be minimized. Roth's novel is written in a conventional, realistic style, takes pains to characterize its colorful minor characters, and is traditionally introspective, exploring the protagonist's Oedipal preoccupations. Dworkin's work, on the other hand, is composed in short fragments, which

insistently repeat key phrases and entire incidents, creating a poetic, incantatory style, pays as little attention to peripheral characters as the story will allow, often not naming or describing them at all, and takes anything but an introspective and psychoanalytic approach to its protagonist. My intention in comparing the two novels is not to interpret one in terms of the other but to reveal structures of narrative and desire that the books share, despite all their differences.

4. Frank Lentricchia has effectively criticized this approach, which is characteristic of what he calls the "conservative fictionalist tradition" (*After* 31), for alienating the reader from any valid grounds of action. "Self-consciousness, then, by producing an awareness of the fictiveness of fictions, produces the knowledge which saves us from being caught up in the net of moral relations" (57).

5. For a related critique of this aspect of Brooks's book, see Winnett.

6. This book is coauthored with Ulysse Dutoit, but for convenience, I refer to it by Bersani's name alone. This practice is justified by two considerations. First, most of the arguments about narrative, violence, and desire are elaborations of positions that Bersani has taken in earlier works. Second, passages and examples in the sections with which I shall be dealing (chiefly those on narrative and on psychoanalysis) are reprinted with only minor changes from an article that Bersani published under his own name.

7. For a discussion of Bersani's recent work that shares some of the same perspectives as this one, see Caserio ("Mobility").

8. Contributions to that project are beginning to appear. See Dollimore (*Sexual*) and Traub (*Desire* and "[In]significance").

9. Carole-Anne Tyler has documented the "(thinly disguised?) misogyny" (38) that still informs Bersani's essay, despite his protests at the end that he is "not arguing for a complicity with misogynist and homophobic fantasies" ("Rectum" 221–2).

10. For recent work by D. A. Miller elaborating these issues in the context of film, see "Anal *Rope*." Other narrative theorists who work to historicize gay desire include Joseph Boone and Caserio.

11. A fine essay by the late Thomas Yingling relates the "ongoing histories in which AIDS unfolds (variously comprised of the viral, the personal, the communal, the national, and the global)" (292) to questions of "postmodern governance" of the sort I explored in Chapter 1. His comments about the gap between the "apprehension" of AIDS "on bodies, in friends, in news reports, in changing populations, behaviors, and rituals" and the "comprehension of the disease" (292) could be used as a commentary on Barnett's story.

Chapter 4

1. The term "minority" is not meant to equate the social or cultural position of groups as various as African-Americans, Latinas, Asian-Americans, and Native Americans or to submerge the differences between male and female experience within these groups. One needs to keep in mind the different historical forms racism has taken in each case, ranging from slavery, to military conquest, to genocide. Equally, one needs to be aware of what the sociologist Deborah King has called the "multiple jeopardy" of women of color, who suffer "interactive oppressions" from race, gender, and class. But the word "minority" does indicate the shared fact of difference—and, in many cases, exclusion—from the dominant culture. JanMohamed and Lloyd make a similar point about the usage of this term in their introduction to *The Nature and Context of Minority Discourse* (1990): "Cultures designated as minorities have certain shared experiences by virtue of their similar antagonistic relationship to the dominant culture, which seeks to marginalize them all" (1).

2. These last two examples are drawn from an article by Michiko Kakutani that remarks on this trend in the fiction of 1989. Like most commentators, she interprets this phenomenon as a conservative sign, a "nostalgia for the days when old-fashioned storytelling was possible, when stories and lives seemed to possess coherent beginnings, middles and ends" (18).

3. Allen writes: "*Cousin-brother* is used at Laguna to describe the relationship between maternal cousins who are more like siblings than cousins in their kinship system" (*Sacred* 278n12).

4. According to Bevis, "the first assumption of tribalism is that the individual is completed only in relation to others, that man is a political animal (lives through a relationship to a village-state), and the group which must complete his 'being' is organized in some meaningful way" (587). Silko's presentation of Tayo's grandmother confirms Bevis's interpretation of tribalism: "An old sensitivity had descended in her, surviving thousands of years from the oldest times, when the people shared a single clan name and they told each other who they were; they recounted the actions and words each of their clan had taken, and would take; from before they were born and long after they died, the people shared the same consciousness" (70). Swan notes the importance of ritual in structuring many aspects of the novel, from the characters to the symbolic geography.

5. Lincoln notes that "There are 43 uranium mines, 5 mills, and 31 mining companies digging up Indian lands in the Four Corners area. . . . The Jackpile open-pit uranium mine, on the Laguna Reservation, is the largest in the country" (284n25). Los Alamos, where atomic scientists

work, is in the center of Pueblo territory, and White Sands, where the first atomic bomb was tested, is nearby to the south.

6. Works by Anaya, as well as by other Chicano novelists, will be discussed in the next chapter. For a definition of *cuentos* and a discussion of Anaya that compares his "cross-generic" sense of form with that of Silko, see Dasenbrock.

7. For discussions of the importance of storytelling in the African-American tradition, see Bernard Bell, Callahan, Valerie Smith, Wilentz, and Willis. Smith emphasizes the connection between narrative and community in the work of Toni Morrison; Callahan and Wilentz stress the oral character of African-American narrative. Both of these issues will be important topics later in this chapter.

8. In *Zami* see p. 22. Bambara's novel contains a scene from a Japanese-American internment camp during World War II that presents an ironic reflection of Tayo's experiences as a Japanese POW in *Ceremony*. Bambara writes of the "stories keeping the people in the camps alive while the bill in Congress to sterilize the women of the camps got voted down by one vote" (222). Silko writes: "[Tayo] made a story for all of them, a story to give them strength. The words of the story poured out of his mouth as if they had substance, pebbles and stone extending to hold the corporal up, to keep his knees from buckling" (11).

9. A related strategy would have been to focus on storytelling in white ethnic writing. As Mark Shechner pointed out to me in correspondence, Jewish novelists such as Roth and Ozick mentioned above, or Isaac Bashevis Singer, are as much "minority" writers as are the novelists treated in this chapter, and they certainly stress the importance of oral or traditional narrative forms.

10. JanMohamed and Lloyd argue that "a collective subjectivity" is characteristic of minority communities: "the collective nature of all minority discourse . . . derives from the fact that minority individuals are always treated and forced to experience themselves generically. Coerced into a negative, generic subject-position, the oppressed individual responds by transforming that position into a positive, collective one" (9–10). Although I think this argument simplifies the complex subject positions actually assumed by individual members of minority communities, it does indicate another reason for focusing on minority writers in this chapter.

11. For illuminating discussions of quilting and the recipe, see Ferrero et al. and Leonardi, respectively. The contemporary African-American artist Faith Ringgold combines painting with oral narrative and quilting in her powerful "story quilts." In an interview Ringgold explains: "I write stories that go with my paintings; little stories based on experiences I have

heard about, and out of my experiences of being a black woman in America" (2). A good introduction to the artist's work is Thalia Gouma-Peterson.

12. Barbara Christian has emphasized the ways in which "this exploration of new forms based on the black woman's culture" has "revitalized the American novel" (*Black* 185).

13. This creation myth appears in the poem from Silko's novel quoted earlier. Grandmother spider, the Thought-Woman, possesses the power of creation through words. As she names something, it appears, and everything that happens is part of an ongoing story she is telling. Grandmother spider is a central figure in Native American mythology. According to Allen, "She is the Old Woman Spider who weaves us together in a fabric of interconnection. She is the Eldest God, the one who Remembers and Re-members. . . . All tales are born in the mind of Spider Woman, and all creation exists as a result of her naming" (*Sacred* 11, 119). For more on this figure, see also Lincoln (237) and Scarberry.

14. The terms are Eagleton's ("Capitalism" 63, 70), but similar charges have been brought by others on the left, notably Habermas (*Philosophical* 4), as well as by liberals such as Goodheart and Rorty. My criticism of Lyotard owes much to Rorty's essay "Habermas and Lyotard on Postmodernity" (163, 174); his desire to split the difference between the two thinkers captures my own sense of the need to discriminate between the sociologist and the anarchist in Lyotard (who himself acknowledges that *The Postmodern Condition* is "very strongly marked by sociology" ["Interview" 277]). Eagleton's essay, on the other hand, indiscriminately categorizes as "postmodernism" the irrationalist element in Lyotard and other theorists.

15. Arnold Krupat, who has harsh words for what he takes to be Lyotard's implicit politics, nevertheless agrees about this feature of oral storytelling. Using contemporary Native American cultures as his example, Krupat writes: "Contemporary singing and storytelling goes on in communities that use those performances as means of affirming and validating their identities as communities — communities, which, insofar as they are traditionally oriented, do not separate those stories from their performers, audiences, and occasions" (187).

16. Karl Kroeber turns to oral narratives from Native American traditions to make a similar point about the social function of storytelling: "The principle that a story 'means' in terms of a specific situation within which it is *used*, and at whom it is aimed, is virtually unrecognized by narratolgists" (5). Kroeber is not entirely correct, however, when he asserts that this topic has been overlooked. James Phelan and Peter J. Rabinowitz usefully emphasize the position of the audience of narratives. Feminists

such as Susan Sniader Lanser and Robyn Warhol have stressed the role of women's voices in narrative for creating community. Cohan and Shires discuss the ways in which the address of narrative to readers or viewers positions them as subjects (149–75). Finally, a new book by Ross Chambers employs many of the same ideas from de Certeau that I draw on to argue for the "oppositional" uses of narrative (6–14).

17. A poem John Ashbery published in the *New Yorker* in 1990 reveals a clear understanding of these issues, as well as considerable ambivalence about them. The poem compares the collective character of ancient ballads with the "collective euphoria" that is making "the world as we know it" look to the "shaman or priest for comfort and counsel." It begins: "Research has shown that ballads were produced by all of society / working as a team." In the third section, the poem continues:

> It remains for us to come to terms with *our* commonalty.
> Small wonder that those at home sit nervous by the unlit grate.
> It was their choice, after all, that spurred us to feats of the imagination.
> It remains for us to come to terms with our commonalty
> and in so doing deprive time of further hostages.

Ashbery's doubts about this new dispensation show up throughout the poem, as in these lines from the fourth and final section: "To end the standoff that history long ago began / must we thrust ever onward, into perversity?"

18. See Habermas ("Modernity" and *Philosophical*). For good discussions of the debate between Habermas and Lyotard, see not only the Rorty essay mentioned above but also a piece by Martin Jay in the same volume and Huyssen (199–206).

Chapter 5

1. My understanding of Anzaldúa's work and of the concept of border zones in general is indebted to Rosaldo and to José David Saldívar's critique of recent cultural studies of Chicano literature ("Limits").

2. This myth is discussed at more length in "The Politics of Contemporary Fiction" in the prior chapter. Often cultural praxis and issue-oriented protest are combined, of course. A novel that argues movingly for the necessity of engaging in both forms of politics is George Dennison's *Luisa Domic*.

3. There are differences as well as similarities between Girard and Burkert. For a helpful comparison of the two, see Mack (3–32). The volume that Mack introduces contains papers by both theorists, as well as illuminating conversations between them.

4. For accounts of the residual interest in the sacred in Durkheim and Mauss, see Detienne and Vernant (13–20) and Mack (1–2).

5. Feminists have criticized his influential theory of desire, first elaborated in *Deceit, Desire, and the Novel* (1961), for a similar universalizing tendency. Girard takes the male heterosexual subject as an unchanging norm and leaves sexual differences and historical variation out of the equation. See Kofman, Moi, Jacobus, and Sedgwick (*Between Men* 21–7).

6. There is beginning to be a sophisticated body of criticism on DeLillo (see LeClair and Lentricchia, *Introducing Don DeLillo*). A commentary that stresses the political dimension in DeLillo's fiction is Morris's suggestive treatment of *The Names*.

7. Julia Kristeva has described the way in which even counterhegemonic groups fall prey to the scapegoating mechanism: "As with any society, the countersociety is based on the expulsion of an excluded element, a scapegoat charged with the evil of which the community duly constituted can then purge itself" ("Women's Time" 479). Like Girard, whom she cites, Kristeva sees only one possible outcome of this process, the reinforcement of an unchanging "symbolic contract" (Kristeva 480). Naylor and Morrison, I am arguing, envision other possible outcomes.

8. In a darkly comic twist on this motif, Denis Johnson stages the following conversation between his narrator and a CIA agent that has been pursuing her through Nicaragua:

> "And in order to feel more secure," [the agent says,] "the most paranoid entity in the hemisphere, you know who I'm talking about, it *must* do everything in its power to mess up the balance around here."
>
> "You mean the U.S.," [the narrator answers.]
>
> He looked at me, quite obviously baffled. "God!" he laughed. "Why don't you stop being ridiculous? I mean the Castro government in *Cuba*" (109).

9. For the rest of the chapter I focus on Chicanas, and writers from the Caribbean working in English. These groups, and especially the former, have been important to the emerging field of "border studies" (see Allen, "'Border' Studies"). Writers exploring other borderlands could have been included with equal justice. For example, the works of Cubans, Puerto Ricans, and other Latino peoples living in the United States would have enriched this discussion. But I have restricted my scope in order to emphasize the specific historical and political circumstances of the writers that I do consider.

10. Although not as well known as her first book, *Brown Girl, Brownstones* (1959), this quiet novel amply repays the critical attention it has begun to receive (see Busia; Christian, *Black* 149–58; Collier; McCluskey;

Wilentz 99–115). Busia and Wilentz call this work a "diaspora novel," a term that presents a different but clearly valuable view of the "journey" going on in this text. My argument about the shape of U.S. culture leads me to emphasize Avey's movement between the islands and the States, but it is not meant to deny the importance of the larger movement of diaspora that grounds the powerful representations in the novel of African-derived cultural forms.

11. In fact, Marshall strives to relate these factors to the ritual, point by point, perhaps concerned that the conventions of psychological realism, which govern much of the novel, are incompatible with the more transformative romance conventions of Avey's experiences on Carriacou.

12. My thinking about Chicano fiction was initially stimulated by Ramón Saldívar's article and several others collected in Lattin's *Contemporary Chicano Fiction*. (Saldívar's article has since been expanded in his important critical study, *Chicano Narrative*.) Further orientation in the field came from books by Sommers and Ybarra-Frausto, Moraga and Anzaldúa, Tatum, Shirley and Shirley, Calderon and Saldívar, and José Saldívar (*Dialectics of Our America*), and from the interviews conducted by Bruce-Novoa.

13. Alvina E. Quintana's essay on this novel relates it to some of the ethnographic themes I have been stressing.

14. My concentration on mixed regional heritages in this argument leads me to neglect an equally important theme in Anzaldúa's work, that of her lesbian identity. For a discussion of *Borderlands/La Frontera* that brings out this latter theme, see Saldívar-Hull (210–17).

15. José Saldívar objects to what he sees as an overemphasis on "interlinguistic play" in Fischer's characterization of Chicano writing, a consequence, Saldívar maintains, of the anthropologist's omnivorous "culture-collecting," his habit of appropriating "'exotic' discourses, facts, and meaning" ("Limits" 253–5). I agree with Saldívar about the importance of situating cultural studies in "local knowledge and local history" (253) and think his point, drawn from the work of Lorna Dee Cervantes, that "men do more code switching" than women (254), merits further study. (Anzaldúa's views, quoted in the text, and the new collection of stories by Sandra Cisneros would suggest otherwise.) Nevertheless, there must be a place for research that investigates the relations among different cultures. Such studies are one way to respond to Saldívar's call for "other histories which are placed in local frames of awareness on the one hand and situated globally, geopolitically on the other hand" (255).

The analysis in this chapter has concentrated on some of the similarities and differences between anglophone literature of the Caribbean and Chicano writing in English, on the one hand, and each of those literatures and the Anglo fictions set in these regions, on the other hand. A different project might look at Roberto Fernández Retamar's effort to define a common agenda for the Chicano, the Latin American, and the Caribbean (Retamar 4; see also Jameson, "Foreword" ix). Retamar chooses José Martí's phrase "our *mestizo* America" as "the distinctive sign" of the post-colonial culture of the entire region, "a culture of descendants, both ethnically and culturally speaking, of aborigines, Africans, and Europeans" (4). The shared interests of the area are symbolized by the prize for fiction given by Casa de las Américas, the Cuban publishing house he heads, which has been won by the Chicano novelist Rolando Hinojosa.

16. The late Arturo Islas's novel *Migrant Souls* (1990), however, pays similarly close attention to how differing class positions can influence the creation of specific rituals of everday life.

17. For a history of the relations between these communities, see Montejano. I am indebted to José Saldívar's writings for this reference and for his interpretation of Hinojosa's fiction generally (see both "Limits" and "Rolando"). See also the essays he has collected in *The Rolando Hinojosa Reader* and one by Gonzales-Berry in Lattin.

Chapter 6

1. I am not the first commentator to identify these shared themes. Nancy Walker notes that the "process of classification into periods has already begun" for women's fiction of the sixties and seventies (4). Walker quotes Nora Johnson's 1988 article "Housewives and Prom Queens, 25 Years Later," which characterizes the feminist fiction of the early seventies in terms similar to those used here. Versions of this literary history also underwrote a more troubling critical procedure, the exclusion of women's writing from virtually all theories of postmodern fiction, until quite recently. For feminist studies determined to challenge this exclusion, see Hutcheon (1988), Hite (1989), Waugh (1989), Marshall (1992), and Linda Kauffman (1992).

2. The differences among women, chronicled in this chapter and in earlier ones as well, indicate some of the problems involved in speaking of *the* women's community. The diversity of women along lines of race, class, sexuality, age, and politics is one of the most prominent themes in feminist criticism of the last decade. On this topic, see, for example, Christian (*Black Feminist Criticism*), Haraway, Lorde (*Sister Outsider*), Rich, Showalter, and Walker (*In Search of Our Mothers' Gardens*).

3. Support for this view also crops up in some novelists' journalism and interviews. In 1985 Godwin provoked controversy by reviewing Sandra Gilbert and Susan Gubar's *Norton Anthology of Literature by Women* negatively in the *New York Times Book Review*. The issue, as Godwin framed it, was whether women's writing should be included in such a collection on the basis of its intrinsic literary merit or because of its status as representative of a female literary tradition. Prominent feminist literary critics responded with a range of arguments that underscored the conclusion that there is no realm of literary value that is gender free. Controversy of this sort inevitably polarizes people, leading them to pose issues in stark either-or terms. Women writers of both fiction and criticism, however, have developed a discourse on such issues too nuanced to be assessed on the basis of positions taken in a single debate. The question of community, I will argue, is a good example of such an issue, one that has developed beyond some of the oppositions in which the topic was initially framed.

4. There are differences between the two endings, however. Gordon's protagonist is motivated by a guilt that the novel identifies as Catholic in origin, whereas Godwin's Episcopalian heroine is motivated first by a hunger for knowledge, then by sympathy and understanding. Gordon's protagonist must wrench herself away from the past that the old woman represents by making a "final payment" of $20,000, and she needs the support of her two closest women friends to complete her escape. Godwin's protagonist maintains that her stay with the old people is only temporary.

5. When the narrator asks the woman whom her mother had run away with years before if they had been lovers, she answers that they were "basically" "straight." Their relationship, however, certainly fits within what Adrienne Rich has called the "lesbian continuum." The passage that explores this aspect of their relationship most explicitly talks of their "love" for one another and the physical nature of their "attraction" (371).

6. Other participants in this dialogue include the philosopher Charles Taylor; the historians Christopher Lasch and Elizabeth Fox-Genovese; the political theorists Michael Sandel, Michael Walzer, and Roberto Unger; the legal scholars James Boyd White, Mary Ann Glendon, Frank Michelman, Cass R. Sunstein, and Suzanna Sherry; and the interdisciplinary group of social theorists who were Bellah's coauthors on *Habits of the Heart*, Richard Madsen, William M. Sullivan, Ann Swidler, and Steven M. Tipton. There are many differences among these authors, which in some contexts would deserve as much attention as their similarities. The themes I discuss below, however, seem widely enough shared to represent a common contrast with the views held by postmodernists and advocates of multiculturalism.

7. Although these authors criticize community in similar terms, their concerns may arise from different sources. Stacey and Young write from a socialist feminist perspective; Martin and Mohanty write within the contexts of lesbian and postcolonial feminisms.

8. Elshtain has written pieces critical of both MacIntyre's and Bellah's versions of communitarianism. See Elshtain, "Citizenship" and "Thinking."

9. Among the many feminist discussions of this relationship in literature, Hirsch's book *The Mother/Daughter Plot* has been especially helpful to me.

10. Indeed, the narrative of female college friends who share the trials of life over the years has become an established convention. It structures Adams's *Superior Women* and Marita Golden's *A Woman's Place* (1986).

Conclusion: Literature without Masterpieces

1. This sketch of pluralism draws on Sunstein (1542–7) and Lowi (95).

2. For a related call for an alternative conception of pluralism, see Sullivan. What she calls "normative pluralism" rejects "any quest for agreement upon a single common good, and locates social interaction and value formation principally in settings other than citizenship. Normative pluralism thus envisions an ongoing and desirable role for groups that are social but not public — groups intermediate between individuals and the state" (1714).

3. Froula (323), Fowler, and Harris persuasively argue for the multiplicity of canons. Harris titles a section of his article "The Ultimate Function of Canons Is to Compete" (118) and concludes, "If the Canon no longer lives, the reason is that it never did; there have been and are only selections with purposes. If anything has been clarified by the last twenty years of critical alarms and excursions, it is the multiplicity of possible purposes" (119). For the existence of canons in areas other than literature, see the articles collected in Clayton, Elshtain, and Schulz.

4. This last point comes from a challenging paper by my student Adriane Stewart.

References

Adams, Alice. *Superior Women*. New York: Knopf, 1984.

Allen, Paula Gunn. *The Sacred Hoop: Recovering the Feminine in American Indian Traditions*. Boston: Beacon P, 1986.

Allen, Paula Gunn. "'Border' Studies: The Intersection of Gender and Color." In Gibaldi. 303-19.

Allen, Paula Gunn, ed. *Studies in American Indian Literature*. New York: MLA, 1983.

Alpers, Svetlana. "Describe or Narrate? A Problem in Realistic Representation." *New Literary History* 8 (1976): 15-40.

Anaya, Rudolfo A. *Heart of Aztlan*. 1976. Albuquerque: U of New Mexico P, 1988.

Andrews, William L. *To Tell a Free Story: The First Century of Afro-American Autobiography, 1760-1865*. Urbana: U of Illinois P, 1986.

Anzaldúa, Gloria. *Borderlands/La Frontera: The New Mestiza*. San Francisco: Spinsters/Aunt Lute, 1987.

Arac, Jonathan. *Critical Genealogies: Historical Situations for Postmodern Literary Studies*. New York: Columbia UP, 1987.

Arac, Jonathan, ed. *After Foucault: Humanistic Knowledge, Postmodern Challenges*. New Brunswick, NJ: Rutgers UP, 1988.

Arac, Jonathan and Barbara Johnson, ed. *Consequences of Theory*. Baltimore: Johns Hopkins UP, 1991.

Arendt, Hannah. "Communicative Power." In Lukes. 59-74.

Ariès, Philippe and André Béjin, ed. *Western Sexuality: Practice and Precept in Past and Present Time*. Trans. Anthony Forster. New York: Blackwell, 1985.

Ariès, Philippe and Georges Duby, ed. *Histoire de la vie Privée*. Paris, 1985.

Aronowitz, Stanley. "Postmodernism and Politics." In Ross, *Universal*. 46–62.

Ashbery, John. "Hotel Lautréamont." *The New Yorker* (Oct. 1, 1990): 44–5.

Atwood, Margaret. *Surfacing*. New York: Simon & Schuster, 1972.

Atwood, Margaret. *Bodily Harm*. New York: Simon & Schuster, 1982.

Auerbach, Nina. *Communities of Women: An Idea in Fiction*. Cambridge, MA: Harvard UP, 1978.

Auerbach, Nina. *Woman and the Demon: The Life of a Victorian Myth*. Cambridge, MA: Harvard UP, 1982.

Auster, Paul. *Moon Palace*. New York: Viking, 1989.

Awkward, Michael. *Inspiriting Influences: Tradition, Revision, and Afro-American Women's Novels*. New York: Columbia UP, 1989.

Baker, Houston A., Jr. *Blues, Ideology, and Afro-American Literature: A Vernacular Theory*. Chicago: U of Chicago P, 1984.

Baker, Houston A., Jr. "In Dubious Battle." In Cohen. 363–9.

Bal, Mieke. *Reading "Rembrandt": Beyond the Word-Image Opposition*. Cambridge: Cambridge UP, 1991.

Bambara, Toni Cade. *The Salt Eaters*. 1980. New York: Vintage, 1981.

Banks, Russell. *Continental Drift*. New York: Harper & Row, 1985.

Barnett, Allen. *The Body and Its Dangers and Other Stories*. New York: St. Martin's P, 1990.

Barrett, Andrea. *Secret Harmonies*. 1989. New York: Washington Square P, 1991.

Barth, John. "The Literature of Exhaustion." *The Atlantic Monthly* 220/2 (1967): 29–34.

Barth, John. *The Tidewater Tales*. New York: Putnam's, 1987.

Barthes, Roland. *Mythologies*. Trans. Annette Lavers. 1957. New York: Hill and Wang, 1982.

Barthes, Roland. "Introduction to the Structural Analysis of Narratives." Trans. Stephen Heath. 1966. In *Image-Music-Text*. New York: Hill and Wang, 1977. 79–124.

Barthes, Roland. *S/Z*. Trans. Richard Miller. 1970. New York: Hill and Wang, 1974.

Barthes, Roland. "The Struggle with the Angel." 1971. In *Image-Music-Text*. 125–41.

Barthes, Roland. "From Work to Text." 1971. In *Image-Music-Text*. 155–64.

Baxandall, Michael. *Patterns of Intention: On the Historical Explanation of Pictures*. New Haven, CT: Yale UP, 1985.

Bell, Bernard W. *The Afro-American Novel and Its Tradition*. Amherst: U of Massachusetts P, 1987.

Bell, Daniel. *The Coming of Post-Industrial Society: A Venture in Social Forecasting*. New York: Basic Books, 1976.

Bell, Daniel. *The Cultural Contradictions of Capitalism*. New York: Basic Books, 1978.

Bell, Daniel. "The New Class: A Muddled Concept." In *The New Class?* Ed. B. Bruce-Briggs. New York: McGraw-Hill, 1981.

Bellah, Robert N. "The Idea of Practices in *Habits*: A Response." In Reynolds and Norman. 269–88.

Bellah, Robert N., Richard Madsen, William M. Sullivan, Ann Swidler, and Steven M. Tipton. *Habits of the Heart: Individualism and Commitment in American Life*. New York: Harper & Row, 1986.

Bellow, Saul. *Mr. Sammler's Planet*. New York: Viking P, 1970.

Bellow, Saul. *Humboldt's Gift*. 1975. New York: Avon Books, 1976.

Benhabib, Seyla and Drucilla Cornell. *Feminism as Critique*. Minneapolis: U of Minnesota P, 1987.

Benjamin, Jessica. "The Bonds of Love: Rational Violence and Erotic Domination." In *The Future of Difference*. Ed. Hester Eisenstein and Alice Jardine. New Brunswick, NJ: Rutgers UP, 1985. 41–70.

Benjamin, Jessica. "A Desire of One's Own: Psychoanalytic Feminism and Intersubjective Space." In *Feminist Studies/Critical Studies*. Ed. Teresa de Lauretis. Bloomington: Indiana UP, 1986. 78–101.

Bennett, William. "To Reclaim a Legacy: Report on the Humanities in Higher Education." Washington, DC: National Endowment for the Humanities, 1984.

Berger, Peter, Brigitte Berger, and Hansfried Kellner. *The Homeless Mind: Modernization and Consciousness*. New York: Vintage Books, 1974.

Bernstein, Richard J., ed. *Habermas and Modernity*. Cambridge, MA: MIT P, 1985.

Bersani, Leo. *A Future for Astyanax: Character and Desire in Literature*. Boston: Little, Brown, 1976.

Bersani, Leo and Ulysse Dutoit. *The Forms of Violence: Narrative in Assyrian Art and Modern Culture*. New York: Schocken Books, 1985.

Bersani, Leo. "Is the Rectum a Grave?" In Crimp. 197–222.

Bevis, William. "Native American Novels: Homing In." In *Recovering the Word: Essays on Native American Literature*. Ed. Brian Swann and Arnold Krupat. Berkeley: U of California P, 1987. 580–620.

Bible, The Jerusalem. Garden City, NY: Doubleday, 1968.

Bloom, Allan. *The Closing of the American Mind: How Higher Education Has Failed Democracy and Impoverished the Souls of Today's Students*. New York: Simon & Schuster, 1987.

Boon, James. *Other Tribes, Other Scribes: Symbolic Anthropology in the Comparative Study of Cultures, Histories, Religions and Texts.* Cambridge: Cambridge UP, 1982.

Boone, Joseph A. "Mappings of Male Desire in Durrell's Alexandria Quartet." *South Atlantic Quarterly* 88 (1989): 73–106.

Boswell, John. *Christianity, Social Tolerance, and Homosexuality: Gay People in Western Europe from the Beginning of the Christian Era to the Fourteenth Century.* Chicago: U of Chicago P, 1980.

Boswell, Robert. *The Geography of Desire.* New York: Knopf, 1989.

Bourdieu, Pierre. *Outline of a Theory of Practice.* 1972. Cambridge: Cambridge UP, 1977.

Bové, Paul A. *Intellectuals in Power: A Genealogy of Critical Humanism.* New York: Columbia UP, 1986.

Bové, Paul A. *In the Wake of Theory.* Hanover, NH: Wesleyan UP, 1992.

Bradley, David. *The Chaneysville Incident.* New York: Harper & Row, 1981.

Bremond, Claude. "The Logic of Narrative Possibilities." *New Literary History* 11 (1980): 387–411.

Brilliant, Richard. *Visual Narrative: Storytelling in Etruscan and Roman Art.* Ithaca, NY: Cornell UP, 1984.

Bromwich, David. *Politics by Other Means: Higher Education and Group Thinking.* New Haven, CT: Yale UP, 1992.

Brooks, Peter. *Reading for the Plot: Design and Intention in Narrative.* New York: Knopf, 1984.

Brown, Norman O. *Life Against Death: The Psychoanalytic Meaning of History.* Wesleyan, CT: Wesleyan UP, 1959.

Brown, Peter. *The Body and Society: Men, Women, and Sexual Renunciation in Early Christianity.* New York: Columbia UP, 1988.

Brown, Rosellen. *The Autobiography of My Mother.* New York: Doubleday, 1976.

Brown, Rosellen. *Civil Wars.* New York: Knopf, 1984.

Bruce-Novoa, Juan D. *Chicano Authors: Inquiry by Interview.* Austin: U of Texas P, 1980.

Bruner, Jerome. "The Narrative Construction of Reality." *Critical Inquiry* 18 (1991): 1–21.

Bryson, Norman. *Looking at the Overlooked: Four Essays on Still Life Painting.* Cambridge, MA: Harvard UP, 1990.

Burkert, Walter. *Homo Necans: The Anthropology of Ancient Greek Sacrificial Ritual and Myth.* Trans. Peter Bing. 1972. Berkeley: U of California P, 1983.

Burkert, Walter. "The Problem of Ritual Killing." In Hamerton-Kelly. 149–88.

Busia, Abena P. "What Is Your Nation?: Reconnecting Africa and Her Diaspora through Paule Marshall's *Praisesong for the Widow.*" In Wall. 196–211.

Butler, Judith. *Gender Trouble: Feminism and the Subversion of Identity.* New York: Routledge, 1990.

Butler, Judith. "Imitation and Gender Insubordination." In Fuss, *Inside.* 13–31.

Calderón, Héctor and José David Saldívar. *Criticism in the Borderlands: Studies in Chicano Literature, Culture, and Ideology.* Durham, NC: Duke UP, 1991.

Callahan, John F. *In the African-American Grain: The Pursuit of Voice in Twentieth-Century Black Fiction.* Urbana: U of Illinois P, 1988.

Caserio, Robert L. "Mobility and Masochism: Christine Brooke-Rose and J. G. Ballard." *Novel* 21 (1988): 292–310.

Caserio, Robert L. "Supreme Court Discourse vs. Homosexual Fiction." *South Atlantic Quarterly* 88 (1989): 267–99.

Castillo, Ana. *The Mixquiahuala Letters.* Binghamton, NY: Bilingual P/Editorial Bilingüe, 1986.

Chabram, Angie. "Conceptualizing Chicano Critical Discourse." In Calderón and Saldívar. 127–48.

Chambers, Ross. *Room for Maneuver: Reading (the) Oppositional (in) Narrative.* Chicago: U of Chicago P, 1991.

Chase, Cynthia. "The Decomposition of the Elephants: Double-Reading *Daniel Deronda.*" *PMLA* 93 (1978): 215–27.

Chase, Joan. *During the Reign of the Queen of Persia.* 1983. New York: Ballantine Books, 1984.

Cheney, Lynne V. "Humanities in America: A Report to the President, the Congress, and the American People." Washington, DC: National Endowment for the Humanities, 1988.

Chodorow, Nancy. *The Reproduction of Mothering: Psychoanalysis and the Sociology of Gender.* Berkeley: U of California P, 1978.

Christian, Barbara. *Black Feminist Criticism: Perspectives on Black Women Writers.* New York: Pergamon P, 1985.

Christian, Barbara. "The Race for Theory." In Newton and Hoffman. 67–80.

Cisneros, Sandra. *The House on Mango Street.* 1984. Houston, TX: Arte Público P, 1985.

Cisneros, Sandra. *Woman Hollering Creek and Other Stories.* New York: Random House, 1991.

Clayton, Jay. "Dickens and the Genealogy of Postmodernism." *Nineteenth-Century Literature* 46 (1991): 181–95.

Clayton, Jay, Jean Bethke Elshtain, and H.-J. Schulz, ed. *Disciplines and the Canon*. (forthcoming).

Clayton, Jay and Eric Rothstein. "Figures in the Corpus: Theories of Influence and Intertextuality." In Clayton and Rothstein. 3-36.

Clayton, Jay and Eric Rothstein, ed. *Influence and Intertextuality in Literary History*. Madison: U of Wisconsin P, 1991.

Clifford, James. *The Predicament of Culture: Twentieth-Century Ethnography, Literature, and Art*. Cambridge, MA: Harvard UP, 1988.

Clifford, James. "Introduction: Partial Truths." In Clifford and Marcus. 1-26.

Clifford, James. "On Ethnographic Allegory." In Clifford and Marcus. 98-121.

Clifford, James and George E. Marcus, ed. *Writing Culture: The Poetics and Politics of Ethnography*. Berkeley: U of California P, 1986.

Cohan, Steven and Linda M. Shires. *Telling Stories: A Theoretical Analysis of Narrative Fiction*. New York: Routledge, 1988.

Cohen, Ralph, ed. *Literacy, Popular Culture, and the Writing of History*. Special Issue of *New Literary History* 18 (1987): 237-468.

Coles, Robert. *The Call of Stories: Teaching and the Moral Imagination*. Boston: Houghton Mifflin, 1989.

Collier, Eugenia. "The Closing of the Circle: Movement from Division to Wholeness in Paule Marshall's Fiction." In Evans. 295-315.

Colwin, Laurie. *Family Happiness*. New York: Knopf, 1982.

Connolly, William E. "Forms of Power." In *The Terms of Political Discourse*. Lexington, MA: Heath, 1974. 86-137.

Connolly, William E. *Politics and Ambiguity*. Madison: U of Wisconsin P, 1987.

Cooper, J. California. *Family*. New York: Doubleday, 1991.

Corbin, Alain. *The Foul and the Fragrant: Odor and the French Social Imagination*. Cambridge, MA: Harvard UP, 1986.

Cornell, Drucilla. "The Feminist Alliance with Deconstruction." In *Beyond Accommodation: Ethical Feminism, Deconstruction, and the Law*. New York: Routledge, 1991. 79-118.

Cover, Robert. "Forward: *Nomos* and Narrative." *Harvard Law Review* 97 (1983): 4-68.

Covington, Vicki. *Gathering Home*. New York: Simon & Schuster, 1988.

Crimp, Douglas, ed. *AIDS: Cultural Analysis/Cultural Activism*. Cambridge, MA: MIT P, 1988.

Culler, Jonathan. *The Pursuit of Signs: Semiotics, Literature, Deconstruction*. Ithaca, NY: Cornell UP, 1981.

Culler, Jonathan. *Framing the Sign: Criticism and Its Institutions*. Norman: U of Oklahoma P, 1988.

Dalton, Clare. "An Essay in the Deconstruction of Contract Doctrine." *Yale Law Journal* 94 (1985): 997–1114.

Danto, Arthur C. *Narration and Knowledge*. New York: Columbia UP, 1985.

Dasenbrock, Reed Way. "Forms of Biculturalism in Southwestern Literature: The Work of Rudolfo Anaya and Leslie Marmon Silko." *Genre* 21 (1988): 307–20.

Davidson, Arnold I. "Sex and the Emergence of Sexuality." *Critical Inquiry* 14 (1987): 16–48.

De Certeau, Michel. *The Practice of Everyday Life*. Trans. Steven Rendall. 1974. Berkeley: U of California P, 1984.

Deleuze, Gilles and Félix Guattari. *Anti-Oedipus: Capitalism and Schizophrenia*. Trans. Robert Hurley, Mark Seem, and Helen R. Lane. 1972. Minneapolis: U of Minnesota P, 1983.

Delgado, Richard. "Storytelling for Oppositionists and Others: A Plea for Narrative." *Michigan Law Review* 87 (1989): 2411–41.

De Lauretis, Teresa. "Desire in Narrative." In *Alice Doesn't: Feminism, Semiotics, Cinema*. Bloomington: Indiana UP, 1984. 103–57.

De Lauretis, Teresa, ed. *Feminist Studies/Critical Studies*. Bloomington: Indiana UP, 1986.

De Lauretis, Teresa. "Sexual Indifference and Lesbian Representation." *Theatre Journal* 40 (1988): 155–77.

De Lauretis, Teresa. "Queer Theory: Lesbian and Gay Sexualities, An Introduction." *Differences* 3:2 (1991): iii–xviii.

DeLillo, Don. *The Names*. New York: Knopf, 1982.

De Man, Paul. *Allegories of Reading: Figural Language in Rousseau, Nietzsche, Rilke, and Proust*. New Haven, CT: Yale UP, 1979.

D'Emilio, John. *Sexual Politics, Sexual Communities: The Making of a Homosexual Minority in the United States, 1940–1970*. Chicago: U of Chicago P, 1983.

Dennison, George. *Luisa Domic*. New York: Harper & Row, 1985.

Der Derian, James and Michael J. Shapiro. *International/Intertextual Relations: Postmodern Readings of World Politics*. Lexington, MA: Heath, 1989.

Derrida, Jacques. *Of Grammatology*. Trans. Gayatri Chakravorty Spivak. 1967. Baltimore: Johns Hopkins UP, 1976.

Derrida, Jacques. "Like the Sound of the Sea Deep within a Shell: Paul de Man's War." *Critical Inquiry* 14 (1988): 590–652.

Detienne, Marcel and Jean-Pierre Vernant. *The Cuisine of Sacrifice among the Greeks*. Trans. Paula Wissing. Chicago: U of Chicago P, 1989.

Doctorow, E. L. *Billy Bathgate*. New York: Random House, 1989.

Doerr, Harriet. *Stones for Ibarra*. New York: Viking, 1984.

Dollimore, Jonathan. "Introduction: Shakespeare, Cultural Materialism and the New Historicism." In *Political Shakespeare: New Essays in Cultural Materialism*. Manchester: Manchester UP, 1985.

Dollimore, Jonathan. *Sexual Dissidence: Augustine to Wilde, Freud to Foucault*. Oxford: Clarendon P, 1991.

Dorris, Michael. *A Yellow Raft in Blue Water*. New York: Henry Holt, 1987.

D'Souza, Dinesh. *Illiberal Education: The Politics of Race and Sex on Campus*. New York: Free P, 1991.

Durkheim, Emile. *The Elementary Forms of the Religious Life*. Trans. Joseph Ward Swain. 1915. New York: Free P, 1965.

Dworkin, Andrea. *Ice and Fire*. New York: Weidenfeld and Nicolson, 1986.

Eagleton, Terry. *Literary Theory: An Introduction*. Minneapolis: U of Minnesota P, 1983.

Eagleton, Terry. *The Function of Criticism: From "The Spectator" to Post-Structuralism*. London: Verso P, 1984.

Eagleton, Terry. "Capitalism, Modernism and Postmodernism." *New Left Review* 152 (1985): 60–73.

Edelman, Lee. "Seeing Things: Representation, the Scene of Surveillance, and the Spectacle of Gay Male Sex." In Fuss, *Inside*. 93–116.

Ehrenreich, Barbara. "On Feminism, Family and Community." *Dissent* 30 (1983): 103–6.

Elias, Norbert. *The Civilizing Process*. Trans. Edmund Jephcott. New York: Pantheon Books, 1978. 2 vols.

Elshtain, Jean Bethke. *Public Man, Private Woman: Women in Social and Political Thought*. Princeton, NJ: Princeton UP, 1981.

Elshtain, Jean Bethke. "Feminism, Family, and Community." *Dissent* 29 (1982): 442–9.

Elshtain, Jean Bethke. "Citizenship and Armed Civic Virtue: Some Critical Questions on the Commitment to Public Live." In Reynolds and Norman. 47–55.

Elshtain, Jean Bethke. "Thinking Traditions: Reflections on the Present/Past." In Clayton, Elshtain, and Schulz.

Epstein, Julia and Kristina Straub. "Introduction: The Guarded Body." In *Body Guards: The Cultural Politics of Gender Ambiguity*. Ed. Epstein and Straub. New York: Routledge, 1991. 1–28.

Erdrich, Louise. *Love Medicine*. New York: Holt, Rinehart & Winston, 1984.

Erdrich, Louise. *The Beet Queen*. New York: Henry Holt, 1986.

Erdrich, Louise. *Tracks*. New York: Henry Holt, 1988.

Estrich, Susan. "Rape." *Yale Law Journal* 95 (1986): 1087–1184.

Evans, Mari. *Black Women Writers (1950-1980)*. Garden City, NY: Doubleday, 1984.

Fabian, Johannes. *Time and the Other: How Anthropology Makes Its Object*. New York: Columbia UP, 1983.

Faderman, Lillian. *Surpassing the Love of Men: Romantic Friendship and Love between Women from the Renaissance to the Present*. New York: Morrow, 1981.

Febvre, Lucien. "*Civilisation*: Evolution of a Word and a Group of Ideas." Trans. K. Folca. In *A New Kind of History: From the Writings of Febvre*. Ed. Peter Burke. London: Routledge & Kegan Paul, 1973. 219-57.

Febvre, Lucien. "Sensibility and History: How to Reconstitute the Emotional Life of the Past." In *A New Kind of History*. 12-26.

Ferguson, Thomas and Joel Rogers. *Right Turn: The Decline of the Democrats and the Future of American Politics*. New York: Hill and Wang, 1986.

Ferrero, Pat, Elaine Hedges, and Julie Silber. *Hearts and Hands: The Influence of Women and Quilts on American Society*. San Francisco: Quilt Digest P, 1987.

Fischer, Michael M. J. "Ethnicity and the Post-Modern Arts of Memory." In Clifford and Marcus. 194-233.

Fish, Stanley. *Doing What Comes Naturally: Change, Rhetoric, and the Practice of Theory in Literary and Legal Studies*. Durham, NC: Duke UP, 1989.

Flynt, Candace. *Mother Love*. New York: Farrar, Straus & Giroux, 1987.

Foley, Barbara. "The Politics of Deconstruction." *Genre* 17 (1984): 113-34.

Forty, Adrian. *Objects of Desire: Design and Society, 1750-1980*. New York: Pantheon Books, 1986.

Foucault, Michel. *The History of Sexuality. Volume I: An Introduction*. Trans. Robert Hurley. 1976. New York: Vintage Books, 1980.

Foucault, Michel. *Power/Knowledge: Selected Interviews and Other Writings 1972-1977*. Trans. Colin Gordon, Leo Marshall, John Mepham, and Kate Soper. Ed. Colin Gordon. New York: Pantheon Books, 1980.

Fowler, Alastair. "Genre and the Literary Canon." *New Literary History* 11 (1979): 97-119.

Fraser, Nancy. *Unruly Practices: Power, Discourse, and Gender in Contemporary Social Theory*. Minneapolis: U of Minnesota P, 1989.

Friedman, Susan Stanford. "Weavings: Intertextuality and the (Re)Birth of the Author." In Clayton and Rothstein. 146-80.

Friedman, Susan Stanford. "Post/Poststructuralist Feminist Criticism:

The Politics of Recuperation and Negotiation." *New Literary History* 22 (1991): 465–90.

Froula, Christine. "When Eve Reads Milton: Undoing the Canonical Economy." *Critical Inquiry* 10 (1983): 321–47.

Fuss, Diana. *Essentially Speaking: Feminism, Nature and Difference.* New York: Routledge, 1989.

Fuss, Diana, ed. *Inside/Out: Lesbian Theories, Gay Theories.* New York: Routledge, 1991.

Gaines, Ernest J. *A Gathering of Old Men.* 1983. New York: Vintage Books, 1984.

Gallie, W. B. "Essentially Contested Concepts." *Proceedings of the Aristotelian Society* 56 (1955–6): 167–98.

Gardner, John. *On Moral Fiction.* New York: Basic Books, 1978.

Gardner, John. *Freddy's Book.* New York: Knopf, 1980.

Garner, Shirley Nelson, Claire Kahane, and Madelon Sprengnether. *The (M)other Tongue: Essays in Feminist Psychoanalytic Interpretation.* Ithaca, NY: Cornell UP, 1985.

Gasché, Rodolphe. *The Tain of the Mirror: Derrida and the Philosophy of Reflection.* Minneapolis: U of Minnesota P, 1986.

Gates, Henry Louis, Jr. *Figures in Black: Words, Signs, and the "Racial" Self.* New York: Oxford UP, 1987.

Gates, Henry Louis, Jr. *The Signifying Monkey: A Theory of Afro-American Literary Criticism.* New York: Oxford UP, 1988.

Gates, Henry Louis, Jr. "'What's Love Got to Do with It?': Critical Theory, Integrity, and the Black Idiom." In Cohen. 345–62.

Gates, Henry Louis, Jr. "Good-bye, Columbus? Notes on the Culture of Criticism." *American Literary History* 3 (1991): 711–27.

Gates, Henry Louis, Jr. *Loose Canons: Notes on the Culture Wars.* New York: Oxford UP, 1992.

Gay, Peter. *The Bourgeois Experience: Victoria to Freud.* 2 vols. New York: Oxford UP, 1984–6.

Geertz, Clifford. *The Interpretation of Cultures.* New York: Basic Books, 1973.

Geertz, Clifford. *Local Knowledge: Further Essays in Interpretive Anthropology.* New York: Basic Books, 1983.

Genovese, Eugene D. "Heresy, Yes—Sensitivity, No." *The New Republic* 204:15 (April 15, 1991), 30–5.

Gibaldi, Joseph. *Introduction to Scholarship in Modern Languages and Literatures.* 2nd ed. New York: MLA, 1992.

Gibbons, Kaye. *Ellen Foster.* Chapel Hill, NC: Algonquin, 1987.

Gibbons, Kaye. *A Cure for Dreams.* Chapel Hill, NC: Algonquin, 1991.

Gilligan, Carol. *In a Different Voice: Psychological Theory and Women's Development.* Cambridge, MA: Harvard UP, 1982.

Girard, René. *Deceit, Desire, and the Novel: Self and Other in Literary Structure.* Trans. Yvonne Freccero. 1965. Baltimore: Johns Hopkins UP, 1961.

Girard, René. *Violence and the Sacred.* Trans. Patrick Gregory. 1972. Baltimore: Johns Hopkins UP, 1977.

Girard, René. "Generative Scapegoating." In Hamerton-Kelly. 73–145.

Glendon, Mary Ann. *Rights Talk: The Impoverishment of Political Discourse.* New York: Free Press, 1991.

Godwin, Gail. *A Mother and Two Daughters.* New York: Viking P, 1982.

Godwin, Gail. "Review of *The Norton Anthology of Literature by Women: The Tradition in English.*" *New York Times Book Review* (April 28, 1985): G-13.

Godwin, Gail. *A Southern Family.* New York: Morrow, 1987.

Godwin, Gail. *Father Melancholy's Daughter.* New York: Morrow, 1991.

Goldberg, Michael. *Theology and Narrative: A Critical Introduction.* Nashville, TN: Abingdon P, 1982.

Golden, Marita. *A Woman's Place.* New York: Doubleday, 1986.

Gonzales-Berry, Erlinda. "*Estampas del Valle*: From *Costumbrismo* to Self-Reflecting Literature." In Lattin. 149–61.

Goodheart, Eugene. "Writing and the Unmaking of the Self." In *Contemporary Literature and Contemporary Theory.* Ed. Jay Clayton and Betsy Draine. Special Issue, *Contemporary Literature* 29 (1988): 438–53.

Gordon, Mary. *Final Payments.* New York: Random House, 1978.

Gordon, Mary. *The Company of Women.* New York: Random House, 1980.

Gordon, Robert W. "Critical Legal Histories." *Stanford Law Review* 36 (1984): 57–126.

Gould, Lois. *Such Good Friends.* New York: Random House, 1970.

Gould, Lois. *A Sea Change.* New York: Simon & Schuster, 1976.

Gouma-Peterson, Thalia. "Faith Ringgold's Narrative Quilts." *Arts Magazine* 61:5 (1987): 64–9.

Graff, Gerald. *Literature against Itself: Literary Ideas in Modern Society.* Chicago: U of Chicago P, 1979.

Graff, Gerald. *Professing Literature: An Institutional History.* Chicago: U of Chicago P, 1987.

Graff, Gerald. *Beyond the Culture Wars: How Teaching the Conflicts Can Revitalize American Education.* New York: Norton, 1992.

Greimas, Algirdas Julien. *On Meaning: Selected Writings in Semiotic Theory.* Trans. Paul J. Perron and Frank H. Collins. 1970, 1976. Minneapolis: U of Minnesota P, 1987.

Grumbach, Doris. *The Ladies.* New York: Dutton, 1984.

Habermas, Jürgen. "Hannah Arendt's Communications Concept of Power." 1975. In Lukes. 75–93.

Habermas, Jürgen. "Modernity versus Postmodernity." Trans. Seyla Ben-Habib. 1980. *New German Critique* 22 (1981): 3-14.

Habermas, Jürgen. *The Theory of Communicative Action*. Trans. Thomas McCarthy. 1981. Boston: Beacon P, 1984-7. 2 vols.

Habermas, Jürgen. *The Philosophical Discourse of Modernity*. Trans. Frederick Lawrence. 1985. Cambridge, MA: MIT P, 1987.

Hall, Stuart, et al. *Policing the Crisis: Mugging, the State, and Law and Order*. London: Macmillan, 1979.

Halperin, David M. *One Hundred Years of Homosexuality*. New York: Routledge, 1989.

Hamacher, Werner, Neil Hertz, and Thomas Keenan. *Responses: On Paul de Man's Wartime Journalism*. Lincoln: U of Nebraska P, 1989.

Hamerton-Kelly, Robert G., ed. *Violent Origins: Walter Burkert, René Girard, and Jonathan Z. Smith on Ritual Killing and Cultural Formation*. Stanford, CA: Stanford UP, 1987.

Haraway, Donna J. *Simians, Cyborgs, and Women: The Reinvention of Nature*. New York: Routledge, 1991.

Harris, Wendell V. "Canonicity." *PMLA* 106 (1991): 110-21.

Hartog, Hendrik. "Pigs and Positivism." *Wisconsin Law Review* (1985): 899-935.

Hebidge, Dick. *Subculture: The Meaning of Style*. New York: Routledge, 1979.

Hinojosa, Rolando. *Claros Varones de Belken/Fair Gentlemen of Belken County*. Trans. Julia Cruz. Tempe, AZ: Bilingual P/Editorial Bilingüe, 1986.

Hinojosa, Rolando. *Klail City*. Houston, TX: Arte Público P, 1987.

Hirsch, E. D. *Cultural Literacy: What Every American Needs to Know*. Boston: Houghton Mifflin, 1987.

Hirsch, E. D. "The Primal Scene of Education." *New York Review of Books* 36:3 (March 2, 1989): 29-34.

Hirsch, Marianne. *The Mother/Daughter Plot: Narrative, Psychoanalysis, Feminism*. Bloomington: Indiana UP, 1989.

Hite, Molly. *The Other Side of the Story: Structures and Strategies of Contemporary Feminist Narrative*. Ithaca, NY: Cornell UP, 1989.

Homans, Margaret. *Bearing the Word: Language and Female Experience in Nineteenth-Century Women's Writing*. Chicago: U of Chicago P, 1986.

Hubert, Henri and Marcel Mauss. *Sacrifice: Its Nature and Function*. Trans. W. D. Halls. 1898. Chicago: U of Chicago P, 1964.

Hunter, James Davison. *Culture Wars: The Struggle to Define America*. New York: Basic Books, 1991.

Hutcheon, Linda. *A Poetics of Postmodernism: History, Theory, Fiction*. New York: Routledge, 1988.

Huyssen, Andreas. *After the Great Divide: Modernism, Mass Culture, Postmodernism*. Bloomington: Indiana UP, 1986.

Irving, John. *The World According to Garp*. New York: Dutton, 1978.

Islas, Arturo. *Migrant Souls*. New York: Morrow, 1990.

Jacobus, Mary. "Is There a Woman in This Text?" *New Literary History* 14 (1982): 117–41.

Jacoby, Russell. *The Last Intellectual: American Culture in the Age of Academe*. New York: Farrar, Straus & Giroux, 1987.

Jameson, Fredric. *The Political Unconscious: Narrative as a Socially Symbolic Act*. Ithaca, NY: Cornell UP, 1981.

Jameson, Fredric. "Postmodernism and Consumer Society." In *The Anti-Aesthetic: Essays on Postmodern Culture*. Ed. Hal Foster. Port Townsend, WA: Bay P, 1983. 111–25.

Jameson, Fredric. "Foreword." In Retamar. vii–xii.

JanMohamed, Abdul R. and David Lloyd. "Introduction: Toward a Theory of Minority Discourse: What Is to Be Done?" In JanMohamed and Lloyd. 1–16.

JanMohamed, Abdul R. and David Lloyd, ed. *The Nature and Context of Minority Discourse*. New York: Oxford UP, 1990.

Jay, Martin. "Habermas and Modernism." In Bernstein. 125–39.

Jen, Gish. *Typical American*. Boston: Houghton Mifflin, 1991.

Johnson, Barbara. *A World of Difference*. Baltimore: Johns Hopkins UP, 1987.

Johnson, Charles. *Oxherding Tale*. Bloomington: Indiana UP, 1982.

Johnson, Denis. *The Stars at Noon*. New York: Knopf, 1986.

Johnson, Nora. "Housewives." *New York Times Book Review* (20 March 1988): 1+.

Jones, Gayl. *Corregidora*. New York: Random House, 1975.

Jong, Erica. *Fear of Flying*. New York: Holt, Rinehart & Winston, 1973.

Joyce, Joyce A. "The Black Canon: Reconstructing Black American Literary Criticism." In Cohen. 335–44.

Joyce, Joyce A. "'Who the Cap Fit': Unconscionableness in the Criticism of Houston A. Baker, Jr. and Henry Louis Gates, Jr." In Cohen. 371–84.

Kakutani, Michiko. "Storytellers Inside Stories Escape the Limits of Reality." *New York Times* (May 31, 1989): 15+.

Kauffman, Janet. *Collaborators*. New York: Knopf, 1986.

Kauffman, Linda S. *Special Delivery: Epistolary Modes in Modern Fiction*. Chicago: U of Chicago P, 1992.

Kelman, Mark. *A Guide to Critical Legal Studies*. Cambridge, MA: Harvard UP, 1987.

Kenan, Randall. *A Visitation of Spirits*. New York: Grove P, 1989.

Kennedy, Duncan. *Legal Education and the Reproduction of Hierarchy: A Polemic Against the System*. Cambridge, MA: Afar P, 1983.

Kennedy, Duncan and Karl E. Klare. "A Bibliography of Critical Legal Studies." *Yale Law Journal* 94 (1984): 461-90.

Kennedy, John F. "From the Address of President John F. Kennedy at the Dedication of the Robert Frost Library, Amherst College, October 26, 1963." In *Of Poetry and Power*. Ed. Erwin Glikes and Paul Schwaber. New York: Basic Books, 1964. 135-7.

Kenney, Susan. *In Another Country*. New York: Viking Press, 1984.

Kermode, Frank. *The Sense of an Ending: Studies in the Theory of Fiction*. New York: Oxford UP, 1967.

Kernan, Alvin B. *The Imaginary Library: An Essay on Literature and Society*. Princeton, NJ: Princeton UP, 1982.

Kernan, Alvin B. *Printing Technology, Letters and Samuel Johnson*. Princeton, NJ: Princeton UP, 1987.

Kernan, Alvin. *The Death of Literature*. New Haven, CT: Yale UP, 1990.

Kimball, Roger. *Tenured Radicals: How Politics Has Corrupted Higher Education*. New York: Harper & Row, 1990.

King, Deborah K. "Multiple Jeopardy, Multiple Consciousness: The Context of a Black Feminist Ideology." *Signs* 14 (1988): 42-72.

Kingston, Maxine Hong. *Tripmaster Monkey: His Fake Book*. New York: Knopf, 1989.

Kofman, Sarah. "The Narcissistic Woman: Freud and Girard." *Diacritics* 10 (1980): 36-45.

Kolodny, Annette. "Dancing Through the Minefield: Some Observations on the Theory, Practice, and Politics of Feminist Literary Criticism." In Showalter, *New Feminist Criticism*. 144-67.

Kosinski, Jerzy. *Blind Date*. Boston: Houghton Mifflin, 1977.

Kosinski, Jerzy. *Passion Play*. New York: St. Martin's P, 1979.

Kristeva, Julia. *Desire in Language: A Semiotic Approach to Literature and Art*. Trans. Thomas Gora, Alice Jardine, and Leon S. Roudiez. Ed. Leon S. Roudiez. 1969. New York: Columbia UP, 1980.

Kristeva, Julia. "Women's Time." In *Critical Theory Since 1965*. Ed. Hazard Adams and Leroy Searle. Tallahassee: U Presses of Florida, 1986. 471-84.

Kroeber, Karl. *Retelling/Rereading: The Fate of Storytelling in Modern Times*. New Brunswick, NJ: Rutgers UP, 1992.

Krupat, Arnold. *Ethnocriticism: Ethnography History Literature*. Berkeley: U of California P, 1992.

Lacan, Jacques. *Écrits: A Selection*. Trans. Alan Sheridan. 1966. New York: Norton, 1977.

LaCapra, Dominick. *History and Criticism*. Ithaca, NY: Cornell UP, 1985.

LaCapra, Dominick. *Soundings in Critical Theory*. Ithaca, NY: Cornell UP, 1989.

Laguerre, Michel S. *Voodoo and Politics in Haiti*. New York: St. Martin's P, 1989.

Lanser, Susan Sniader. *Fictions of Authority: Women Writers and Narrative Voice*. Ithaca, NY: Cornell UP, 1992.

Lanternari, Vittorio. *The Religions of the Oppressed*. New York: Knopf, 1963.

Laplanche, Jean. *Life and Death in Psychoanalysis*. Trans. Jeffrey Mehlman. 1970. Baltimore: Johns Hopkins UP, 1976.

Lasch, Christopher. "The Communitarian Critique of Liberalism." In Reynolds and Norman. 173–84.

Lattin, Vernon E. *Contemporary Chicano Fiction: A Critical Survey*. Binghamton, NY: Bilingual P/Editorial Bilingüe, 1986.

LeClair, Tom. *In the Loop: Don DeLillo and the Systems Novel*. Urbana: U of Illinois P, 1987.

Leithauser, Brad. *Hence*. New York: Knopf, 1989.

Lentricchia, Frank. *After the New Criticism*. Chicago: U of Chicago P, 1980.

Lentricchia, Frank. *Criticism and Social Change*. Chicago: U of Chicago P, 1983.

Lentricchia, Frank, ed. *Introducing Don DeLillo*. Durham, NC: Duke UP, 1991.

Leonardi, Susan J. "Recipes for Reading: Summer Pasta, Lobster à la Riseholme, and Key Lime Pie." *PMLA* 104 (1989): 340–7.

Levinson, Sanford and Steven Mailloux. *Interpreting Law and Literature: A Hermeneutic Reader*. Evanston, IL: Northwestern UP, 1988.

Lévi-Strauss, Claude. *The Savage Mind*. 1962. Chicago: U of Chicago P, 1966.

Lincoln, Kenneth. *Native American Renaissance*. Berkeley: U of California P, 1983.

Liu, Alan. "The Power of Formalism: The New Historicism." *ELH* 56 (1989): 721–71.

Liu, Alan. "Local Transcendence: Cultural Criticism, Postmodernism, and the Romanticism of Detail." *Representations* 32 (1990): 75–113.

Lopez, Gerald P. "Lay Lawyering." *UCLA Law Review* 32 (1984): 1–60.

Lorde, Audre. *Zami: A New Spelling of My Name*. Freedom, CA: Crossing P, 1982.

Lorde, Audre. *Sister Outsider*. Freedom, CA: Crossing P, 1984.

Lowi, Theodore. "The Public Philosophy: Interest-Group Liberalism." In *The Bias of Pluralism*. Ed. William E. Connolly. New York: Atherton P, 1969. 81–122.

Lukes, Steven. "Introduction." In Lukes. 1–18.

Lukes, Steven, ed. *Power*. New York: New York UP, 1986.

Lukinsky, Joseph. "Law in Education: A Reminiscence with Some Footnotes to Robert Cover's *Nomos and Narrative.*" *Yale Law Journal* 96 (1987): 1836–59.

Lyotard, Jean-François. *The Postmodern Condition: A Report on Knowledge.* Trans. Geoff Bennington and Brian Massumi. 1979. Minneapolis: U of Minnesota P, 1984.

Lyotard, Jean-François and Jean-Loup Thebaud. *Just Gaming.* Trans. Wlad Godzich. 1979. Minneapolis: U of Minnesota P, 1985.

Lyotard, Jean-François. "An Interview" (Conducted by Willem van Reijen and Dick Veerman). Trans. Roy Boyne. *Theory, Culture & Society* 5 (1988): 277–309.

MacIntyre, Alasdair. *After Virtue: A Study in Moral Theory.* Notre Dame, IN: U of Notre Dame P, 1981.

Mack, Burton. "Introduction: Religion and Ritual." In Hamerton-Kelly. 1–70.

MacKinnon, Catharine A. *Feminism Unmodified: Discourses on Life and Law.* Cambridge, MA: Harvard UP, 1987.

Marcus, George E. and Michael M. J. Fischer. *Anthropology as Cultural Critique: An Experimental Moment in the Human Sciences.* Chicago: U of Chicago P, 1986.

Marcus, Jane. "Still Practice A/Wrested Alphabet: Towards a Feminist Aesthetic." *Tulsa Studies in Women's Literature* 3 (1984): 79–97.

Marshall, Brenda K. *Teaching the Postmodern: Fiction and Theory.* New York: Routledge, 1992.

Marshall, Paule. *Praisesong for the Widow.* New York: Putnam's, 1983.

Marshall, Paule. *Daughters.* New York: Atheneum, 1991.

Martin, Biddy and Chandra Talpade Mohanty. "Feminist Politics: What's Home Got to Do with It?" In De Lauretis, *Feminist.* 191–212.

Mason, Bobbie Ann. *In Country.* New York: Harper & Row, 1985.

Mason, Theodore O., Jr. "The Novelist as Conservator: Stories and Comprehension in Toni Morrison's *Song of Solomon.*" *Contemporary Literature* 29 (1988): 564–81.

Matsuda, Mari J. "Public Response to Racist Speech: Considering the Victim's Story." *Michigan Law Review* 87 (1989): 2320–81.

McCaffery, Larry. *The Metafictional Muse: The Works of Robert Coover, Donald Barthelme, and William H. Gass.* Pittsburgh: U of Pittsburgh P, 1982.

McCloskey, Donald N. *If You're So Smart: The Narrative of Economic Expertise.* Chicago: U of Chicago P, 1990.

McCluskey, John, Jr. "And Called Every Generation Blessed: Theme, Setting, and Ritual in the Works of Paule Marshall." In Evans. 316–34.

McDowell, Deborah E. "Negotiating between Tenses: Witnessing Slavery After Freedom—*Dessa Rose.*" In McDowell and Rampersad. 144–63.

McDowell, Deborah E. and Arnold Rampersad. *Slavery and the Literary Imagination*. Baltimore: Johns Hopkins UP, 1989.

McFague, Sallie. *Speaking in Parables: A Study in Metaphor and Theology*. Philadelphia: Fortress P, 1975.

McMillan, Terry. *Mama*. New York: Washington Square P, 1987.

McRae, Diana. *All the Muscle You Need*. San Francisco: Spinsters/Aunt Lute, 1988.

Merod, Jim. *The Political Responsibility of the Critic*. Ithaca, NY: Cornell UP, 1987.

Michelman, Frank. "Law's Republic." *Yale Law Journal* 97 (1988): 1493–1538.

Miller, D. A. "*Cage aux folles*: Sensation and Gender in Wilkie Collins's *The Woman in White*." *Representations* 14 (1986): 107–36.

Miller, D. A. *The Novel and the Police*. Berkeley: U of California P, 1988.

Miller, D. A. "Anal *Rope*." In Fuss, *Inside*. 119–41.

Miller, D. A. *Bringing Out Roland Barthes*. Berkeley: U of California P, 1992.

Miller, J. Hillis. "Narrative and History." *ELH* 41 (1974): 455–73.

Miller, J. Hillis. *Fiction and Repetition: Seven English Novels*. Cambridge, MA: Harvard UP, 1982.

Miller, J. Hillis. *The Ethics of Reading*. New York: Columbia UP, 1987.

Miller, J. Hillis. *Versions of Pygmalion*. Cambridge, MA: Harvard UP, 1990.

Miller, Nancy. *Subject to Change: Reading Feminist Writing*. New York: Columbia UP, 1988.

Miller, Sue. *The Good Mother*. New York: Harper & Row, 1986.

Miller, Sue. *Family Pictures*. New York: Harper & Row, 1990.

Mills, C. Wright. *The Power Elite*. New York: Oxford UP, 1956.

Mink, Louis O. "History and Fiction as Modes of Comprehension." *New Literary History* 1 (1970): 541–58.

Minow, Martha. "Words and the Door to the Land of Change: Law, Language, and Family Violence." *Vanderbilt Law Review* 43 (1990): 1665–1700.

Mohanty, Chandra Talpade. "Under Western Eyes: Feminist Scholarship and Colonial Discourses." In Mohanty, Russo, and Torres. 51–80.

Mohanty, Chandra Talpade, Ann Russo, and Lourdes Torres, ed. *Third World Women and the Politics of Feminism*. Bloomington: Indiana UP, 1991.

Moi, Torril. "The Missing Mother: The Oedipal Rivalries of René Girard." *Diacritics* 12 (1982): 21–31.

Momaday, N. Scott. *The Ancient Child*. New York: Doubleday, 1989.

Montejano, David. *Anglos and Mexicans in the Making of Texas, 1836–1986*. Austin: U of Texas P, 1987.

Moraga, Cherríe and Gloria Anzaldua. *This Bridge Called My Back: Writings by Radical Women of Color*. 2nd ed. New York: Kitchen Table/ Women of Color P, 1983.

Morris, Matthew J. "Murdering Words: Language in Action in Don DeLillo's *The Names*." *Contemporary Literature* 30 (1989): 113-27.

Morrison, Toni. *Sula*. New York: Knopf, 1974.

Morrison, Toni. *Song of Solomon*. New York: Knopf, 1977.

Morrison, Toni. "An Interview" (Conducted by Nellie McKay). *Contemporary Literature* 24 (1983): 413-29.

Mouffe, Chantal. "Radical Democracy: Modern or Postmodern?" In Ross, *Universal*. 31-45.

Naylor, Gloria. *The Women of Brewster Place*. 1982. New York: Penguin Books, 1983.

Naylor, Gloria. *Mama Day*. New York: Ticknor & Fields, 1988.

Newton, Judith and Nancy Hoffman, ed. *Feminism and Deconstruction*. Special Issue. *Feminist Studies* 14 (1988) 3-192.

Nicholson, Linda J., ed. *Feminism/Postmodernism*. New York: Routledge, 1990.

Okin, Susan Moller. *Justice, Gender, and the Family*. New York: Basic Books, 1989.

Otto, Whitney. *How to Make an American Quilt*. New York: Villard Books, 1991.

Ozick, Cynthia. *The Messiah of Stockholm*. New York: Knopf, 1987.

Phelan, James. *Reading People, Reading Plots: Character, Progression, and the Interpretation of Narrative*. Chicago: U of Chicago P, 1989.

Phillips, Caryl. *A State of Independence*. New York: Farrar, Straus & Giroux, 1986.

Phillips, Jayne Anne. *Machine Dreams*. New York: Dutton, 1984.

Piercy, Marge. *Fly Away Home*. New York: Summit Books, 1984.

Plaza, Monique. "Our Damages and Their Compensation: Rape: The Will Not to Know of Michel Foucault." *Feminist Issues* 1:3 (1981): 25-35.

Poovey, Mary. "Feminism and Deconstruction." In Newton and Hoffman. 51-66.

Posner, Richard. *Law and Literature: A Misunderstood Relation*. Cambridge, MA: Harvard UP, 1988.

Poster, Mark. *Foucault, Marxism and History: Mode of Production versus Mode of Information*. Cambridge, UK: Polity Press, 1984.

Poulantzas, Nicos. *Political Power and Social Classes*. Trans. Timothy O'Hagan. 1968. London: New Left Books, 1975.

Propp, Vladimir. *Morphology of the Folktale*. Trans. Laurence Scott. 1928. Austin: U of Texas P, 1979.

Pryse, Marjorie and Hortense J. Spillers. *Conjuring: Black Women, Fiction, and Literary Tradition*. Bloomington: Indiana UP, 1985.

Quintana, Alvina E. "Ana Castillo's *The Mixquiahuala Letters*: The Novelist as Ethnographer." In Calderón and Saldívar. 72–83.

Rabine, Leslie Wahl. "A Feminist Politics of Non-Identity." In Newton and Hoffman. 11–32.

Rabinowitz, Peter J. *Before Reading: Narrative Conventions and the Politics of Interpretation*. Ithaca, NY: Cornell UP, 1987.

Radhakrishnan, R. "Toward an Effective Intellectual: Foucault or Gramsci?" In Robbins, *Intellectuals*. 57–99.

Retamar, Roberto Fernández. *Caliban and Other Essays*. Trans. Edward Baker. Minneapolis: U of Minnesota P, 1989.

Reynolds, Charles H. and Ralph V. Norman, ed. *Community in America: The Challenge of "Habits of the Heart."* Berkeley: U of California P, 1988.

Rich, Adrienne. "Compulsory Heterosexuality and Lesbian Existence." *Signs* 5 (1980): 631–60.

Ricoeur, Paul. *Time and Narrative*. Trans. Kathleen McLaughlin, David Pellauer, and Kathleen Blamey. Chicago: U of Chicago P, 1984–8. 3 vols.

Ringgold, Faith. "Black Artists in a 'Catch-22.'" *Daily Tennessean* (June 18, 1989): F-1+.

Robbins, Bruce. "Oppositional Professionals: Theory and the Narratives of Professionalization." In Arac and Johnson. 1–21.

Robbins, Bruce. "Death and Vocation: Narrativizing Narrative Theory." *PMLA* 107 (1992): 38–50.

Robbins, Bruce, ed. *Intellectuals: Aesthetics, Politics, Academics*. Minneapolis: U of Minnesota P, 1990.

Robertson, Mary Elsie. *Family Life*. New York: Atheneum, 1987.

Robinson, Marilynne. *Housekeeping*. New York: Farrar, Straus & Giroux, 1980.

Roof, Judith. *A Lure of Knowledge: Lesbian Sexuality and Theory*. New York: Columbia UP, 1991.

Rorty, Richard. *Consequences of Pragmatism (Essays: 1972–1980)*. Minneapolis: U of Minnesota P, 1982.

Rorty, Richard. "Habermas and Lyotard on Postmodernity." In Bernstein. 161–75.

Rosaldo, Renato. "Anthropological Commentary." In Hamerton-Kelly. 239–56.

Rosaldo, Renato. *Culture and Truth: The Remaking of Social Analysis*. Boston: Beacon P, 1989.

Ross, Andrew. *No Respect: Intellectuals and Popular Culture*. New York: Routledge, 1989.

Ross, Andrew, ed. *Universal Abandon? The Politics of Postmodernism*. Minneapolis: U of Minnesota P, 1988.

Roth, Philip. *The Professor of Desire*. New York: Farrar, Straus & Giroux, 1977.

Roth, Philip. *The Counterlife*. New York: Farrar, Straus & Giroux, 1986.

Russell, Bertrand. *Power: A New Social Analysis*. London: Allen & Unwin, 1975.

Ryan, Michael. *Marxism and Deconstruction: A Critical Articulation*. Baltimore: Johns Hopkins UP, 1982.

Ryan, Michael. *Politics and Culture: Working Hypotheses for a Post-Revolutionary Society*. Baltimore: Johns Hopkins UP, 1989.

Ryan, Michael. "Social Violence and Political Representation." *Vanderbilt Law Review* 43 (1990): 1771–85.

Sahlins, Marshall. *Culture and Practical Reason*. Chicago: U of Chicago P, 1976.

Said, Edward W. *Beginnings: Intention and Method*. New York: Basic Books, 1975.

Said, Edward W. *Orientalism*. 1978. New York: Vintage Books, 1979.

Said, Edward W. *The World, the Text, and the Critic*. Cambridge, MA: Harvard UP, 1983.

Said, Edward W. "Representing the Colonized: Anthropology's Interlocutors." *Critical Inquiry* 15 (1989): 205–25.

Saldívar, José David. "Rolando Hinojosa's *Klail City Death Trip*: A Critical Introduction." In Saldívar, *Rolando*. 44–63.

Saldívar, José David. "Towards a Chicano Poetics: The Making of the Chicano-Chicana Subject, 1969–1982." *Confluencia: Revista Hispánica de Cultura y Literatura* 1:2 (1986): 10–17.

Saldívar, José David. "The Limits of Cultural Studies." *American Literary History* 2 (1990): 251–66.

Saldívar, José David. *The Dialectics of Our America: Genealogy, Cultural Critique, and Literary History*. Durham, NC: Duke UP, 1991.

Saldívar, José David, ed. *The Rolando Hinojosa Reader: Essays Historical and Critical*. Houston, TX: Arte Público P, 1985.

Saldívar, Ramón. "Dialectic of Difference." In Lattin.

Saldívar, Ramón. *Chicano Narrative: The Dialectics of Difference*. Madison: U of Wisconsin P, 1990.

Saldívar-Hull, Sonia. "Feminism on the Border: From Gender Politics to Geopolitics." In Calderón and Saldívar. 203–20.

Sallis, John, ed. *Deconstruction and Philosophy: The Texts of Jacques Derrida*. Chicago: U of Chicago P, 1987.

Sanchez, Thomas. *Mile Zero*. New York: Knopf, 1989.

Sandel, Michael J. *Liberalism and the Limits of Justice*. Cambridge: Cambridge UP, 1982.

Sanders, Dori. *Clover*. Chapel Hill, NC: Algonquin Books, 1990.

Sayles, John. *Los Gusanos*. New York: HarperCollins, 1991.

Scarberry, Susan J. "Grandmother Spider's Lifeline." In Allen, *Studies*. 100–7.

Schafer, Roy. "Narration in the Psychoanalytic Dialogue." *Critical Inquiry* 7 (1980): 29–54.

Schele, Linda and Mary Ellen Miller. *The Blood of Kings: Dynasty and Ritual in Maya Art*. Fort Worth, TX: Kimbell Art Museum, 1986.

Schlegel, John Henry. "Notes Toward an Intimate, Opinionated, and Affectionate History of the Conference on Critical Legal Studies." *Stanford Law Review* 36 (1984): 391–411.

Schwartz, Lynne Sharon. *Disturbances in the Field*. New York: Harper & Row, 1983.

Schwarz, Daniel R. *The Case for a Humanistic Poetics*. Philadelphia: U of Pennsylvania P, 1991.

Scott, Charles E. *The Language of Difference*. Atlantic Highlands, NJ: Humanities P International, 1987.

Scott, Joan W. "Deconstructing Equality-Versus-Difference: Or, the Uses of Post-structuralist Theory for Feminism." In Newton and Hoffman. 33–50.

Sedgwick, Eve Kosofsky. *Between Men: English Literature and Male Homosocial Desire*. New York: Columbia UP, 1985.

Sedgwick, Eve Kosofsky. *Epistemology of the Closet*. Berkeley: U of California P, 1990.

Shacochis, Bob. *Easy in the Islands*. New York: Crown, 1985.

Shacochis, Bob. *The Next New World*. New York: Crown, 1989.

Shange, Ntozake. *Sassafrass, Cypress and Indigo*. New York: St. Martin's P, 1982.

Shapiro, Michael. "Dissolving the Political Economy Canon: The Smithian Narrative at the End of Modernity." In Clayton, Elshtain, and Schulz.

Sherry, Suzanna. "Civic Virtue and the Feminine Voice in Constitutional Adjudication." *Virginia Law Review* 72 (1986): 543–616.

Shirley, Carl R. and Paula W. Shirley. *Understanding Chicano Literature*. Columbia: U of South Carolina P, 1988.

Shorter, Edward. *The Making of the Modern Family*. New York: Basic Books, 1975.

Showalter, Elaine. "A Criticism of Our Own: Autonomy and Assimilation in Afro-American and Feminist Literary Theory." In Warhol and Herndl. 168–88.

Showalter, Elaine, ed. *The New Feminist Criticism: Essays on Women, Literature, and Theory*. New York: Pantheon, 1985.

Shulman, Alix Kates. *Memoirs of an Ex-Prom Queen*. New York: Knopf, 1972.

Silber, Joan. *Household Words*. New York: Viking, 1980.

Silko, Leslie Marmon. *Ceremony*. 1977. New York: New American Library, 1978.

Singer, Joseph. "Real Conflicts." *Boston University Law Review* 69 (1989): 1–129.

Smiley, Jane. *Ordinary Love and Good Will*. 1989. New York: Ballantine Books, 1991.

Smith, Lee. *Family Linen*. New York: Putnam's, 1985.

Smith, Paul. *Discerning the Subject*. Minneapolis: U of Minnesota P, 1988.

Smith, Valerie. *Self-Discovery and Authority in Afro-American Narrative*. Cambridge, MA: Harvard UP, 1987.

Smith-Rosenberg, Carroll. "The Female World of Love and Ritual: Relations between Women in Nineteenth-Century America." *Signs* 1 (1975-6): 1–29.

Sommers, Joseph and Tomás Ybarra-Frausto. *Modern Chicano Writers: A Collection of Critical Essays*. Englewood Cliffs, NJ: Prentice-Hall, 1979.

Spence, Donald P. *Narrative Truth and Historical Truth: Meaning and Interpretation in Psychoanalysis*. New York: Norton, 1982.

Spillers, Hortense J. "Cross-Currents, Discontinuities: Black Women's Fiction." In Pryse and Spillers. 249–61.

Spivak, Gayatri Chakravorty. "Translator's Preface." In Derrida, *Of Grammatology*. ix–lxxxvii.

Spivak, Gayatri Chakravorty. "Three Women's Texts and a Critique of Imperialism." *Critical Inquiry* 12 (1985): 243–61.

Spivak, Gayatri Chakravorty. "Imperialism and Sexual Difference." 1986. In *Contemporary Literary Criticism: Literary and Cultural Studies*. 2nd ed. Ed. Robert Con Davis and Ronald Schleiter. New York: Longman, 1989. 517–29.

Spivak, Gayatri Chakravorty. "Acting Bits/Identity Talk." *Critical Inquiry* 18 (1992): 770–803.

Stacey, Judith. "Are Feminists Afraid to Leave Home? The Challenge of Conservative Pro-Family Feminism." In *What Is Feminism?* Ed. J. Mitchell and A. Oakley. New York: Pantheon Books, 1986. 208–37.

Stewart, Adriane. "Affirmation and the Rhetorical Utopia in Poststructuralist and Minority Discourse." (Unpublished manuscript).

Stone, Lawrence. *The Family, Sex and Marriage in England, 1500–1800*. New York: Harper & Row, 1977.

Stone, Robert. *A Flag for Sunrise*. New York: Knopf, 1981.

Sullivan, Kathleen M. "Rainbow Republicanism." *Yale Law Journal* 97 (1988): 1713–23.

Sunstein, Cass R. "Beyond the Republican Revival." *Yale Law Journal* 97 (1988): 1539–90.

Swan, Edith. "Laguna Symbolic Geography and Silko's *Ceremony.*" *American Indian Quarterly* 12 (1988): 229–49.

Tan, Amy. *The Joy Luck Club.* New York: Putnam's, 1989.

Tanner, Tony. *Adultery in the Novel: Contract and Transgression.* Baltimore: Johns Hopkins UP, 1979.

Tatum, Charles M. *Chicano Literature.* Boston: Twayne, 1982.

Taussig, Michael T. *The Devil and Commodity Fetishism in South America.* Chapel Hill: U of North Carolina P, 1980.

Taussig, Michael. *Shamanism, Colonialism, and the Wild Man: A Study in Terror and Healing.* Chicago: U of Chicago P, 1987.

Taylor, Charles. "Language and Human Nature." In *Human Agency and Language.* Vol. 1 of *Philosophical Papers.* Cambridge: Cambridge UP, 1985.

Theroux, Paul. *The Mosquito Coast.* Boston: Houghton Mifflin, 1982.

Tichi, Cecelia. *Electronic Hearth: Creating an American Television Culture.* New York: Oxford UP, 1991.

Todorov, Tzvetan. *The Poetics of Prose.* Trans. Richard Howard. 1971. Ithaca, NY: Cornell UP, 1977.

Tompkins, Jane. *Sensational Designs: The Cultural Work of American Fiction, 1790–1860.* New York: Oxford UP, 1985.

Torres, Lourdes. "The Construction of the Self in U.S. Latina Autobiographies." In Mohanty, Russo, and Torres. 271–87.

Traub, Valerie. "The Ambiguities of 'Lesbian' Viewing Pleasure: The (Dis)articulations of *Black Widow.*" In Epstein and Straub. 305–28.

Traub, Valerie. *Desire and Anxiety: Circulations of Sexuality in Shakespearean Drama.* London: Routledge, 1992.

Traub, Valerie. "The (In)significance of 'Lesbian' Desire in Early Modern England." In *Erotic Politics: Desire on the Renaissance Stage.* Ed. Susan Zimmerman. London: Routledge, 1993. 150–69.

Treichler, Paula A. "AIDS, Homophobia, and Biomedical Discourse: An Epidemic of Signification." In Crimp. 31–70.

Turner, Victor. *The Ritual Process: Structure and Anti-Structure.* 1969. Ithaca, NY: Cornell UP, 1979.

Tushnet, Mark. "Critical Legal Studies and Constitutional Law: An Essay in Deconstruction." *Stanford Law Review* 36 (1984): 623–48.

Tyler, Anne. *Dinner at the Homesick Restaurant.* 1982. New York: Berkley Books, 1983.

Tyler, Anne. *Saint Maybe.* New York: Knopf, 1991.

Tyler, Carole-Anne. "Boys Will Be Girls: The Politics of Gay Drag." In Fuss, *Inside.* 32–70.

Tyler, Stephen A. "Ethnography, Intertextuality, and the End of Description." In *The Unspeakable: Discourse, Dialogue, and Rhetoric in the Postmodern World.* Madison: U of Wisconsin P, 1987.

Ungar, Roberto. *Politics: A Work in Constructive Social Theory*. Cambridge: Cambridge UP, 1987. 3 vols.

Unger, Douglas. *El Yanqui*. New York: Harper & Row, 1986.

Veeser, H. Aram, ed. *The New Historicism*. New York: Routledge, 1989.

Vizenor, Gerald. "Trickster Discourse." In *Narrative Chance: Postmodern Essays on Native American Indian Literature*. Albuquerque: U of New Mexico P, 1989.

Walker, Alice. *Meridian*. 1976. New York: Pocket Books, 1977.

Walker, Alice. *The Color Purple*. New York: Washington Square P, 1982.

Walker, Alice. *In Search of Our Mothers' Gardens*. San Diego: Harcourt Brace Jovanovich, 1983.

Walker, Cheryl. "Feminist Literary Criticism and the Author." *Critical Inquiry* 16 (1990): 551-71.

Walker, Nancy A. *Feminist Alternatives: Irony and Fantasy in the Contemporary Novel by Women*. Jackson: UP of Mississippi, 1990.

Wall, Cheryl A., ed. *Changing Our Own Words: Essays on Criticism, Theory, and Writing by Black Women*. New Brunswick, NJ: Rutgers UP, 1989.

Wallace, Ronald. "Introduction." In *Vital Signs: Contemporary American Poetry from the University Presses*. Madison: U of Wisconsin P, 1989. 3-40.

Walzer, Michael. *Spheres of Justice: A Defense of Pluralism and Equality*. New York: Basic Books, 1983.

Warhol, Robyn R. *Gendered Interventions: Narrative Discourse in the Victorian Novel*. New Brunswick, NJ: Rutgers UP, 1989.

Warhol, Robyn R. and Diane Price Herndl, ed. *Feminisms: An Anthology of Literary Theory and Criticism*. New Brunswick, NJ: Rutgers UP, 1991.

Watney, Simon. *Policing Desire: Pornography, AIDS and the Media*. Minneapolis: U of Minnesota P, 1987.

Waugh, Patricia. *Feminine Fictions: Revisiting the Postmodern*. London: Routledge, 1989.

Weber, Max. "Domination and Legitimacy." In *Economy and Society*. Ed. Guenther Roth and Claus Wittich. 2 vols. Berkeley: U of California P, 1978. 941-55.

Weeks, Jeffrey. *Sex, Politics and Society: The Regulation of Sexuality since 1800*. London: Longman, 1981.

Welch, James. *Winter in the Blood*. New York: Harper & Row, 1974.

Welch, James. *Fools Crow*. New York: Viking, 1986.

West, Cornel. "The Role of Law in Progressive Politics." *Vanderbilt Law Review* 43 (1990): 1797-1806.

West, Robin. "Jurisprudence and Gender." *University of Chicago Law Review* 55 (1988): 1-72.

White, Hayden. *Metahistory: The Historical Imagination in Nineteenth-Century Europe*. Baltimore: Johns Hopkins UP, 1973.

White, Hayden. "The Value of Narrativity in the Representation of Reality." *Critical Inquiry* 7 (1980): 5–27.

White, Hayden. *The Content of the Form: Narrative Discourse and Historical Representation*. Baltimore: Johns Hopkins UP, 1987.

White, James Boyd. *Heracles' Bow: Essays on the Rhetoric and Poetics of the Law*. Madison: U of Wisconsin P, 1985.

Wideman, John Edgar. *Reuben*. 1987. Harmondsworth: Penguin Books, 1988.

Wilentz, Gay. *Binding Cultures: Black Women Writers in Africa and the Diaspora*. Bloomington: Indiana UP, 1992.

Williams, Patricia J. "Alchemical Notes: Reconstructing Ideals from Deconstructed Rights." *Harvard Civil Rights-Civil Liberties Law Review* 22 (1987): 401–33.

Williams, Raymond. *Marxism and Literature*. Oxford: Oxford UP, 1977.

Willis, Susan. *Specifying: Black Women Writing the American Experience*. Madison: U of Wisconsin P, 1987.

Wilson, B. R. *Magic and the Millennium: A Sociological Study of Religious Movements of Protest Among Tribal and Third World Peoples*. London: Heinemann, 1973.

Winnett, Susan. "Coming Unstrung: Women, Men, Narrative, and Principles of Pleasure." *PMLA* 105 (1990): 505–18.

Wolin, Sheldon S. "On the Theory and Practice of Power." In Arac, *After Foucault*. 179–201.

Wuthnow, Robert, James Davison Hunter, Albert Bergesen, and Edith Kurzweil. *Cultural Analysis: The Work of Peter L. Berger, Mary Douglas, Michel Foucault, and Jürgen Habermas*. London: Routledge & Kegan Paul, 1984.

Yingling, Thomas. "AIDS in America: Postmodern Governance, Identity, and Experience." In Fuss, *Inside*. 291–310.

Young, Iris Marion. "The Ideal of Community and the Politics of Difference." In Nicholson. 300–23.

Zimmerman, Bonnie. "What Has Never Been: An Overview of Lesbian Feminist Criticism." In Showalter, *New Feminist Criticism*. 200–24.

Author Index

Subject Index

African-American studies: and agency,
102; and civic republicanism, 96–97;
and community, 99–106, 114,
163n.7, 166n.7; and Critical Race
Theory, 57–58; and identity politics,
25, 162n.1, 163n.10; and narrative,
58–59, 93, 97–99, 102, 104–6, 163n.7,
n.8, 163n.11; and oral literature, 93–
95, 163n.7, n.11; and ritual, 95–96,
98–99, 114, 166n.7; and theory, 33–
34, 57–58, 127, 158n.4. *See also specific writers*
Agency, 102; liberal, 6–7, 27–28, 30;
postmodern, 27, 30, 46–47, 53–59,
126–29, 152–53
Anthropology: and border zones, 109–
10; and Clifford, 122–23; culture in,
8, 28–29, 119–20, 122, 127–29; and
Fischer, 125–27; and functionalism,
112–13, 119; and Girard, 119; and interpretive turn, 11, 127–29; and narrative, 11, 95, 120, 128–29; and Oedipus complex, 82; and postmodern
ethnography, 119–20, 122, 125–29;
and practice theory, 21, 128; ritual
in, 110–12, 119–20; and Rosaldo,
119–20, 127
Art history, 12
Asian-Americans: and identity politics,
25, 162n.1; writing of, 93, 98, 105–6

Babel. *See* Culture, in postmodern era
Border zones, 109–10, 135, 166n.9; and
the Caribbean, 114–16, 120–23,
167n.15; and Latin America, 114–18,
123–27, 167n.15

Canons, 30–31, 52, 95, 147–53; and
community, 150–51; conflict among,
150–51; multiplicity of, 150–51,
170n.3
Capitalism. *See* Culture, in postmodern
era
Chicanos/Chicanas: and code switching, 108, 124–25, 167n.15; and deconstruction, 160n.19; and identity politics, 25, 162n.1, 163n.10; writing of,
123–27, 166n.9, 167n.12. *See also
specific writers*
Civic republicanism, 20, 132–33, 149,
156n.14, 169n.6; and African-
Americans, 96–97. *See also* Communitarianism; Community
Communitarianism: and civc republicanism, 132–33, 169n.6; definitions
of, 133–35, 144; and feminism, 133,
136–38; and identity politics, 134; vs.
liberalism, 133–35; and narrative,
133–35; vs. postmodernism, 133–35;
and practice, 133–35; and subject,
133–34